Dear John, I Love Jane

WOMEN WRITE ABOUT LEAVING MEN FOR WOMEN

Editors
Candace Walsh
& Laura André

Foreword by
Dr. Lisa M. Diamond,
author of *Sexual Fluidity*

SEAL PRESS

Dear John, I Love Jane
Women Write About Leaving Men for Women

Copyright © 2010 by Candace Walsh and Laura André

Published by
Seal Press
A Member of the Perseus Books Group
1700 Fourth Street
Berkeley, California

"First Date With Ann" from *What It's Like To Live Now* by Meredith Maran, copyright © 1995 by Meredith Maran. Used by permission of Bantam Books, a division of Random House, Inc.

"Wedding Gown Closet," © 2010 Katherine A Briccetti, is an adaptation from *Blood Strangers*, published by Heyday Books.

Library of Congress Cataloging-in-Publication Data

Dear John, I love Jane : women write about leaving men for women / edited by Candace Walsh and Laura André.
 p. cm.
 ISBN 978-1-58005-339-6
1. Women–Sexual behavior. 2. Bisexuality. 3. Man-woman relationships. 4. Interpersonal relations. I. Walsh, Candace. II. André, Laura, 1965-
 HQ29.D37 2010
 306.76'5082–dc22
 2010010375

Cover design by Kate Basart/Union Pageworks
Interior design by Tabitha Lahr
Printed in the United States of America
Distributed by Publishers Group West

If I didn't define myself for myself, I would be crunched into other people's fantasies for me and eaten alive.
—Audre Lorde

Contents

Foreword

Dr. Lisa M. Diamond

his gripping collection of first-person narratives will undoubtedly expand and deepen your understanding of women's sexuality, whether you are gay, straight, or somewhere in between. As someone who has been studying women's erotic and affectional changes and transformations for over fifteen years, I am jumping for joy to see such stories on printed pages. Journeys such as these usually remain untold, unexplored, and uninvestigated, drowned out by the more familiar and predictable coming out stories that recount continuous, early-appearing, and readily identifiable same-sex attractions. The women in this volume have followed notably different—and remarkably diverse—routes to same-sex love and desire. Their single point of commonality is their compelling defiance of societal expectations about how women are "supposed" to discover, experience, interpret, and act on same-sex desires. Instead of tortured childhoods, these women report sudden and surprising adult experiences of same-sex desire—sometimes after ten, twenty, or thirty years of heterosexuality—which turn their worlds upside down. Listening to these women recount the perplexing bliss of their first same-sex affairs, coupled with the doubt, disapproval, and disrespect they suffered at the hands of friends and family, offers an utterly new perspective on women's erotic lives.

There are statements in these stories that bowled me over because they so strongly resemble statements I've heard from the lesbian, bisexual, questioning, and heterosexual women I've been interviewing over the past fifteen years.

- I wish I had realized earlier that I didn't want to be like those girls so much as I just wanted them.
- I'm not attracted to women . . . but I'm falling in love with this person.
- I knew I had shifted from being a "straight" girl. Where along the continuum I landed, I wasn't sure yet.
- Inside, a part of me still wavered about whether my changing sexuality was sparked because of who she was, as my friend, or because she is a woman.
- I've always felt like I was somewhat of a fraud in the gay community. Where was my gay history?
- In three short months, I had gone from A (a hopelessly straight girl) to Z (hopelessly in love with a woman).

Quite simply, voices and experiences like these have been missing from our popular *and* scientific understandings of female sexuality, and the twists and turns that sexuality takes over the life course. Instead, when women make unexpected mid-life transitions to same-sex love and desire, when they fall madly in love with "just this one woman," they find themselves discounted and dismissed as inauthentic by the larger gay community because they have no long childhood struggles with nascent same-sex desires to report, no adolescent self-hatred. Some of them—glory be—enjoyed or continue to enjoy relationships with husbands and boyfriends. What's *that* about?

The truth is that these journeys are far more common than most people think, and they deserve our full attention. These women's candor is refreshing, revelatory, and deeply important to our attempts to understand and validate same-sex love and desire in all its miraculous forms. These women have bravely explored every edge of the supposed boundary dividing queer from straight, before from after, truth from falsehood, self from façade, and girl from woman. They have shown that the closer one gets to the boundary, the more ephemeral it appears to be, shifting and mutating like a smoke ring before our very eyes. In the end, each of these women makes her own peace with identity, desire, kinship, community, partnership, and self, sometimes with a lover by her side, sometimes alone. Each journey has its own logic and truth, its own "deep structure" imprinted in memory, desire, sweat, salt, and the powerful bond between two women who cannot resist one another, despite the horrified shock of everyone around them.

The past looms large in these narratives. As one woman's ex-boyfriend says, matter-of-factly, "History is important." History *is* important, but where is it to be found? Which past matters? Which experiences should we rely upon as signposts for the future? These women steadfastly resist the impetus to erase or discount past identities, desires, relationships, but instead choose the harder role of integration, moving toward a future that can contain contradiction, fluidity, change, and dynamism. As one woman boldly claims, "You won't find me re-writing history to say that I was gay all along. I was straight. Now I am gay. I won't insult my past self by saying I was in denial or confused." It takes guts to hold this line and to speak one's truth to a society that doesn't understand it.

To be clear, men are not villains here. In contrast to the classic stereotype of men as uniformly blocking their wives' and girlfriends' processes of sexual questioning, we meet a notably different cast of male characters in these women's stories. There are men tortured by the loss of women who couldn't fully love them back; men who give their lovers lessons in their own bodies, lessons that will eventually lead these women into the arms of other women. As one husband told his wife as she wrestled with blossoming same-sex desires, "Sometimes when you encourage people to be all they can be, you get a little more than you bargained for." Some of the men in these narratives resist and denounce; others relinquish and mourn, affirm and accept. Watching women as they struggle to reconcile the past, current, and future roles of these complex men in their lives is one of the most fascinating and original gifts of this collection.

No matter what your own history, this book will challenge and expand your notion of what it means to be (for lack of a better, broader term) queer: Queer women come out at fifteen, at eighteen, at forty, and at sixty. Queer women live openly and in secret. Queer women get and stay married to (open-minded) men. Queer women settle down with the first woman they ever kissed. Queer women have children with men, with women, with both. Queer women play the field. Queer women make lifelong commitments. Queer women keep questioning. Queer women strike out into new and unfamiliar territory. As one woman says, "You never know where love and honesty will take you." This book is a series of unique journeys through love and honesty (with plenty of lust, sweat, fumbling, and ecstasy thrown in) that has much to teach us about the nature of female affection and eroticism. We owe all of the participants a debt of gratitude for their candor, and for allowing us to listen and learn.

Introduction

Candace Walsh and Laura André

*W*hen we met each other two years ago (on Match.com), we immediately noticed a shared love of language and books. And almost since that time, we've been working on books together. As is often the case with new lovers, our early conversations touched upon our respective romantic histories. Candace had recently left her husband of seven years and was dating women for the first time. Laura, who had never dated men (well, there was that guy from band in tenth grade), had also never dated a woman who had Candace's heterosexual bona fides (traditional wedding, children from that marriage). We had lots to discuss and learn. We had been living on two different planets and were about to touch down on a third.

It was a particular kind of conversation. Not two women sharing our long lists of ex-girlfriends, or a woman talking to a man about her divorce—it was a conversation that more and more women are having on private and public levels. Cynthia Nixon, Wanda Sykes, Meredith Baxter, Carol Leifer, and countless others have left the fold of heterosexual identity to enter into or pursue same-sex relationships. It used to be the punch line of a joke if a man's last girlfriend or wife left him and went on to partner with a woman. Now it is just something that happens—something that doesn't cast either party as a villain or a laughingstock. The instance of a woman leaving a man for a woman has more visibility and is becoming less of a shocker (although it remains a curiosity because it challenges so many commonly held truisms about what women want).

It's a relationship that reflects circumstances our society is now absorbing more frequently. As Dr. Lisa Diamond's recent ground-breaking book, *Sexual Fluidity,* makes clear, women's sexual desire and identity are not only capable of shifting, they do shift. Instead of standing on the outside looking in, this book is made up of intimate perspectives shared from inside women's lives. Diamond's research has given us a new language to talk about our capacity to love. The women in this book are writing from a deeper understanding of their emotional and sexual territory.

Love is seen as a soft, romantic thing, but it can also be as leveling as an earthquake. It can rework and redefine people's lives in ways they never imagined. It's the reason why people move halfway around the world, get married, and expose themselves to rejection and ridicule—or delight. It can make us act like fools, or make us wise with the knowledge of what's important and what is superfluous. This book is a series of love stories, bursting with all of the passion, uncertainty, self-discovery, and sacrifice that make up the truly good ones.

CANDACE: There were a series of physical steps that led me out of my marriage: loading my station wagon with "what would you grab in a slow-burning fire" items (journals, clothing, children's books, sippy cups, a tin of smoked paprika, and all of my Joan Didion books); signing the three-month lease on my rented casita; buying groceries that were put away in a new refrigerator and cabinets. Key among these steps was my Internet search for books on women leaving men for women. Women who "jumped the fence," "went gay," "were lesbians all along," or "betrayed their vows." What I was doing felt radical in the contexts of both the straight community I was leaving behind and the lesbian community that seemed like a distant shore on the horizon. The ground under my feet was a no-man's-land between two territories. Would they be hostile? Friendly? Guarded? A mix?

LAURA: You have the double whammy of processing your divorce and coming to terms with your sexuality. It gives new meaning to the term "disorienting."

CANDACE: I wanted to get my bearings—to read stories by women who had gone down the same path I was walking with my fingers crossed. I ordered *And Then I Met This Woman* and *From Wedded Wife to Lesbian Life*, which were well-done and gave me hope, but were also rooted in a different time. Many of the contributors came out in the '70s and '80s, when society was a lot less accepting. Mothers often ran the risk of losing their kids in divorce court if their sexuality came up. (Not that we're completely out of the woods—recently, a friend told me about her new relationship, and then told me to keep it in confidence, since her girlfriend was going through a custody battle.)

A number of the women in this book had to confront the drama of telling their parents about the shift in their sexuality. Parents do still disown their kids or become estranged from them due to their sexuality, but it's becoming more rare to encounter that level of judgment. Categorically disapproving of gay people is becoming more and more universally tacky, right up there with walking around Wal-Mart dressed in a muscle shirt and bike shorts.

LAURA: While some of the writers found a sense of community online and in books, others felt terribly alone as they struggled to deal with the changes they were going through. And even those who found community online still had to live their offline life at a certain level of isolation.

CANDACE: I wanted to be in a room surrounded by women who were now on the other side, and had stories to tell. A support group, or a retreat, that involved a tall stacked-stone fireplace, and tumblers of shiraz. A klatch of smart, sparkling women like the ones who gathered at Meryl Streep's character's house in *It's Complicated*. I wanted to dish.

What was your first time like? What did your mother say? How long did you wait to tell her? Does she even know? Did you lose any female friends who were afraid you were going to start vibing them (oh, please)? Are you now in a relationship with one of your female friends? Are long-time lesbians not taking you seriously? Isn't it weird that men try to pick you and your girlfriend up when you go out to restaurants?

LAURA: That last bit actually happened to us.

CANDACE: It was another round of adolescence. How to flirt. How to date. Sexual experience: zero. Everything old is new again. I was on a different planet where everything seemed mostly the same, except that little differences tipped me off to the fact that I couldn't go home again. I had to craft a new home out of pieces of my old life and my new one.

As the editor of *Ask Me About My Divorce: Women Open Up About Moving On* (Seal Press, 2009), I knew full well that if I couldn't find the book I wanted to read, I could take a stab at creating it. Every editor wonders whether her anthology idea is a quirk or a bellwether, especially if it comes from a personal place. Laura had generously joined me in the trenches of pulling together *Ask Me About My Divorce* and I knew I didn't want to edit another book without her.

LAURA: I was really happy—and relieved—when the submissions started rolling in. I wasn't sure that there would be that many women out there who were willing to sit down and write essays detailing their experiences. After all, we're talking about major life changes here, and it's not always easy to write well about them. But as soon as I started reading the essays, I forgot about the quantity and began getting lost in the individual stories that were being told. Real lives, unfolding and caroming and being recorded right here, as potential elements of our book. I began to see how it was falling into place, and it was powerful.

CANDACE: I thought there'd be enough submissions. Not a deluge, but *enough*. And that if they were not top-notch in the writing department but story-driven, I could work them up. Well, we got a deluge (130), and we had more than enough to choose from; we selected the ones that were the most powerfully written. But I have to say, Laura's anxiety fueled her posting of the call for submissions all over the Internet. She spent days. And it paid off.

Before we submitted the book proposal, we sat together and watched the March 2009 *Oprah* episode on women leaving men for other women. Guests included Dr. Lisa Diamond, who patiently explained women's sexual fluidity to the puzzled host and a millions-strong televised audience, and Micki Grimland, raised Baptist and married for twenty-four years to her husband, mom of three, declaiming her personal truth: she left that husband (still a dear friend), because she realized that she was a lesbian. Little did we know that Diamond and Grimland would accede so happily and graciously to contribute to our project. It wasn't just my story. It was a conflation of timing, a bouquet of high-profile women's decisions at a particular point of same-sex relationship acceptance, and a deeper understanding of women's fluid sexuality, which historically had been woefully under-researched.

LAURA: Coming from an academic background, I can say that we're seeing the fruition of what seemed solely theoretical twenty years ago. The idea that sexuality can be pegged to simple binaries (straight/gay, men/women), and that those binary pairs are absolute, has been completely dissolved by the notion of sexual fluidity. The essayists in this book are living proof that sexuality can change over time, often against our will. The women in this book didn't set out to dismantle their marriages and relationships; the last thing they wanted was to hurt their husbands or boyfriends. This switching doesn't happen voluntarily, which will frustrate those who believe that sexual orientation is a choice, like ordering from a catalog. The cultural lesbianism that some have adopted is separate from this core thing that happened to these writers: falling in love with a woman. Theory aside, what it comes down to is actual lived experience, and through these personal essays, we have first-person accounts—primary source material—not of queer theory, but of queerness itself.

CANDACE: These are not love stories with templates that are delivered to girls from Walt Disney, these are not women who found their princes. We are told, in this book, that we can keep our whole selves *and* still find love. Or it finds us. We are awakened with a kiss, a look, a job interview, or a "non-date." Something in our destinies rips us out of what's comfortable, expected, and rubber-stamped. We are given a choice. Will we follow bliss? Or hunker down and live a conciliatory lie?

I was hungry for a story that didn't make me suspect, or a liar, that didn't cast a third of my life into the "mistake" or "do-over" category. I found my tribe. Like many of the women in this book, I hold my children close, close enough to model an example of authenticity while also feeling moments of uncertainty and even anxiety (isn't that an indication that I'm not sleepwalking through life?). My children love my partner ardently. I have expanded their definition of what love looks like. Recently, my five-year-old son saw my Valentine's Day present for Laura, wrapped in pink tissue paper. "Who's that for?" he asked. "That's for Laura," I said. "Oh, good," he replied.

LAURA: Recently Candace told me that she was glad I never doubted her. The truth is, I didn't ever question her commitment to finding a woman to fulfill her, regardless of the fact that she once identified as straight. I knew what she gave up. One doesn't walk away from full-blown heterosexual privilege on a whim. It surprised me how many of the essays in the book refer to people who were suspicious that a woman who once loved a man could never love a woman as fully. That she must be experimenting, playing around, not serious.

The whole idea that women leaving men for women is some sort of a trendy, hot thing to do is patronizing and dismissive. This book is not about BFFs frenching in bars to turn on their boyfriends. Especially in today's climate, which is still—despite much progress—patently homophobic.

CANDACE: And downright punishing, when you know what you're missing. The women in this book once benefited from heterosexual privilege. We had the married income tax status, the pensions waiting for us, the right to be at our beloved's bedside in the hospital. The frosty-white wedding albums filled with unequivocally supportive friends and relatives. We walked away.

LAURA: As Jennifer Baumgardner notes in the epilogue to this book, women taking charge of their sexual identity is a specifically feminist gesture, one that is sure to ruffle a few conservatives' feathers. But the truly immoral thing is to deny one's real identity, whether it has been simmering for years or it's newly sprung. I admire the women in this book so much, as they're really brave to have done what they've done, and then write about it so honestly.

One of the funny things about dating Candace is how, at the beginning, she was more out than I was in public. I've always been a lesbian, but I was used to being very low-key in public. And here she comes along, fresh from the hetero fold, wanting to hold hands, call me "honey," and give me little kisses in public, and I stiffened up, which I feel bad about. I think those experiences opened both of our eyes to how heterosexual privilege operates in terms of public displays of affection. Many of the writers in the book express dismay that they don't feel comfortable holding hands with their female partners in public—that simple, spontaneous gestures like that are something they miss from their previous relationships with men.

CANDACE: Women who come out in their thirties or forties have a lot in common with high school girls coming out today into an environment that's comparatively accepting. They may have a lack of self-consciousness about holding hands or being affectionate in public, which reveals evidence about the nature of their relationship.

I noticed the awareness of a growing reflexive restraint, and felt it to be a damming up, a hemming in, of the flow of my romantic impulses. I am not a neuroscientist, but that can't be preferable to the kind of freedom and safety heterosexual couples take for granted.

LAURA: Another thing that was a big shocker for me was getting used to the kids. I thought I had chosen a life without children, and I was content with that. Falling in love with Candace not only meant having to confront my fear of children; it also meant letting go of my life as I thought it would look like. So, while I never left a man for a woman, I did have to switch my identity to someone who finds herself at children's music recitals and ice skating lessons, and that made me more empathetic to the *"Oh my God, I can't believe this is my life"* emotion that so many of our writers express.

But as a result, my definition of family has expanded and I'm getting to experience what it means to love and be loved by two amazing children. Many of the essays in this book express a similar salient joy in having it all work out (including new partners who take the kid thing on with a ton of grace and enthusiasm), despite what seem like insurmountable challenges.

It also meant having a third adult figure—the kids' dad—in the "family." I must say it is sometimes strange to be hanging out with Candace's ex-husband. But then again, that's very lesbian of us, to be friends with our exes. There are quite a few essayists in the book who have managed to preserve good relationships with their ex-husbands or former male partners. After the crisis and fallout, it seems that it's worth it for many women who've left men for women to hang on to the parts of those relationships that they can salvage. In fact, a few of the writers are still married to their husbands, still trying to rework their concept of marriage to absorb their newfound identities.

CANDACE: My ex-husband and I are active coparents to our two children. As a result, we probably talk more than we did when we were married—because instead of floating along on autopilot, we're negotiating who's picking up the kids from school Thursday, where the snow pants are, and how we're going to swing music lessons. I'm glad that we have an open and honest dialogue. We're much more authentic with each other now that we aren't invested in preserving something that was so fragile. It's meaningful to have continuity with a person I've known for a decade. And our children benefit from sensing warmth between the two adults who brought them into this world.

LAURA: This is more than a book of essays by women who've left men for women. I've come to think of it as a massive coming-out story, written collectively by a group of women who've finally found their voices.

CANDACE: Their stories diverge from the Michigan Womyn's Music Festival, gold star, accepted, "pure lesbian" narrative (example: "As a girl I was a tomboy . . . I didn't date in high school and had *Teen Beat* posters of Nancy McKeon in a secret scrapbook").

LAURA: Women have always left men for other women, it's just that now enough barriers have fallen, enough taboos have been smashed, for them to be able to tell their stories and share their struggles as a matter of course. In these twenty-seven essays, you'll find stories from women who have always known they were different, but tried to make a go at the straight life, earning the approval of society and their families, but betraying themselves in the process. You'll also find your fair share of essays by women who were hit over the head with their sexuality when they least expected it, or even wanted it. These women, who always considered themselves straight, had to deal with the cataclysmic revelation that they fell in love with someone of the same sex. And while coming out to friends, family, and strangers is hard enough, coming out to one's self is the most difficult and powerful step of all.

While some of the writers found great relief in finally identifying as lesbian—and shouting it from the rooftops, so to speak—others eschewed that and any other label, preferring to think of themselves and their identity without having to name it. Naming is such a powerful political tool for both empowering and marginalizing people; it's easy to see how one might choose carefully in selecting or refusing labels.

CANDACE: Especially after spending a lifetime unfettered by such categorization.

LAURA: What it comes down to in these essays, however, is love. Having the freedom to follow and express love is the single uniting heart of these essays. Despite the obstacles and deterrents, these women found, as Katherine Briccetti writes in her essay, "the pull toward bliss was too great."

Undoing Everything

Erin Mantz

I had prepared myself for the Saturday night couples' dinner invitations to stop arriving, for the Evites to moms' nights out to end. I braced myself to be unofficially banned from the most powerful PTA committees, to be shunned at the neighborhood pool club and shut out of family barbeques hosted by my sons' friends' parents. I dreamed of longtime friends literally turning their back on me, and my closest thirtysomething friends shaking their heads in disgrace and walking away. At the grocery store and in the gym, people would turn and stare, I thought, and say "She was married to a guy but now she's with a woman. She *must* be insane!"

And then it happened: nothing. At least, not to my face. Not yet.

Falling in love with a woman at thirty-nine may have turned my life upside down, but the friends and family all around me are still standing.

When your life is tightly wrapped up with a bow before you turn forty, the thought of unraveling it on purpose is almost impossible to comprehend. Your name is on a mortgage for a nice suburban home. You have a husband of eleven years, two sons, an SUV, and a community where lots of people know your name. You get lost in day-to-day plans of playdates and Disney vacation dreams, and pound on the granite kitchen countertops trying to decide what to throw together for dinner. You're a lot like everyone else. You fit in. That was me.

I was just another person in line for a latte at the neighborhood Starbucks.

Then I fell in love with a woman. I was shocked and I was immediately absolute. I wanted to be with her for the rest of my life. And for a brief moment, I would think, *there's too much to undo.*

Trendy it is, women falling in love with other women for the first time in their lives. A short while after it happened to me, the topic was hot on *Oprah* and in various magazines. I never set out to be a trendsetter, had never identified with "Girls Gone Wild" or set out to shock people (though I admit the shock factor has been rather fun). I just wanted to be happy. I wanted to be with the person I realized I loved, who happened to be a woman. I didn't want to have to undo everything. But I began to.

As I broke the news to my friends near and far, in order of emotionally closest and those perceived to be most loyal, I went through a kind of steeling of my soul each night before the conversations. I'd wake up several times in the middle of the night and feel a kind of panic and a sense of resolve at the same time. During the days, I felt like I was floating through a foreign world or acting in a Lifetime movie, because what was happening was so unexpected, so crazy, so senseless, so selfish, that I didn't even know how to articulate it. "I just love her," I said.

And they simply said, "As long as you're happy." A few bold ones asked, "How did this happen?" (Good question. I had no idea. It just happened. My therapist suggested a great answer after this question arose more and more: "Say 'I have no idea,'" she urged. "Because you don't!") "I don't know," with a smile, a shrug, and a raise of the eyebrow became my well-rehearsed reaction. It was actually something I could laugh about later, as I recounted conversation after conversation to my girlfriend.

Every person I told hung in there. They hung on my every word as I broke the news. Many thought they'd heard wrong when I said a woman's name. I'd have to repeat myself and watch as their eyes got big as saucers. Some said, "It's 2009!" to kind of justify it. But every single friend who stood by me—and I mean every single one did—said, "As long as you're happy, that's what matters. You seem *happy*."

I had, undoubtedly and tremendously, underestimated my friends' ability to deal with my news. I had been getting ready for the disgust and discrimination, which I knew would come from strangers, and which I had anticipated from friends. But I was the one who was reeling and changing. They were staying the same.

I was still their friend. But I didn't feel like myself as I unraveled my marriage and everything that came along with it. Facebook connections with old boyfriends became reassurances of the old me—something, I guess, I'm still looking for. I searched profile pictures of old boyfriends—one particularly good-looking one from college, who I once thought I could have married—and tried to analyze everything. Was I the same person then? Am I still me? If I saw him today, would I feel anything? Would I have anyway?

For all the statements I heard while breaking the news to friends, the one that hit me hardest was something I had never stopped to face. "Aren't you scared?" one asked me. Of course I was scared. I had been terrified for months and months. I was still terrified. But it never stopped me from moving forward. I didn't let it get to me every day. That night, however, her question replayed in my mind, and I had a moment thinking *Oh my G-d. This really is scary. Am I really making this choice?*

But I found my soul mate. I had always felt *something* was missing from my life. Never, ever, did I think I would find it. I hadn't even known what I was looking for.

I'm in love with a woman, but so many little things haven't changed. I still go to work and walk my dog. I try to go running three times a week and eat better, and I worry about my kids getting sick. I take my kids to the park and run out of milk just like everybody else. I received two Evites from other moms in my community last week. I didn't have to undo everything!

But, the big things are coming undone. Big vacations and lofty retirement goals as I'd envisioned them, and a chance to give my young sons a "normal" life—I've let all that go. A sense of place in the world I knew and the ease of being just like everybody else is gone now. And, amazingly, I am living with that, because the rewards of really being in love make it all worthwhile. It isn't even a contest.

The weight of the big things feels like a thousand rocks on my shoulders some days. But nobody can really relate to those moments of panic and awe, except my girlfriend, who is carrying the same. But, here's the reality: Undoing everything isn't something that happens at once. It will be reflected in random moments, not just this year, but always, and it's something I can't anticipate or complete. I am living with an enormous bet that what I'm getting will be so much more than what I'm giving up. Yet, I will never ever really know, will I? Living with *that*—that's going to be the hard part.

Running from the Paper Eye

Susan White

*M*y mother's hatred for her sister goes back to the chicken: an Easter chick dyed cotton-candy blue. My mother told me this story to squash my fondness for my aunt, Big Joan.

Under the oppressive Tennessee sun, the two girls in their homemade white dresses spent the afternoon in their backyard playing with their chicks. Probably because she handled it too much—and because of the chemicals saturating its miniature body—Joan's green chick swooned into death before supper. After the burial behind the swing set, Joan stood on top of the rust-red picnic table glaring down at my mother's chick, Lucy, who pecked each speck on the smooth, cement sidewalk. My mom squatted by the screen door, calling Lucy to her. The chick cocked its head, shrugged its wing nubs, and waddled toward my mother. Joan jumped from the table. The bones popped and crunched. Thick darkness leaked from the blue beneath Joan's new Sunday shoes.

So what came before the chicken? An egg. And then a zygote. And then a child. But then another child. And they are sisters, right? Same last name, dark hair, nose, and accent.

But, according to my mother, they had nothing but differences on the inside. She insists that Joan ruined her childhood. My mom learned not to count her chicks, lest they be flattened beneath Joan's fierce feet.

When I was old enough to know that parents cry and lie, I asked Joan how she remembered the Easter deaths. She claimed the unfortunate blue chick's demise was an accident. With a brash smoker's laugh, she said, "Your mother is the victim in all her stories." She stood, running her hands down her linen pants. "And I'm always the villain." Winking at me, she added, "Some people need a villain."

I admire Joan's certainty. Her swaggering speech. She was, after all, a high school basketball star in the '50s who sported a flat top. Now she is a retired personnel director of the Arlington school system. She hatched no children. She is what no one talked about until I came right out and asked: a lesbian.

I thought I was a boy the first few years of my life. Born between brothers, I wore my hair short, played shirtless and shoeless in the neighborhood, and tried to pee standing up. My mother called me to the Formica kitchen table, showed me a picture book, and gave me an anatomy lesson. I believed she cast a spell on me with strange, magical words to turn me into a girl that day. But at that age, I begged my mom to leave my sandwich whole, believing I would have less if she cut it. My larva brain saw the world in cartoon terms. A few weeks earlier, I had attempted to release all the characters inside by dropping a large rock on the malfunctioning TV left in our yard. After epic battles of forcing party dresses over my head, my mother eventually convinced me I was born a female. Years later, another female was born into our family.

Easter came before my sister. The night before the first ovulating moon of spring, my swollen mother hid eggs around our front yard. The next morning, three eager kids grabbed the baskets filled with green plastic grass that lay waiting for us on the living room floor. We ran down the unswept stone steps into our yard, which was littered with dyed eggshells and chocolate wrappers. Our dogs had found the hidden treasures first. A couple of days later, one of those dogs, a chow-shepherd mix with a half-black tongue, killed the rabbit our uncle gave us. Slung it around and snapped its neck. It was a limp Easter.

On Earth Day, Anne was born. She always knew she was a girl. Mom did not need to work her magic. Anne sprouted fiery hair, rekindled from two generations past on my mother's side, which her green and yellow dresses complemented. She delighted my grandmother by actually taking the dolls she gave her out of the box. (There is a Christmas picture of me aiming my brother's BB gun at a doll standing upright in its package.)

I was probably fifteen; I had written my name in my grandmother's carpet, rubbing the fibers the wrong way with a yellow-green comb.

"Mother will have a fit," Joan said.

"But I can fix it easily," I said.

Joan sat on the organ bench. "Doesn't matter. That shit drives her crazy—rubbing things the wrong way."

My parents laughed in agreement.

And I felt compelled to comb the carpet to its submissive state. As I uncombed my name, I heard my father speak to Joan as if I weren't there: "She looks up to you." Leaning toward her, using his English-teacher voice, he added, "She *identifies* with you."

Despite (or perhaps because of) dreams of sexual encounters with females that left me sick and terrified in the morning light, I married. Married my best male friend, whom I had dated for two years. College was over. He had a job and was renting a house. I walked right through those open doors.

I was at my parents' house a few months before the wedding when Big Joan called to confirm the date with my mother prior to booking her flight. I picked up the phone in my sister's room, lay on my back, my eyes settling on the closet I used to sleep in at night when I was scared—when the room was mine—and talked to Joan. My mother, who can never talk long to Joan, hung up her phone before I even flipped to my side and pulled at a thread coming loose from the comforter.

"Are you the only one on the phone now, Susan?" she asked.

"Hello? Yep, it appears so," I said, breaking the thread and releasing it to the carpet.

"You know you don't want to do this," she said.

"Do what?" I asked, looking into the full-length mirror with butterfly stickers on the bottom.

"Marry a man."

My heart snagged. "Of course I do," I said, turning away from the mirror.

"You sure about that?"

"I love Wes," I said.

Wes blames our divorce on the poison oak. Sure, let the plant take the fall. A natural disaster.

He warned me not to climb the rocky embankment. He was afraid I'd fall. But I grabbed onto plants that grew between the rocks when toeholds crumbled and tumbled. I reached the top, stood triumphant on the ledge. He looked up, sunlight bouncing off his glasses. He didn't wave back.

The day before I flew to New Mexico for a six-week summer session of graduate school, Wes refused to touch my raised, red skin. Intimacy was not worth risking his future discomfort. He would not believe that poison oak is spread by leaf, not skin. After our divorce, he told me that he believed if he'd rubbed his body all over my poisoned skin that night we'd still be married. I find it amusing that in his mind's plotline of our tragedy, the poison oak is the peripeteia.

In New Mexico I studied words, while Wes and I withheld ours from each other. Our phone calls and emails were sparser than the grass on the mesa—where I ran each morning pretending to be free.

My skin cleared, and I rubbed it against a woman's. New Mexico, New Me. Grace is her name, and I am not making that up.

Grace and I ran together—in the promising mornings—and she spoke lapidary phrases polished by her stunning brain. Good god, I was electrified. I was alive. One night, we sat close to one another in a crowded hot tub as she spoke only to me, describing her recently published book. Here, next to me, was this brilliant woman I could hold, lick, bite, caress, kiss until I cried. I laid my hand on her smooth, bare thigh. The others could not see our contact beneath the warm, bubbling surface. They could not feel the tingling sensations that thrilled and pained me. We swam in the pool to cool. Raced each other the length of the pool. I think she won.

Our hair still damp, we lay on a blanket atop the mesa—stars pulsating all around us. Our shoulders touched. And as she laughed about the ledge being named for Dinty Moore—the beef stew cowboy—I kissed her neck that shone like bone. She rolled on top of me. Vanilla-scented lotion, cool skin, warm mouth. Waves and waves of heat. I brushed the back of my hand between her legs, and when she moaned, my fears of homosexuality melted away in a frothy lava rush.

Wes picked me up from the airport. Though we could see each other's faces, the distance remained. My brain remained on Grace. I relished long car drives when Wes read in the passenger seat and I could relive the feel and scent of her. The Internet brought me closer to my affair, until Wes discovered my notebook of printed infidelity. Before he confronted me, he plastered our apartment's cinderblock walls with pieces of computer paper, each one proclaiming something about me he loved. Wes convinced me that I was in love with Grace's writing accomplishments, not Grace. I tossed the notebook into the rusted Dumpster and pronounced all contact with Grace over. I believed that I could throw that part of me away.

He stopped crying. Sat at a desk in our cramped apartment and made a giant eye out of construction paper. The only other art project I had seen him undertake was when we painted bright, intricate designs on our plastic, thrift store headboard. We ditched that headboard when we moved to Georgia and bought a grownup bed. The eye, he told me, was to watch over us. The iris was green, and the lashes were thick, black, and rectangular. The pupil, dilated. He used double-sided tape to stick the eye to the wall above our cherry headboard. It wasn't long before the tape dried out and the eye fell behind our bed. Within three months, our marriage dried out. Again.

⚬

But we traveled to Asheville, North Carolina, together. He had his master's in accounting, and we both had the quixotic notion that a new setting would put the adhesion back on the eyeball of our commitment. I craved the mountains. Having grown up on the Cumberland Plateau in Tennessee, I believe the elevation is good for the spirit. The Georgian humidity had worn me down into its red soil.

So I convinced two schools in Asheville that they wanted me to teach their students: one was a day school and the other was a boarding school. Wes had no trouble landing an accounting job, and he had definite ideas about which job I should accept. Though I wanted to teach at the day school, he insisted I take the job at the boarding school, as room and board would be free. Wes is the man, after all, who convinced me to sleep in our car on long trips rather than paying for a hotel room. The same man who stuck dated labels beneath light fixtures to prove that I had foolishly squandered money on light bulbs marketed to be longer-lasting. So we moved our mismatched furniture into the girls' dormitory where I would have countless duties. I taught ninth-grade English and coached cross-country and track.

My first morning at the school, I ran the cross-country course and lost myself near the horse stables. I ran into a clearing and faced a huge, wooden throne. A man in blue jeans and a striped button-down shirt sat on it. He was completely still. He did not budge as I walked toward him to ask him for directions back to the school buildings. Blood soaked the wood behind his mangled head.

The newspaper article said he was found at a clearing on Asheville School campus; a clearing that Camp Hollymont uses in the summer. He had shot himself in the head the day before he was found. There was no mention of me, and the headmaster told me I was not to discuss the unfortunate man with any other faculty members, and certainly not with the students who would be arriving in a couple of weeks.

I learned the campus and neighboring trails well, thanks to other teachers who were distance runners. Four of us formed a running group. I did not discover any more dead bodies on these group runs, but I did discover Becky. Since she was married with two young kids and a baby, I was not too concerned that I found her sexy. Though I had thrown away the printed proof of my attraction to women, I ran behind Becky, watching her muscles move beneath her tight skin. I found reasons to touch her curly, blond hair. I lay awake at night thinking of ways I could amuse or impress her. I convinced myself that a crush was allowable, though it did make sex with Wes even less bearable.

One February night at dusk, I was at the track, counting out steps for my J-run to the high jump. Having been told that I would coach this event during track season, I had watched a couple of videos and a practice at the local college. Though I felt uncomfortable practicing this event on the wide-open track, I needed to be able to do what I would soon instruct others to do.

After I cleared the lowest height a few times, clapping and cheering startled me. I sat up on the blue landing cushion and saw her. Tall, lithe Becky. She had a way of finding me.

Though she wore jeans, I coaxed her to the blacktop before the high jump. I showed her how to run the J formation and marked off her steps with a little rock. She ran through the marks but stopped before the bar. Again and again, I showed her how to throw her body over the bar.

She told me, "This is outside my comfort zone."

My sweat drying in the coolness of the approaching evening, I felt charged—like I did on the mesa with Grace. Becky didn't jump that night.

I was off duty that Friday. The two of us went to a bar—a cheesy bar where two guys who brought their own pool sticks tried to pick us up. We were there because it was across the street from the campus. We both wanted to drink. I ripped the cardboard coaster into pieces as I confessed my attraction to her. She told me she wanted me too, but she was a mother. We had made the J-run together. Before she took me to my dorm, she parked her car by the stables—not far from the throne where I had seen the dead man. We kissed. I thought nothing could make me stop kissing Becky. I kissed her with a three-year hunger, and she opened. So soft, so lovely. So illicit.

Our affair blazed. We reached for each other whenever we could. Made love in my apartment between classes, on the wrestling mat late at night, in the woods mid-run, and in the headmaster's bathroom during a spring faculty party. Her back against the door. My hands pushing up her blue dress. Her mouth on my neck. My fingers in her warmth. One night, we drove to the new soccer complex. I lay on top of her in the back seat of her minivan. Police lights discovered us. We sat up. The policeman asked us where our boyfriends were. Had they run off into the woods? He would not believe that no men had been with us. That we could be there in the back seat together. Alone.

Wes found a blond, curly hair on our sheet. A CD player was plugged into the wall next to the bed. Shaking, he asked. I told. Everything. I asked him to leave me. He was gone within the week. The dean of faculty asked me if our small apartment contributed to our separation. Just the small space I had tried to exist in since puberty, I thought.

I adopted Zora from the pound after Wes moved out. Becky and her daughter helped me pick out a medium-size female with about three breeds in her. She has tweed-looking fur covered with big black spots on her back to match her black head and her right hind leg. The employees were calling her Beatrice, so the first thing I did was upgrade her name to Zora. When the volunteer rubbed Zora's belly, he showed me a woman-symbol tattoo beneath her fur. I thought she was a feminist miracle dog, but he explained veterinarians often make this tattoo to eliminate the guessing game of whether or not pets have been fixed. Since she'd already been spayed, I got to take her that day.

I was in love with Becky and she with me, but the little shoes by her front door broke my heart. Wes was hurt. Angry. We didn't talk much by phone. Only once in person. He did not tell Becky's husband, Pete, anything. He did tell me to think about her family. I told Becky it was over because of the little shoes. She disagreed. Yes, she had a family—was a mother and a wife—but she would decide what was right for her. She came to me at night. Crawled into my bed. We agreed we could not leave each other.

She told Pete. Then she called me to tell me she told Pete. Pete, the assistant headmaster, told the headmaster. The headmaster told me I had four hours to get off campus. Called me a sinner. A homewrecker. Told me I was sick and could possibly teach again once I got help. I still had a handwritten note he put in my box a week earlier in which he expressed how thankful he was for my teaching and coaching. That parents and students had nothing but positive reports. In closing, he'd written that he hoped I would stay with the school a long, long time. I left that note in his school mailbox along with the keys he told me to return. I was the corpse in the woods who needed to disappear to keep the campus from being tainted.

I loaded all I could fit into my Jeep. Zora sat in the passenger seat. And we drove to Becky's friend's house because I had nowhere else to go. Becky was fired, too. Pete begged her to stay with him, but she rented a house. They told their kids they were separating. I called my parents and siblings. Told them I was fired and gay. And I was as out as out can be. I was an outcast. My family offered nothing but love, but I lost every friend I had in Asheville, except Becky. I was not just out, I was inside out. Raw. I was a scandal. But I was still in love, and Becky and I played pool with Big Joan at a dive near my parents' house the day after Christmas. The next semester, I got a job at the rival school—the day school that I had applied to before I moved to Asheville.

But Becky's mom sent her Christian pamphlets about the sinfulness of homosexuality and told her she was ruining her and her family's lives. Pete often called her and cried. He is Catholic—one of the reasons for their three kids. And though I got along well with her kids, her daughter wasn't sleeping well.

One night after I timed her kids running the indoor obstacle course I made out of chairs, toys, balls, and canned food, she told me she was going to try to make things work with Pete. I ran seven miles down murky streets and never felt tired—just the pain that I was still alive.

I ran and ran and ran and ran and ran. And running is magical. Eventually I get somewhere. Six years ago, I got to Lucy. We met training for the Boston Marathon.

One night when the snow came down like feathers, I opened a beer because I knew school would be canceled the next day. Lucy, who never misses opportunities, called me and asked if I wanted company. We sat on the couch I had impulsively bought the day before. I drank a second beer as she sipped wine I worried had sat too long since I'd opened it. Her face flushed, and she explained that always happens when she drinks because she is half-Japanese. I had no excuse for my flushed face. I excused myself. Went to the bathroom. I washed my hands and then brushed my teeth. When I joined her on the sofa, she held my face and said, "Do you want to do this?" Yes, I did. Despite a broken marriage, despite the Christian pamphlets, despite losing a job, despite scandals, despite abandonment, despite Becky's relationship with a woman other than me after leaving Pete a second and final time, despite the laws, despite gossip. I wanted Lucy. I wanted me. As we moved on the new couch together, I did not feel the fiery rush of the forbidden. I felt certain. As certain of us as I was that I would have the next day off to remember every detail of our first evening together.

⁓

Lucy and I live together, and I'm thankful each night she presses her breasts and belly against my curled back, rests her tiny toes on my calves. We have three dogs. One of those dogs has a female symbol tattooed on her belly. Zora and I appreciate living cage-free. Each Easter, Lucy and I put chicken and ham inside plastic eggs and hide them around the yard. Our dogs sniff them out. Roll them with their noses. Crack them open with their teeth. Eat the meat and lick the plastic. And as we laugh at their discovery, I feel like a child who has found a way to set characters free.

The Right Fit

Kami Day

One summer when I was about nine, my mother, brother, sister, and I spent a few months in Seattle with my maternal grandparents. My mother asked me to walk to a nearby store to buy her some Tampax, so I did and then carried the box home in full view rather than asking the store clerk for a bag. My mother was mortified—and maybe realizing I had no idea what Tampax were motivated her to have the sex talk with me. I remember we were lying on my grandparents' living room rug as she used all the technically correct terms to describe how sex works. She then told me Heavenly Father had made one man whose penis would fit just perfectly inside my vagina. She wanted me to believe the only man I could have sex with was my husband. I was too young to think about the logistics of making sure every man met the woman he was designed for, and vice versa. And later when I learned what rape was, I thought it must be painful because the rapist was not the man Heavenly Father had designed for the victim. A few years passed before I began to have disturbing questions about women who married more than once, and I remember feeling nauseated when I finally realized people who were not married were having sex, and not always with just one partner. Yes, we were told that when you love someone and are married in the temple, sex is wonderful, but we were also told that sex before marriage is terrible.

What my mother told me about this perfect fit seems extreme, but she was only doing her best to inculcate the teachings of the Mormon Church. She and my father are Mormons, and their parents and grandparents were also Mormons. For almost forty-four years, the church controlled my life. It was part of nearly every decision I made, every breath I took. I had been taught from infancy that the Mormon Church was the only true church, and that being a member was the one way to salvation, to returning to live with Heavenly Father. I was told that I would grow up, fall in love with a worthy Mormon man, get married in the Mormon temple for time (earth time) and all eternity (afterlife time), and have many children. I would find joy in devoting my life to serving my family and the church. I would find motherhood fulfilling and meaningful, and in my old age, I would revel in my grandchildren and look forward to being reunited in the Celestial Kingdom with Jesus Christ, Heavenly Father, and my deceased relatives.

There was a great deal of preaching and teaching about remaining sexually pure until marriage. Sex was connected to love, joy, marriage, and righteousness, but also to misery, sin, loneliness, and uncleanliness. We heard sad stories about young women and men who had defiled their bodies—which we were to think of as temples that housed our spirits—by having premarital sex. These stories were always filled with shame and remorse, creating a disturbing mix of titillation and disgust that washed over the whole idea of sex for me. As a young teenager, I was in the habit of reading whatever was in my parents' bookcase, and I found *Marjorie Morningstar* in their collection of *Reader's Digest Condensed Books*. I carried it to school with me, and as I was reading in class one day, I stopped and closed the book. I had come to the part of the story in which Marjorie has sex for the first time, and the description includes the words "horrible uncoverings . . . and then it was over." As I read those words, I experienced physical sensations I had never felt before—sensations involving pleasure and revulsion. That I still remember the exact words of the passage forty-six years later attests to their power for me. In the following years, I tried to understand why sex would be bad the day before you got married and wonderful the day after. But I was sure it would be true.

So, we Mormon youths thought about sex all the time and felt guilty about our thoughts all the time. In an attempt to protect us from ourselves, church guidelines state that we are not to date until we are sixteen, and necking and petting are taboo. Like most people, young Mormons are not able to adhere to such guidelines, so they are tortured with guilt about their weakness. I was no exception. I dated a few boys steadily, and I liked to make out with them, but I came home from my dates feeling sinful and wretched, full of promises to Heavenly Father and myself that I would not give in to temptation again. Of course, I did. However, I did not have much trouble saying no to actual intercourse and remained a virgin until my wedding night on September 24, 1970, one month after my twentieth birthday.

In spite of all that talk about sex, though, I don't remember anyone at church ever mentioning homosexuality. No invitations were issued to us young people to explore our sexuality. No consideration seemed to be given to the possibility that there might be gays and lesbians among us. The first time I heard the word "homosexual" out loud was from the lips of my mother when I was about fifteen. I danced in a ballet company, and one of our principal dancers was Henry; somehow (the story is hazy), Henry got into trouble with one of his male art students. My mother explained to me that Henry was gay—homosexual. Her explanation was direct and unencumbered, as I recall, by judgment or moralizing. She said some men loved other men and Henry was one of those men. She did not say anything about women, and I would be several years older before I realized women could be gay too. I did not even make the connection between Henry's story and the relationship I had with my friend Sharon when I was thirteen.

For about six months during my eighth-grade year, Sharon and I got together every Friday night. As time went on, we began to pretend we were on a date. One of us would be the boy and one would be the girl. At first one of us would put an arm around the other one, or we held hands, but soon we escalated to making out. Truthfully, Friday nights could not come soon enough for me; if we spent the night together, we slept in the same bed and eventually had all our clothes off. We pretended to have sex, still thinking of one of us as the boy and one of us as the girl. We couldn't really have straight sex of course, and we didn't know girls *could* have sex. In our minds, we were practicing making out for when we had boyfriends and for when we had sex with our husbands. And we were sure we would have the same feelings when we were married to the men of our dreams. We carried on this junior high friendship, punctuated by hot and heavy make-out sessions, but we did not talk about our relationship. And somehow we sensed it was important that no one knew what we were doing. We didn't know about lesbians, but we knew we would be in trouble if anyone caught us. I had some inkling then that I was different, but I could not articulate why I did not fit in, and I certainly did not attribute my difference to my sexual orientation. Years later, after I came out to my parents, my mother admitted that she had never known what to do with me.

In the fall of 1969, when I was a sophomore at the University of Utah, I began dating the man who would be my husband for twenty-three years. Up until he asked me out, he had only dated cheerleaders and sorority girls, so my long blond hair and dancer's body made me exotic; and I think he was as fascinated by my serious, non-bubbly personality as I was by his happy-go-lucky Mormon one. He was the kind of man every Mormon girl wants to marry: former missionary, clean cut, funny, athletic, attentive, cute. He wanted lots of children and he planned to become a dentist so he could support them. He declared his love for me. How could I not marry him? I was almost twenty, the time had come for me to take on the role I had been taught was my destiny, and here was John to marry me. He was a member of the Sigma Chi fraternity, so we got "pinned" in November, became engaged in February of 1970, and married later that year. The path of our relationship did not deviate from the one expected in the Mormon culture, and to any observer, we were the right fit for each other—the perfect couple.

But our dating, and the months leading up to our wedding, were fraught with contention that was soon to be sharpened by the pain of rejection and guilt. After all the positive attention we got on the day of our marriage, I had to get in the car and drive away with my new husband for our honeymoon. Years later, my mother told me she had seen me through the car window, sitting very still, staring straight ahead. I looked trapped. But I don't think she was surprised by that. A few weeks earlier, I had gone to her room, sat on her bed, and told her I wasn't sure I wanted to get married. Her words to me were, "The invitations are out." She believed I was just nervous about the big step I was taking, that I would be fine once the wedding was over. And I wanted desperately to believe that too. I clearly had my doubts or I would not have expressed them to my mother, but I clung to the belief that having sex with my husband once we were married would make me fall in love with him. I wanted to be in love with him—someone who loved me, loved children, lived a faithful Mormon life. Love, marriage, sex—I had been taught these things went together. I had not really experienced a longing for sexual intercourse, but I believed that as soon as I had sex, I would like it and I would be an enthusiastic partner.

After our reception, my new husband and I drove to Park City, Utah, for our first night as husband and wife. My mother had bought me a light-blue negligée, and John and I were both excited to finally experience the big event we had been saving ourselves for. I know it sounds incongruous to say I felt trapped and yet looked forward to having sex, but I was sure I would love sex and therefore all my misgivings about getting married would magically disappear. But we were woefully unprepared. John had not known how babies were made until he was a senior in high school, and the only advice he got about lovemaking was from his older sister: "Take your time." I knew the mechanics of what was going to happen, but nothing about the fine points of pleasure. So, neither of us had any experience—we thought it would just come to us naturally.

What I remember about that night was the darkly paneled, unfamiliar, downstairs room that reminded me of a cheap motel. I remember the physical discomfort, the stickiness and stiffness, the too-bright bathroom light. I was shocked to discover that intercourse hurt, but worse, that it was messy. I lay awake that night as John slept, thinking about the movies I'd seen in which people had sex. In *Butterfield 8*, Elizabeth Taylor just gets up and gets dressed—I didn't see her wipe herself off—and no one had told me I'd have to sleep on the wet side of the bed. No one had told me about the feeling of violation, either. Or the sense of suffocation. Or the stark loneliness of lying under someone while he labors to an ecstatic conclusion in which you have no part except to be the receptacle. We both had all the right parts anatomically, but we did not fit together. There was little sense of "give," of comfort, of rightness. John woke me for sex three more times that night, and I kept thinking of bumper cars. I finally got up, filled the tub with water, and tried to figure out how to hold the douche bag (a gift from my mother) aloft so the Massengill would flow down the tube into my vagina, thus flushing me out. I imagined a lifetime of this distasteful operation. When I was squeaky clean, I dried off and got back into bed. I lay there in the dark, thinking about the life I had made for myself.

Morning finally came and we headed to Jackson Hole, Wyoming. I had convinced myself that after the first experience with sex it would get better, and I was actually looking forward to trying again. The sex didn't get better, though, and the car trip back to Salt Lake City a few days later was long and quiet. We had decided to live in John's parents' house while they were out of the country, so it was there, about a week later, that we had our first conversation about divorce. We stood in his parents' bedroom, their bed between us. I don't remember who brought up the possibility of ending our marriage—I suspect John did in hopes that I would ridicule such a suggestion. When I didn't—I do faintly remember feeling a glimmer of hope—he insisted that we would not break his mother's heart by divorcing, that we had been married in the temple for time and all eternity so divorce was not an option. He pointed out how young we were—he was twenty-two, I was twenty—we were inexperienced newlyweds, but we had a lifetime to learn to make each other happy. Heavenly Father would help us if we honored our temple vows and kept the commandments. I was humbled. I just needed to have more faith, so I resolved to try harder. And every day from then on, I awoke with that resolution.

Six years later, John and I were living in Texas, where he was stationed with the Navy. By then, we had three children, and on the surface, we were a happy little Mormon family. On the outside, I was an exemplary Mormon housewife and homemaker; but deep down, I knew I was trying to compensate for my inadequacies as a mother, and that I was not cut out to be a wife either. John and I had sex about once every three weeks, and I had never had an orgasm except for the occasional one that woke me up from a deep sleep. Understandably, John resented the time and energy I put into cooking, canning, sewing, taking care of the boys, and my church jobs because there was very little left over for him. We were both sure I was frigid, so we decided to do something about my problem. He learned of a Navy psychiatrist who specialized in working with sexually dysfunctional couples, and we began seeing him once a week. During the first session, I learned that many women do not have orgasms with intercourse, and I also learned that I needed to be responsible for my own orgasm. Of course, I did not have a clue about how to take on that responsibility, so to help me, the doctor showed John and me a video of a woman masturbating. I watched in amazement—I had not known women could masturbate, and watching that video was one of the most sexually stimulating experiences I'd had in years.

About a week later, using my memories of the video as a guide, I had sex with myself for the first time and discovered my dormant libido. My body did work! I had believed I was doomed to live my life without ever experiencing the pleasure I was sure everyone else in the world enjoyed. My husband had been away, so I greeted him at the door with the good news, and in the following weeks, I taught him how to help me have an orgasm. We believed we had found the solution to the one obstacle to our married bliss, and we were so confident we decided to have another baby.

We continued to visit the psychiatrist for several months, and in the course of our therapy, the doctor also showed us videos of straight couples making love. I found these less enjoyable and not as sexually stimulating as the video of the woman masturbating, and my husband found them embarrassing, so we discontinued our therapy. Shortly after that, I realized I enjoyed having sex with myself more than I enjoyed having it with my husband. Then I found myself imagining making love with a woman, even though I had never even seen a movie in which two women had sex. For some reason, I remember one day in particular: I was dressed in a denim maternity jumper and red knee socks, standing in the middle of the living room, contemplating driving to Corpus Christi to find a female prostitute. Learning how to have an orgasm had made me begin to think of what turned me on the most, and evidently that was women's bodies. So, the frequency of John's and my lovemaking tapered off, and bedtime once again became fraught with tension, guilt, and, sometimes, anger and recrimination. I consented to sex every few weeks out of guilt and obligation, and I lay there hoping it would be over soon. When we did have sex, I envisioned the woman in the video. I did not share these fantasies with anyone, but for the rest of my marriage, which was about fifteen more years, I fantasized about women when I was fantasizing at all.

By June of 1994, those fifteen years had come and gone, and I began a doctoral program. I was forty-four years old. My husband and I had divorced the previous year, and I felt stronger, smarter, and more beautiful than I had ever felt in my life. I no longer woke up every morning with the loop playing over and over in my head that said, "I'll do better today." On the first day of classes, I walked up the hill to campus feeling powerful. That morning, our linguistics class met for the first time, and I have a clear memory of one member of our cohort, Michele, sitting at a desk after class as the rest of us stood around her talking about our reading list. I also have a clear memory of her looking up at me. She held my gaze for just a second or two. Her eyes were green, and I thought, "I'd like to know this person." Lightning did not strike. The earth did not move. It should have, though. In that instant, my life was changed profoundly and irrevocably.

I was fascinated by Michele—I had never known anyone like her. She swore, smoked Camels, drank bourbon, and told dirty jokes. At one point during that first week, I mentioned I was not getting enough hot water to finish my shower in the morning. Michele offered to check out my water heater—it seems she had been a plumber in another life. Knowing that bit of information was strangely exciting to me, and watching her work on my water heater made me feel something I could not define.

A few nights later, Michele and I met in a fellow student's apartment so the three of us could study. When we finished, Michele and I walked to my apartment (we had decided to share a few textbooks to save money, and she needed one to prepare for class the next day). On the way over, she complained of a backache, so I offered to give her a backrub. We were hitting every cliché in the book, but it all felt fresh and dangerous and exciting to me. She lay on the floor of my apartment, and I sat astride her back, making the massage last as long as I could. It began to rain, then pour, so I suggested she hang around—we could do some work until the weather cleared up. She sat at my desk, ostensibly reading a text about research methods, and I sat on the couch, pretending to read about linguistics. When we heard the rain stop, Michele said she'd better go, and she left. I sat on my bed wondering how I was ever going to get any work done that night. I thought I had seen her writing something in the book she was reading, so I leafed through it hoping to find her handwriting. What I found was a yellow sticky note that read "Hey." I turned pages in a frenzy and found nine more notes. The second said "Kami," and the third read "would." The remaining seven read, one word at a time, "it be intimidating to you if I." I was frantic. "Would it be intimidating to you if I *what?*" Michele had given me her phone number, so I punched it in and she answered immediately. "I need to talk to you," I said with no preliminaries. As soon as I heard "Okay, meet me in the oak grove," I was out the door.

The most famous landmark on the campus is the oak grove, a quad surrounded on three sides by old university buildings, criss-crossed by paths, and populated with huge, old oak trees. I ran most of the way to the grove, and when I got there, I saw Michele entering it from the opposite side. We came together like lovers do in those cheesy movie scenes—the only thing missing was the swelling musical soundtrack. Not one to waste time on small talk, I blurted, "I'm in love with you." She walked me back to my apartment and asked if she could kiss me. I was terrified, but I submitted to a small kiss and then backed away. "That's enough," I said. "I have to think about it." She just gave me a look that implied she knew something I didn't know yet and said, "Okay. We'll see."

The next evening I tried to study before Michele arrived, but it was hopeless, and she and I had no illusions about studying together. She kissed me. I liked it. And then we went to bed. We left the lamp on so we could see each other in its warm light, and as we lay on my favorite patchwork quilt, Michele filled my vision and I thought about nothing else. I admit, though, that the details are not clear—I feel more than I remember. Fear, desire, excitement, wonder. Amazement at how our bodies worked together. Delight in Michele's body, so different from my own. Fascination with the matter-of-factness of her desire, her acceptance of her own body and what she wanted and enjoyed, her lack of shame. Relief that I could enjoy sex with another human being so much. My strongest memory of that night is being held very tightly, and even fifteen years later, being held is still one of the things I love in our physical relationship. Her roundness fit my hollows, her parts matched mine. We didn't spend the night together that night, but inside of a week, we were sleeping together every night, spooned in a single bed.

After Michele left, I forced myself to perform the ordinary ablutions of brushing my teeth and washing my face, even though I was feeling so extraordinary. I tried to sleep, but it was a long night. I didn't think about what would happen the rest of the summer, or, indeed, anytime in the future. I didn't think about whether I was a lesbian. I didn't think about what my family would say if they knew I had had sex with a woman. I didn't think about anything but what making love with Michele felt like and how much I wanted to do it again. I finally slept, but I awoke the same way I awoke every morning for the rest of the summer: after a few seconds of blankness, I remembered Michele and I began to feel as if my body was literally buzzing. I was besotted and I was horny, but I was sure there was something more. I knew it might be best if we thought of our relationship as a summer fling, but I didn't believe that was going to be possible.

We successfully completed that first summer of graduate school, but the added curriculum of learning what it was like to have an active libido, learning how to be a lesbian, and learning how to function when all I wanted to think about was Michele and sex with Michele meant I slept and ate little. I wasn't tired and I wasn't hungry. Life outside the confines of the Mormon Church was good; I felt as if the shell that had encased me had cracked open and fallen away. That summer, I didn't attend church meetings, I didn't pay my tithing, I drank coffee and beer, and I had a lot of sex outside marriage with a woman. But I did not feel miserable, lonely, sinful, or unclean. I felt no shame or remorse. And I knew I would no longer greet each day vowing to try harder to be someone I was not.

Fifteen years later, Michele and I are still together. She is my second sex partner, and she will be my last. We share our birthdays, good friends, a love of reading, an enthusiasm for Coen brothers movies and William Trevor novels, and a preference for staying at home in the evening. We earned graduate degrees in the same field, and we write and teach together. And every night, I fall asleep with my head on her shoulder, or we spoon, using only about half the mattress in our double bed. We fit.

Wanting

Vanessa Fernando

I identified as a heterosexual throughout my growing-up years. In elementary school, I had a crush on a boy named Alec; he had a mushroom cut, red hair, and freckles. I wanted a boy to be nice to me, to call me on the phone and ask how I was doing, to hold my hand.

When I was eleven, I fell in love with my dance teacher. Her name was Kelly; she had a long face and green eyes, and her shiny brown hair fell straight to her shoulders. In class she wore spandex tights and leotards and made us spin and move in unison to Janet Jackson's "The Velvet Rope." At night, I'd lie awake, too strung out with craving to fall asleep.

My diary from that time says, "I don't know what's wrong with me. I keep having all these weird feelings about Kelly, about Jennifer Aniston, about Alicia Keys. There's no way I'm a lesbian. But what's wrong with me?"

I also thought about men. My friends and I ripped sexy photographs of male models out of *CosmoGIRL!* magazine and passed them back and forth. We read Judy Blume's *Forever* when no one was watching, shocked at the thought of a boy naming his penis Ralph. We went online and assumed fake identities, posing as older jezebels ready to give the desperate, leering chat-room men what they had been searching for. In our pop-up chat windows we described our DD-breasts and our long blond hair, doubled over in fits of nervous laughter while confronting our own dubious power.

My friends and I never talked about other girls in the visceral terms we reserved for boys, but we admired them. We saw breasts peeking out of spaghetti-strap tank tops and thongs riding up backsides in the hallways at school. We looked at all the so-called perfect bodies around us, and pretended to be disgusted. "They are all so slutty," we'd say. "Such whores."

I wanted to be beautiful so badly. I wanted to be like those girls, the ones that were tall and thin and could spend all summer at the beach, wearing bikinis, being tossed around in the arms of stringy teenage boys. But I wasn't one of those girls. My skin was darker, and I had to pluck my upper lip, and my stomach didn't look like theirs.

I spent years trying to be the kind of girl a boy would want to toss into the air. I wish I had realized earlier that I didn't want to *be* like those girls so much as I just *wanted* them.

Because opposite-sex partnerships are the institutionalized norm, I never questioned the fact that I was destined to share my life with a man. It just was, independently of my musings, a solid fact like puberty or divorce. I thought about men in the dark fantasies of my childhood, daydreaming about an aggressive male sexuality wanting me, craving me. I fantasized about men's impatience and my power to grant or withhold. It was always about them, about those shadowy men in my mind, even as I masturbated at six years old, rubbing my clit against the corner of the bed, hungry for friction.

Everything began to change once I graduated from high school. Needing time away from my mother's townhouse, I scoured the Internet for "roommate wanted" ads. A month after graduation, I went to meet with Sarah, who lived in a squat white plywood building, two levels with three bedrooms upstairs, nestled close together off a corridor littered with dust and cat hair. The room she showed me was painted hot orange, and crammed with end tables and two broken-down television sets.

Sarah spoke quickly, and when she grinned her two front teeth stood at odds, crooked. Her hair was short, dyed red, and stood up in gelled spikes. Next to her, I felt awkward and too young.

"We'll get everything out of there by the time you move in," she said. And then she leaned against the door, stood there and studied me. Her left eyelid was the slightest bit droopy, and her lips were as dark as her hair, chapped. She wore a white tank top and no bra. I felt too conscious of the way her low-slung breasts pressed against the fabric.

We went into the living room. It used to be a bedroom, and so the space was enclosed, crowded. A small bookshelf stood by the door: *Whores and Other Feminists, The Whole Lesbian Sex Book, The Ethical Slut.* I wanted to ask Sarah if she was a lesbian but my mouth wouldn't open, couldn't form the word. A cat, wide and short-haired, lay on top of the bookcase, licking its genitals.

"Do you mind if I smoke?"

I shook my head, even though I minded. Sarah sat down on a worn, green couch and, twisting sideways, pulled a battered tin from her pocket. The lid creaked as it opened; inside were four hand-rolled cigarettes, the tobacco spilling a little. I watched her fingers shake as she lit it. "Come sit down," she said, looking at me. "We should get to know each other if you'll be living here."

I sat down. She asked me how old I was and I told her. She laughed, then. "Do you have a boyfriend?" she asked me.

"No. We broke up," I said. My first-ever boyfriend had been tall and thin and full of bones too big for his frame. He wore ratty jeans and combat boots and let his hair grow long. When I cut off my hair, stopped shaving my arms, and started preaching feminism, he stopped calling.

"Are you straight?"

I nodded. There was a pause, then, and Sarah smiled as though she knew something I didn't. I looked at the white cat, which had jumped off the bookcase and into my lap.

I thought Sarah was the most intriguing woman in the world, because she kept a larger-than-life Rabbit Habit vibrator propped on her bedside table. It was bubblegum pink and swiveled in circles like a carnival ride.

The sex I'd had by that point was perfunctory and a little painful. I'd take off my shirt and my bra, and then he would be aroused, and maneuver his penis past my labial folds and into my vagina with varying degrees of accuracy. I'd lie back and let him push into me, and after a while he would have an orgasm, and I would lay my head on his collarbone and hope that he'd hold me for a little while before falling asleep. I got some satisfaction out of being desired—I felt, for a moment, like the sylphlike girls I'd admired at the beach—but in the quiet moments afterward I felt empty.

Unlike me, Sarah seemed to have a succession of fascinating lovers. There was Roman, a twentysomething genderqueer with close-cropped blond hair and a septum piercing; and Zana, who left her bicycle chained to the fence outside whenever she spent the night. There were also men who came and left quickly, never staying to chat.

Sarah told me that it was better to spread your abundance of love among many people. This was her philosophy of the world: monogamy wasn't righteous, but selfish. Still, there were moments where I caught glimpses of the complications. There were moments when she was angry. Once, I found her sitting quietly at the bottom of the staircase, and when I sat next to her she said, "All men want is pussy. Cunt is fun; cock is work."

I lived with Sarah and worked at a natural foods store, volunteered on the weekends at the anarchist bookstore, and helped organize a feminist music festival. Everyone I met was polyamorous, or queer, or non-normative in some shape or form. They fled the heterosexual trappings—marriage and 2.5 kids—traded the stereotype for radical resistance, chosen families, and polyamory. I met them and I felt jealous that they had somehow managed to extricate themselves from the conveyor belt model of adult life. I couldn't do it. I couldn't be like them; wasn't them. I still believed in the middle-class cult of romance, of happily ever after, despite my own cynicism.

I cut my hair shorter and wore ripped-and-patched clothes in an effort to become more like them, these untouchable queers with purpose and community. At night, I wrote in my journal about how I could never fit in. I was too young to go to bars, and I'd never slept with a woman. I remembered the night in high school when my friend and I wailed that we wished we could be lesbians, because sometimes being in love with men is the most frustrating thing in the world. We'd looked at each other, a sparkle of tension in the air between us, and laughed it off. "Too bad we're straight."

That August, two months after moving in with Sarah, I followed her to a radical queer gathering on Vancouver Island. For a week, the hundreds of participants functioned as a single organizational body, making decisions in consensus-based meetings and cooking all meals communally. The goal of the festival was to put anarchist theory into practice, and work to create a queer community, decentralizing heterosexuality and allowing for an alternative social structure. At the festival, submerged in an entirely new society, I met Lucy.

Lucy was small, with black hair cut bluntly across her forehead; she wore a peaked cap and tight jeans. Her voice was melodic, coquettish. She called me a "dreamboat" in her Brighton accent. We met while waiting in line for supper; we spent the week together, and by the end we were holding hands. Lucy was twenty-nine years old and pursuing a Ph.D. in women's studies, writing her thesis on gender-neutral pronouns. I couldn't believe the way she looked at me—softly, the way I used to look at my boyfriend. She batted her eyelashes and purred at me; it made me feel so masculine, so desired, so in control. I didn't know what to do with the power Lucy gave me.

On the last day of the festival, Lucy left me a note saying that she wanted a kiss goodbye. I was terrified. I contemplated hiding, but before I had the chance I saw her, standing at the edge of the festival grounds with a friend. She was wearing a shirt patterned with tiny hearts. Our eyes met, and we drew together. I pulled her in for a hug, so conscious of the fine bones beneath her skin, savoring the feeling of this stranger now pressed close against me. As we came out of the hug, I leaned close and we kissed; it felt so natural that I was relieved. Lucy looked naughty and interested. The girlish, flirty way she looked at me still felt alien, unexpected. I felt dizzy, drugged. I wanted to move my hands all over her body. I loved, more than anything, the feeling of freedom, of moving through time and space without chains or walls, and just enjoying all the infinite possibilities of being together in that one, simple moment.

I don't want to give the impression that I began to love and desire women because I was imitating Sarah or Lucy. In all honesty, I don't know what shifted. I wouldn't define myself as one of those lesbians who knew since childhood the "truth" about her sexual orientation. But I do feel that I defined myself as a heterosexual because the society in which I grew up never affirmed the other parts of me. I was able to play the heterosexual game. I was able to dress myself up, to play the role of attractive, available female, and so I never let myself experience the vast expanse of my own sexual desire until I found myself in incredibly new territory, where love, relationships, sex, self-definition, gender, and identity became much more multi-dimensional than I would ever have expected.

Today, three years later, I am with the most amazing person in the world. She identifies as a woman, as a lesbian, but I don't think of her in gendered terms. To me, she is my partner in crime. She has a masculine presentation, in the sense that she feels most comfortable wearing clothing tailored for men, and my mother always asks me if this means that she is the man in our relationship. My mother doesn't seem to understand that sex and gender are completely different things, and that dichotomous gender roles do not operate in our relationship.

Occasionally, however, I feel uncomfortable that my gender presentation tends to be more feminine. I wonder if I am dressing this way because it is how I truly feel comfortable, or whether I am still trying to play the role of the desirable girl, suppressing my own wants in order to play the femme to my partner's butch. Am I still trying to be that girl on the beach from my adolescence, beautiful because she is wanted? But then I remind myself that nothing is so simple, and that outward appearances often obscure complex truths. This relationship is unlike anything I have experienced before because of the emphasis my partner and I both place on communication. I now feel comfortable saying no, and saying yes. I am capable, for the first time, of being clear if I am not enjoying a certain sexual act; of articulating my needs; of setting boundaries; of exploring my sexuality in a context that feels safe.

My experience identifying as a heterosexual was always about trying to be the kind of woman I believed would appeal to men. I wanted to be the "right kind of woman": white, skinny, able-bodied, and hungry, with high cheekbones and pursed lips. Now that I identify as queer and am in a relationship with a woman, however, I feel more comfortable expressing and experiencing my own desire. It's true that my current relationship is not affirmed by mainstream society the way it was when I was dating men; my current partner and I are two women of color who love and sexually desire one another, and because of this we frequently attract hostile glances and comments. But existing outside of the heterosexual Hollywood romance script also has the potential to be empowering, because it allows us to live by our own standards, and redefine romance and courtship to suit our own needs. I may not be the "right kind of woman" in society's eyes because I am mixed-race, queer, and don't believe in the binary sex/gender system, but I much prefer living on the margins of "respectability" to the alternative of suppressing my desires, my needs, and my voice. Living as a whole person, and learning to accept my own messy contradictions, is not only politically powerful, but much more sexually satisfying.

Watershed

Veronica Masen

*I*t was dark in the kitchen; the party was loud on the other side of the closed door. We leaned toward each other and I slid my hands up the nape of her neck, into her hair, holding the back of her head, this woman I had known only a short while but with whom I had been flirting shamelessly all night. Our eyes locked, her lips parted and tipped toward mine, and my knees literally went weak. There was a full two- or three-second pause (which feels like forever when you're about to kiss a girl for the very first time, and you're thirty-seven years old, and you have wanted this your whole life, and here she is *right here in your hands*, and it's really going to happen, it's not a dream this time) during which I just let myself revel in the delicious thought of *you're about to do it*. Finally. After all this time, all those men, all that longing, all that want and curiosity and fantasy and imagining: *here she is*. Now. Feel it? Feel your heart slamming against your chest? Feel her breath, slow and shuddery? Feel her cheek brush yours? A little closer. There. Closer. Her lips, on yours; yours, on hers. So soft—a mouth like velvet. The tongue—delicate, polite. Her skin—no stubble, no roughness. My hand slid down her body, her waist, her curves, and came to rest on her hip—no roughness anywhere, no hard, no angles. All soft.

I'm home.

I almost fainted.

That was a year ago.

A year of therapy and tears and sex and kisses and books and arguments and sleepless nights and angst and long phone calls and more passion than I ever knew existed. A year of falling down a rabbit hole, of peeling off my skin, of being thrown off my axis, or any one of a dozen other phrases that would still never come close to describing what it's like to have your whole existence shaken upside down and called into question. It's been a year of wondering and discovering and poking and prodding at my soul, my belief system, my fear, my desires, my identity. I have laughed harder, loved deeper, and cried more this year than any other time in my life. I have wondered if I have finally discovered my true sexuality, or am simply going through my own late-bloomer experimentation phase that everyone else went through in college while I was dutifully studying and living off-campus. I have asked myself the following questions a million times a day, every day: Am I gay? Or is it just her? What should I do? What now? What next? What if? What if I stay married, and stifle my inner lesbian (who, now that I have let her come out and play, might not want to go back inside)? My husband is the greatest guy in the world—what if I break up our family over a temporary sexual revolution and regret it forever? My commitment to our marriage is strong; my desire to provide security, consistency, and dependability to our children is even stronger. How would I feel about myself if I threw all that away for a kiss? But what if it's the most incredible kiss in the whole world? What if it's a kiss that woke up my whole being, made me believe in all the sappy love songs and fireworks and fairy tales? What if I can no longer even contemplate kissing my husband, let alone allow our naked bodies to entangle the way hers and mine have? What if now that seems so wrong, so icky, so intrusive?

Then what?

It really was something I had wanted to do my whole life. Some girls dream of big frothy wedding dresses, traveling the world, skydiving, or having babies. Me? I wanted to kiss a girl.

And by "wanted to kiss," I mean that when I was with boys, I thought of girls. Always have. When I had sex for the first time at sixteen, I closed my eyes to block out the six-pack abs, broad shoulders, and chiseled jaw of the boy on top of me. The drunken escapades and one-night stands of my youth? There was never any desire for the person himself. There was the thrill of being a little trashy and a little rebellious, of racking up a reputation, of throwing it back at them, of letting them know we can be just as crude and uncaring as they can—but there was never the lust that I would hear my friends talk about. When they were oohing and aahing over the volleyball scene in *Top Gun*, I was thinking of Kelly McGillis with her pencil-skirt and clipboard and tousled bedhead hair. (I know. That plus the fact that I later drove a Subaru and listened to the Indigo Girls should have tipped me off.) I have *always* thought the female body was much more beautiful than the male; I have *always* been far more turned on by our magical, slippery little orchid than by their—what *is* that? A puppet? Some sort of sea creature? I have never had an orgasm with a male without thinking of a female. I have never had an orgasm from intercourse. I have faked orgasms to make it be over. When I have had an orgasm with a man, it's usually because I've taken over and done it myself. And it's always easier with my eyes closed, when I can pretend his fingers or mouth are a woman's. I am not turned on by looking at them, their hairy chests, their shape, their size. And don't get me started on testicles—are we really supposed to find those attractive?

You'd think I would have put these pieces together and found me a woman. It's not like I lived in some uptight part of the country. It was Greenwich Village. In the '80s. Everyone was doing everyone and everything, and there was no judgment and much freedom. I had always been a part of the performing arts culture, a world peppered with experimentation and avant-garde practices of all kinds—I may have even been among the minority in the circles in which I traveled: a mousy little hetero pixie surrounded by big Cuban bulldykes and smooth-waxed pretty boys. But I thought that since I lacked the sort of brazen knowledge about my sexuality that they possessed, since I wasn't *sure*, that I must, by default, be straight. That if I *knew*, I would *know*. And since I didn't *know*, I must not be. I didn't have any internalized homophobia, I wasn't worried about what others would think, I just didn't want to be an imposter. I didn't want to take something so real and so personal and trivialize it by trying it on like a costume. I didn't want to use another person as a science experiment or a sex object. I didn't want to take it lightly. I heard the way recreational fence-jumpers were talked about, and it wasn't always pleasant. "Gay" was something you knew in your heart and felt in your bones and would fight to the death for. Something you earned, something you *were*, not something you did, or claimed to be just because you wonder sometimes, just because you find women aesthetically beautiful, just because you feel so much more yourself when you're hanging around with lesbians than with straight women.

I thought sexual orientation was hardwired. Honestly. I didn't get that it could change. Of course I was aware of places, families, or religions where homosexuality was not tolerated (or worse), so I understood why some people stay closeted—but I truly believed that coming out later in life was more a choice to reveal something known, not the unexpected appearance of something new. Most of my gay friends had always known they were gay whether they had spent any time in the closet or not; hence my assumption that people who came out after leading a heterosexual life always *knew* they were gay but denied it (either to themselves or others). Somehow I made it to adulthood without understanding that one could *not know*, that one could speculate and ponder but not conclude, or that one could find one's self all grown up and suddenly in love—or lust, or some combination of the two—with someone of the same sex, and be just as surprised as everybody else that they are, now, as gay as the day is long.

I remember, when I was about twenty years old, telling a lesbian friend of mine that I didn't want to "try it" because I might "like it too much." She gave me The Look (if she had worn reading glasses she would have peered over the top of them) and said, "Honey, it's sex. I think we're *supposed* to like it too much." We had a brief conversation about self-deprivation, self-worth, and why I would deny myself unbearable pleasure. I didn't have any answers then, but now I can see how deep the "I don't deserve happiness" groove is carved into my heart. And that's where the work is now—it's not about sex, it's about love; and it's not about loving *her* or *him*, it's about *me*.

But back to the sex.

If that first kiss almost made me faint, you can imagine what happened the first time I touched her. Or she me. Our first several weeks can only be described as "furtive": there were lots of stolen moments, lots of groping and grinding and grabbing that took place in stairwells and bathrooms and movie theaters, and it was a full two months of these clandestine trysts before we spent our first night together, before we were able to lie naked together, to shower together, to wake up together, to take our time, to slow down and breathe each other in. Everything about her delighted me, and vice-versa. We played with each other's long hair, we traced the lines in our palms, we massaged feet and legs and backs, we made love quickly and slowly and roughly and gently, over and over and over, and I knew I would never tire of it. Though it embarrassed her at first, I loved to lie on my tummy between her legs, open her a little and gaze; alternately licking and looking, entranced by the beauty, amazed by the power and the ache of the desire I felt.

She was so . . . womanly. An hourglass figure, a way of putting on lipstick, lace-trimmed underthings, quick to laugh, quick to cry. I watched as she did her hair and makeup the morning after that first night, and felt like those old photos of the little boys backstage watching the women in the dressing room roll their stockings on. She pointed out that I had the same big-eyed look as them, and asked if I felt about twelve. I said that I did. She nodded, knowingly. She was a couple years older than I was and had been out for quite some time, and while we tried to avoid the teacher-student dynamic, sometimes it appeared in the form of a nod or a look that said she knew what I was feeling, how exhilarating it was to finally be setting that part of me free, what she meant to me.

However, just because she was older and wiser and had been the "top" in her past relationships, didn't mean that I became meek or subservient in ours. We vied for top, and she got to discover the pleasure of yielding, submitting, surrendering. She allowed me to flip her over, to get her on her knees, to let me wear the strap-on in the family—all new things for her. We became sexual playgrounds for one another, exploring, discovering, coloring so far out of the lines that we were making whole new pictures. We gave each other the gift of complete trust, and not just sexually: our hearts, our little spirits, fell in love mind-body-soul. She was a best friend, a confidant, a partner. We could speak volumes just by silently staring into each other's eyes. Hot bubble baths, handheld walks through the park at night in the snow, dessert dates. Private jokes were endless. Orgasms came fast and furious for both of us. "Intense" is an understatement. We were on fire. It was like we were the only two people in the world when we were together; nothing else mattered, nothing else existed.

But that quickly became a problem.

Because things did exist, and they were big things, and I was neglecting them. Two children. A home business. A marriage. A house. My parents. My siblings. My garden. My dogs. My own self-care. I started to feel guilty, sketchy—always hiding, sneaking, making up reasons to go out for the night, emailing her from the train on the days I commuted into the city, bringing the phone into the bathroom with me while I got ready in the morning and talking in hushed whispers under the white noise of the running water. I started to hate the feeling of always covering my tracks. I started to worry about getting caught. I started to tire of the double life. I was on an emotional rollercoaster, but not so much one with ups and downs as one with dizzying spins and inversions and sheer drops. After several months of holding on for dear life, I knew it was time to start making some choices and went about the hard work of cross-examining my sexuality and figuring out what this was: a fling, an awakening, a one-time romp in the hay, or the beginning of a whole new life. I was terrified, but ready to roll up my sleeves and unearth my truth.

So I did what any good soul-searcher does: I headed for the Internet.

I looked up everything I could find online and discovered a ton of resources: I ordered books; I read blogs, articles, and medical journals; I joined a chat room; I connected with a therapist who specializes in women coming out later in life (who herself had been through the same thing), and found a weekly group for married women coming to terms with their gayness (apparently we're everywhere).

I arrived at my first therapy session with tears brimming in my eyes before I even knocked on the door, tears that flowed freely as I spilled my story. She sat before me, this impish mini-lesbian with silver hair cropped close to her head, wisdom and peace emanating from her like a guru, tiny quick mannerisms belying her seventy-plus years of age. She listened with rapt attention, jotted down some notes, and when I was through telling her everything, she leaned forward and said to me, with the faintest almost-wink of a smile, as if we shared a delicious and enchanting little secret:

"Startling, isn't it?"

Indeed.

From there, we dove into my past and inspected my present (I couldn't do future just yet). For a while I was fixated on figuring out if I had always been gay but just never acted on it, if this dalliance was an isolated incident, or if I had undergone some sort of a mid-life shift. Eventually I realized I could make a case for any of those explanations, but ultimately it didn't matter if it had taken the train or a town car. It's arrived, and what am I going to do about it?

Motivated by the guilt brought on by secret-keeping, my husband wondering why I was so moody, and my lover's growing discomfort with my being married and closeted, *What am I going to do about it?* rapidly became *How do I tell my husband?*

And so one night after the kids were sound asleep, I turned off the TV, turned to face him, and told him exactly what my anguish and distance had been about. I told him I was really confused because I still loved him, but not in *that way*, and had no idea what this meant for me or for us. He wasn't mad, and he wasn't shocked. He was understanding and kind and supportive, and instead of heading straight to blame and resentment, we talked about how to move forward from here. Was the marriage over? Or was it just redefined? If so, as what? Did we want an open marriage, or a polyamorous arrangement, or a don't ask/don't tell policy? Did my questioning mean we needed to file for divorce immediately? Did "sexual fluidity" mean that I had cruised over to the other side and might just as easily cruise back someday? He made it clear that he didn't want me to deny or stifle my true self, but that he was just as committed to the non-breakup of our family as I was, and asked if it was possible for these things to exist in harmony, and if so, how? He started therapy. He found a straight-spouse support group, went every week, and created his own network of men in the same situation. We had not been physically intimate for a long time anyway; we agreed to stay that way indefinitely. We had been married nearly seventeen years by then—neither of us wanted to do anything impulsive, and both of us wanted to exhaust every possibility before calling it quits, if that was what needed to happen (which we weren't even sure was the answer).

Meanwhile, I started comparing—not so much her to him, but my life the way it was presently versus what it would be like with her. I started examining that relationship with a critical eye, and found myself thinking: Do I really want to leave *this* for *that?* Was I willing to trade no sex and stability for great sex and instability? She was fun, but not terribly reliable. She was successful and wealthy, but not happy. She was physically attractive, but not spiritually sound. There was a demanding, controlling quality to her that made me feel resentful and rebellious. I didn't like her all-or-nothing attitude about our relationship and she didn't like my not coming out more fully, not leaving my marriage faster, or my need for time and space. She was jealous of my business, my dogs, my children, and my husband. She refused to come to my home because of those things; and I was tired of traveling the hour-plus to hers. Eventually we went from feeling like we had our own secret club to feeling like we were speaking different languages.

The stress and pain of living in secrecy and uncertainty was taking its toll on her and me, our trust, our sanity. When one person is waiting alone on the sidelines tapping her watch and the other has a life so full she feels like she's going to burst, emotions go horribly awry. Over the course of the year we went from the bliss of new love to the tedium of a long, drawn-out breakup between two inherently incompatible people. As I pulled back, she held tighter, and we spiraled into a cycle of push/pull, break up/get back together, ultimatums, misunderstandings, and drama after drama after drama. Finally it ran out of steam, but instead of sadness I felt freedom.

So now I am in limbo. I am celibate, and introspective, and shell-shocked. I would love to have waited until I had a more popular, less ambiguous ending to write my story, to be able to say, "and now I've left my marriage and have a girlfriend and I'm happier than ever!" or "and then I fell in love with my husband all over again and I'm happier than ever!" I would love to be able to tell you that I have all the answers, or at least a definition or a label for my sexuality. There are days I know I am a lesbian, that I always have been and always will be, but for now I am choosing not to honor that part of myself purely out of a sense of responsibility and loyalty to my family. There are flashes of doubt, when I wonder if she was just a really good seducer (she has a pattern of going after married women, and bragged about her "conversion rate") and I was in a ready place to do some exploration. There are times I think she was the great love of my life, and other times I thank my lucky stars I didn't leave the security of my home for the passion of her bed. There are brief moments that I still wonder if my attraction to women was something dormant that came to life, or something brand-new that showed up when she did. (Like I said, "brief." There is too much evidence pointing more toward *dormant* than *new*, and I know that if I were to find myself single, it would be women I would seek out, not men.)

Today my inner world is a maelstrom of anger and sorrow and loss and relief and chaos as I sort out what it all means. But I don't have any regrets. Sometimes I feel a happy bittersweet-sad, as if I had been perfectly content with my cup of Folgers every morning (really—it was fine), and then one day I was handed the most delectable, creamy Caffé Vita breve latte, granules of brown sugar melting into the thick velvety foam, served in a gorgeous Italian china mug with handmade almond biscotti on the side—a delightful gift, but one that renders the Folgers, in comparison, pretty much undrinkable. So the sadness is more of a Smokey Robinson "a taste of honey is worse than none at all" wistful, nostalgic sadness than an emptiness or a grief. It's a feeling that brings me both gratitude and heartache.

On my more melancholy days, I long for the ignorant girl who could swig that black coffee out of a Styrofoam cup and think nothing of it. On my more hopeful days, I know there is a world of designer espresso drinks that I will make my way back to someday. On my still-confused days, I put the whole drink order far back on the shelf and let myself awaken naturally, at my own pace, without trying to decide what I want, what I can or can't have, what I should do, what I want to do, which is better, what I'm willing to fight for, and—these have been the two most interesting questions of the year—what I can live with, and what I can't live without.

Over the Fence

Audrey Bilger

I was thirty-four when I jumped the fence. I didn't put it that way
at the time and only learned this phrase a few months later, when
a friend told me a male colleague had used it to ask her if that's what
had happened—if I'd become a lesbian. At first it seemed like a crass
expression. Were heterosexual women kept behind chain-links? Was there
a line between straight and gay that could only be crossed by leaping?
Having lived as a lesbian for a decade and a half now, I understand better
where the metaphor comes from. Mainstream culture likes to see things in
black and white, with barricades to maintain order and stability. A straight
woman who leaves the fold disrupts the pattern and must chart a new
course. She has to put up her own guideposts and decide which directions
to take.

My adult life so far divides evenly between two marriages and two
ways of being a wife. When I got married the first time, I wanted to make
an honest woman of myself. I had moved in with this man, and marriage
seemed like the way to get back in the good graces of my community. The

second time I married, having lived with my wife-to-be for eleven years, very little in the culture supported our union; in fact, forces were conspiring to eliminate this right. The clock was ticking on Proposition 8—the ballot initiative that would amend the California constitution to ban same-sex marriage—and we had a limited amount of time to get legally hitched. Different sets of pressures at radically different moments in history.

As I've discovered, marriage is never a purely personal matter between two people only (regardless of their genders). It always involves external approval—a license—from the state, and there are actual barriers erected to keep people in their place. Happily ever after may be out of your control. But if you can learn to jump a fence or two, you might find, as I did, your way to a better life.

"Why buy the cow if you can get the milk for free?"

This is what my mother said to me on the phone when I announced, in the spring of 1981, that I was moving in with my boyfriend. It's one thing when you hear a cliché like this as a snide piece of gossip about someone else. It's quite another when you get it from your own mother.

I thought I had to get married. The cultural script at the time—in Oklahoma, at least, which is where I lived then—said that male/female couples ought only to cohabit after they had signed on the dotted line. That's why when my future husband and I got an apartment together, less than a year after we first met, we told everyone we were planning to marry. Soon.

I was twenty years old. I had graduated from a rural high school. Many of my peers were already married. Only a handful went on to college. My family believed firmly in a standard script with assigned gender roles. Girls did household chores; boys did yard work. In terms of marriage, one of my friends' mothers used to put it this way: the husband makes the living, the wife makes the living worthwhile. You got married. You had children. You lived in a house with material goods that signified your level of success. My grandfathers on both sides had been coal miners in West Virginia, and, as first-generation members of the middle class, my parents took social mores seriously.

Conventions can be unbelievably powerful, especially when you're young. The idea that when you meet a man and form an attachment you ought to get married was so firmly entrenched in my worldview that I didn't question it. I ignored warning signs—we failed a compatibility test we took as part of our marriage preparation classes, and we thought that was funny—and focused on the things we had in common. We were philosophy majors, and we were both passionate about music. I loved exploring his seemingly vast record collection, and we were at our best when we talked about ideas or listened to tunes.

I debated whether to keep my own name, and we considered hyphenation. In 1980s Oklahoma, all the women I knew had changed their names, and I worried that having different names might be complicated. I decided to make the change. Once you take your husband's family name, however, you have to confront the dreaded M-R-S. Being called Mrs. made me feel stripped of an individual identity. At the same time, in some circles, I experienced a sense of privilege that accompanied the status of being a straight wife, a membership in a club with other women who had similarly found spouses and who felt proud to have done so. I would eventually come to embrace Ms. as my preferred honorific, but since I shared a name with my husband, there was really no way to enforce this, and I found that few people responded well when I corrected them on it.

The early years of this marriage involved numerous negotiations with the status quo. We liked the idea of gender parity and generally saw one another as equals. It was hard, though, to separate housework from a gendered base. I did the cooking and laundry. We agreed at a certain point that he would do dishes. Even though he was perfectly comfortable doing things like vacuuming floors or cleaning toilets, people would tell me I was lucky to have a husband who "helped out" around the house.

When you're in a heterosexual marriage, everyone takes an interest in your reproductive life. The longer you're married without children, the ruder the questions get about why you haven't had any yet. Married straight couples who don't want kids are viewed with suspicion. We had a good story for the first few years. We both started a Ph.D. program in English in the mid-1980s, and we said we wouldn't have time or money for children until we finished up. Being in school gave us a temporary license to opt out of the baby game, and thanks to birth control, we had a choice.

In my studies, I specialized in women's fiction and joined a faculty/student reading group that met on late afternoons in lounges on campus to talk about feminist theory and the newly emerging field of Women's Studies. I analyzed women's historical oppression and reconsidered the world in relation to gender inequities and other interlocking structures of power and control. As a girl growing up in Oklahoma during the 1970s, my only contact with feminism had been my teachers' expressed horror at the Equal Rights Amendment. (Men and women would have to share public bathrooms! Women would be drafted!) Feminists, I had been taught, were hostile, angry, unpleasant women. Now I understood that feminists were viewed that way by people who didn't like the questions they asked.

Toward the end of graduate school, I pulled ahead of my husband. I finished my dissertation before he did, went on the job market, and took a visiting faculty position at Oberlin College. Once I became the primary earner, he and I reconfigured our domestic world. He started taking on more roles traditionally identified with women. He cleaned, cooked, and shopped for groceries. I taught full-time and went through the stress of ongoing job-hunting, conference participation, and getting articles published. We began to feel an asymmetry in our separate spheres and joked at times about his role as househusband.

In the last movement of our marriage, we moved to California, where I had accepted a tenure-track job. Gender issues loomed large in my work life because the small private college where I worked turned out to be extremely conservative, and there were relatively few female faculty members. When I received a hand-lettered invitation to a college-sponsored event addressed to "Mr. and Mrs. [His name] Bilger," I wrote a polite note asking not to be subsumed under my husband's name. I couldn't believe my claim to a professional title—Professor or Doctor, I had earned them both—would be erased by my employer and that my husband would be given top billing. Imagine my surprise when I got back a petulant note from the wife of the president, who had addressed the invites herself, condescendingly explaining that on formal occasions, I'd best get used to being "Mrs." What had initially seemed like a gauche oversight, a throwback to the pre-1970s, now became the writing on the wall. My job would entail many such unpleasant encounters—with administrators, colleagues, and even students—and this put a strain on my home life.

When I wasn't dealing with problems at work and the demands that came with being an untenured professor, I had other things to keep me busy. While living in Ohio, for recreation, I had learned to play drums. Next to books and writing, music was still an important part of my life, so when I got out West, I helped put together an all-female blues band. Our lead guitarist was (insert drum roll here) a lesbian. She was more than that, of course, but for the purpose of my story, she was the Catalyst.

If this woman were a man, you would say she was a player. And just like the stereotypical male on the prowl, she enjoyed the challenge of seducing straight women. She didn't necessarily want to keep them once she got them, but she loved the pursuit. I'm not saying I was helpless in the face of her prowess, but she did a number of things that made me feel desired and desirable, and at that time in my life, I wasn't getting this kind of attention anywhere else. I fell for her. Hard. I was like an irresponsible teenager. We started seeing more of each other. We played music together. We went running on the track. Step by step, she pried me away from my marriage. I went willingly. As the pursuer, this woman had a masculine energy but she wasn't a man. She put the moves on me, but because she was a woman, this didn't feel like aggression.

In other words, I jumped that fence. Here's how it felt at the time: like my eyes were opened to things I hadn't seen before. When I began to accept to the possibility of being with a woman, I saw the advantages. The intimacy dance was less about seeking commonalities across a gulf of difference than about figuring out how to manage wavelengths and frequencies that were fundamentally similar.

I broke up my marriage. I contended (and to a certain extent believed in the moment) that this was my true nature, that I'd always been closer to women than to men, and that I was fulfilling a kind of destiny. I hadn't felt explicit desire for women before this, but I didn't look too closely at discordant elements in the story because it helped to justify my exit from the marriage. By focusing solely on my shift in sexuality as the barrier that came between us, my ex and I avoided examining the many other things that ought to have separated us sooner.

The day my soon-to-be-ex-husband finished loading his things— including most of the large record collection we had amassed together over the years—into a van and drove away, the woman came over to survey the damage. She said she couldn't stick around right then because her "ex-girlfriend" needed her help. It didn't take long before I learned that this girlfriend was still in the picture and that I was going to be the *other* woman. Suffice it to say, that didn't work out.

In the aftermath of two almost-simultaneous painful breakups, I paused to get my bearings. At this point, I might have crawled back over that fence. Doing so would have certainly been the path of least resistance. I had been warned against being out at work before I got tenure, and it wasn't easy being a closeted lesbian at a school that was, at that time, antifeminist and, in some corners, deeply homophobic. I had already caught the attention of my coworkers—like the one who tried to find out from my friend if I'd turned gay—and had I started dating men, they probably would have just talked about this as a passing phase. Or, I might have recast myself as bisexual—one of a group commonly identified in derogatory terms as "fence-sitters" by a culture that likes to believe there are only two sides to the sexuality story. I could have played the field(s) and taken stock of my options.

In this suspended and in-between phase, I met Cheryl and found my true compass and sense of direction. We tell the story of how we met as if it were mythic—Meant To Be. We were both playing in bands. She's a fierce rhythm guitar player, and proficient, as she likes to say, in "things with strings." I was still with my blues band (we were on our third guitarist at this point). We got a gig at a bookstore where we hadn't played before, and so two of my band mates and I went there one night to see another band we had heard was good and to check out the scene. We stood in the back, trying to figure out whether we'd need to adjust our sound levels for this room and making comparisons between our band and this one.

The female lead singer held center stage, but I found my gaze moving to the left, where the real force behind the band pounded out chords. Cheryl was dynamic; she played and sang with such passion and intensity, I couldn't look away. There were two other players: a male drummer, and a guy who played violin and mandolin. I kept my eye on the guitarist. At the break, I went up and talked to her. I told her we'd be playing there next weekend. I was trying to figure out if she was gay or straight. It seemed like we were flirting, but I couldn't be sure. She laughed at the idea of playing loud music in a bookstore and said something about being careful not to disturb the dictionary-browsers that made me laugh right back. I stayed for the whole show but didn't have the nerve to approach her again after they were done.

The following Saturday, when I saw her from the stage as I played my drums, I was elated. I kept asking my band mates if they thought she might be attracted to me. They were pretty sure she was. Cheryl played it cool and said she was just coming to check out the music, but it wasn't long before I knew—and she will occasionally confess when we recount this tale—she came back for me.

I probably would have married Cheryl right away had that been an option. We started building a life together from our first date on. One thing that works for us as a couple, I think, is that we're in different fields—so we each bring something of our own to the table—but we complement each other and share a set of core values. At my house, when I showed

her what was left of the record collection and told her there was much I
missed, she assured me I would get back everything I had lost. As luck
would have it, she's a collector by vocation, a record producer in the music
business, and her collection even then was by far much bigger than the
one my ex carted off—and it's grown exponentially over the years. She, in
turn, couldn't believe her good fortune in meeting a woman who actually
cared so much about records. To make things even sweeter, we found that
we had remarkably similar taste in music. She's a whip-smart historian of
tunes—a walking encyclopedia with a detailed knowledge of artists, bands,
and records across all genres. The preservation and archive work that she
engages in is actually quite similar to academic endeavors. I learn from
her, and she opens my ears to new sounds. She's also a talented writer,
with a regard for the written word that matches my own. We both have
deep respect for what the other person does, and we always root for one
another to be as creative, motivated, and energized as possible.

In terms of gender roles, I'm definitely more of a femme, whereas
she inclines toward masculine qualities—in a rock 'n' roll kind of way. I
like dresses, makeup, and heels. She prefers jeans, tour T-shirts, and
sneakers. She's athletic. I throw like a girl. We tease each other about our
differences, but they don't become barriers between us. At first it troubled
her that my name hearkens back to my failed marriage, but I believe I've
made it my own, and she understands. She doesn't want me to take her
name, something she might very well ask if she were a he.

Quite frequently I forget we're in a socially stigmatized group. We live
in greater Los Angeles, a place where same-sex couples don't stand out as
much as they do in other parts of the country. When we're out in public,
though—whether for a walk in our neighborhood or on a city street—if we
hold hands or show affection, we have to be aware of our surroundings.
An approaching car or stranger can feel hostile. Because I spent so much
of my life unconsciously benefiting from heterosexual privilege—and
because when I'm out on my own I am probably perceived as straight,
as femmes often are—I continue to be surprised and deeply wounded by
disgusted looks and the occasional comments when they occur. Straight

couples, when they attract attention at all, tend to be applauded and celebrated. Mostly, they're invisible, just part of the way things are.

Same-sex couples like us have to fight to claim the privileges straight ones typically take for granted. Just getting people to take you seriously as a couple can be a challenge. On more than one occasion, Cheryl has had to deal with men who want to know if I have a boyfriend because they think I'm straight—I'm not with a man, so I must be single. The labels available to us when we first got together didn't help. Acquaintances might identify us as roommates or friends, and it was often hard to tell whether people fully got the reality of our connection. Even those who said girlfriend, partner, or life partner often seemed to do so in scare quotes. Coming out was a seemingly endless process.

We've committed to one another in a variety of ways. The year after we met, we exchanged wedding bands we've worn ever since. We contemplated a ceremony but couldn't decide what such an event would add to our relationship. When San Francisco issued same-sex marriage licenses in 2004, we decided against taking the plunge because it seemed improbable that these unions would withstand dissolution—they didn't— and we didn't want to ride that roller coaster. The next year, the state of California granted virtually all the legal rights of marriage to domestic partners, and we registered as such. This gave us tax benefits, and required a bit of paperwork, but otherwise, it wasn't such a big deal. It seemed like a separate-and-partially-equal category.

In 2008, during that brief window when same-sex marriage was declared legal here in California, we finally tied the knot. We were too busy doing what we do best to put time into wedding planning; and with our large circle of friends, there was no way to imagine a simple ceremony. Having gone through that drill once before, and having given much thought to the way the Wedding Industrial Complex puts couples through their paces, I didn't see the point in making too big a fuss over the display. Marriage, I knew from long experience, takes place in the details of everyday life. We signed papers across the table from our minister friend and his husband, and then went to see the movie *Mamma Mia*.

Among the many perks of being a married couple, getting to claim the word "wife" is a daily source of pride. Not only is it far preferable to labels like "partner," "girlfriend," and "lover," it instantly clarifies our status when we refer to one another out in the world. When I say "my wife" to someone I've just met, it's like coming out on speed—they have to get it right away. I've also noticed a profound shift in how I think of the meaning of "wife." Whereas when I was married to a man, the word seemed like the necessarily subordinate half of a male/female-oriented binary, now it is much more powerful—not genderless, but unmoored from a system that privileges men—and, on a day-to-day basis, it's a cause for celebration. In many ways, I'm more of a wife to Cheryl than I was to my ex-husband, and she's more of a husband to me than he was (although I don't use that word to describe her). I do most of the cooking and take pleasure in tending to and nurturing her. She manages our budget and keeps the house in check. She has a job that puts her out in the world more than mine; I'm happiest when I'm working at home. She makes more money and gets greater recognition for her work than I do (she's a two-time Grammy nominee), and she moves in circles of powerful and influential people, where I'm often identified as a "plus one." Yet I don't feel diminished by such things that in a heterosexual marriage might be viewed as just par for the course if she were in fact a man. Her power and status aren't the by-product of gender—the music business is still an old boy's club—and our household interactions revolve around decided preferences and skill sets, rather than prescribed traditional roles.

In an interview I conducted with the English novelist Jeanette Winterson for *The Paris Review* in the late '90s, I asked her to talk about heterosexuality versus lesbianism. "Men," she said, "can really get in the way when you are trying to sort out your life and get on with it. Because they just take up so much space." She continued, "There was a part of me which instinctively knew that in order to be able to pursue my life, which was going to be hard anyway, I would be much better off, either on my own or with a woman. A man would simply get in the way, and I would have to use up energy that I didn't have to spare." In my experience, being with a woman does create more space for my life's adventure, and gives me more energy than I felt when I lived with a man. Even though men are the ones with cultural power and prestige, women are expected to support and protect the male ego in the home. Cheryl and I don't follow that script. We're more fully partners. We run alongside one another.

Thanks to the California Supreme Court decision that upheld marriages performed in 2008 before Proposition 8 took effect, I'm legally married with a wife of my own, and every time we say "wife," Cheryl and I feel proud and affirmed. We've moved beyond the fences that restrict individuals to pre-ordained roles. Lesbian marriages like ours defy outdated notions of women's inferiority to men. We elevate the word "wife" from its subordinate status and transform it into a badge of honor.

Leap of Faith

Libbie Miller

"**H**ey, lady! How are ya?" asks Lori, my perfectly coiffed hairdresser. She bears a striking resemblance to a young Loni Anderson.

"I'm all right. Could be better, could be worse," I reply.

"Just all right? That's the best you can muster?" she teases. Both Lori and I hail from Middle America, where steak and corn are dinnertime staples, and conversation is honest and straightforward. Lori has no trouble filling the conversational space that transpires over a cut and color session. "You know, not once have you ever said you're doing great, or even good," she says. The inflection of her voice changes from carefree to deeply concerned and her volume drops considerably. She circles from the back of the chair, removing the mirror from our discussion, and grabs the armrests of my chair as she looks me right in the eyes. "Are you depressed, Libbie?" I make incoherent noises, meant to be the beginnings of an appropriate response, but I'm coming up empty as I squirm awkwardly in my chair, looking around for the nearest possible escape. A lump rises in my throat as I feel wetness permeate the corners of my eyes. My face reddens as I realize I'm about to cry . . . in public. I flounder for a response that doesn't come. Her delicate, manicured hands rise to her mouth as she slowly shakes her head and says, "Oh, Libbie. I'm so sorry, sweetie." I'm quiet, and so is she, for the duration of my appointment, although my head is swimming with thoughts.

Ballsy, Lori. Ballsy indeed, but dead on, I think to myself as I start my car's engine. It took a blond, size 4, Loni Anderson look-alike to point out the obvious: something I knew was there but dared not address. But now I have no choice. The lid is off and the contents are leaking out uncontrollably. It's time to confront this thing once and for all. I can't continue to ride along as a complacent passenger to my own life. I can see the edge of the cliff that drops into the unknown. I can't keep backing away. And so here comes the burning question. The question that scares the living shit out of me every time it floats to the surface, only to be quickly squelched by something else. Anything else. Ice cream, that marked-down Crate & Barrel sofa, whether I need to pick up dog food. Anything that doesn't start the question with "am" and end in "lesbian."

Inappropriate Things

I remember one day walking through Omaha's Westroads Mall, at the age of fourteen, when my mother and I passed two women holding hands as they peered into a Benetton store window display. We stared at them as we approached and passed them by. My mother hissed, "My God. Get a room," loud enough for only me to hear. I stared at my mother blankly. "It makes me sick to see those people being so inappropriate in public places . . . out there for everyone to see," she said, with such contempt in her voice that it still chills me to the bone. In that moment I wanted to ask her why two women holding hands was any different than a man and a woman holding hands, but instead, I remained quiet and just kept walking.

Sure, my mother mentioned gay male friends of hers who were hairdressers, or fun, flamboyant coworkers every now and then, but not once did I ever hear her use the word "lesbian." Being a lesbian was unfathomable. I was raised in a conservative household; homosexuality was about as far from appropriate as you could get. Though gay men seemed harmless, even humorous, providing the color to some of my mother's more entertaining stories, lesbians were another subject entirely. They were far too inappropriate to recognize, let alone talk about.

The moment in the mall was about as much as she'd ever said, but it was more than enough for me to understand that being a lesbian was a vulgar thing. And that moment is undoubtedly the reason my mother stepped in to create distance between Karen, my best friend in high school, and me. I shared a more intense connection with her than anyone I'd ever known.

I lived to make Karen happy, and wanted to be around her as much as I possibly could. We spent almost every day after school in her bedroom listening to Dave Matthews Band, Bush, Candlebox, Oasis . . . the list goes on. Karen's love for alternative music sparked my own; a passion that still lives in me to this day. We talked about the prettiest girls in school, and obsessed about Craig, Karen's crush, as we lay side-by-side in her bed, slowly rubbing each other's arms in what we called "tickle-scratchies." "Do my back?" she requested one day as she removed her Phish T-shirt, rolled onto her stomach, and reached behind to unlatch her bra. With my hands trembling and my heart racing I reached for her beautiful naked back, taking in the warm glow of her olive skin. "You can sit on my legs if you want," she said as her big brown eyes met mine. There was a Fourth of July fireworks celebration happening in my underpants. It was exhilarating . . . and dangerous.

I didn't spend much time dwelling on what those afternoons with Karen meant. I knew they touched on the borders of highly risqué behavior, but that made it even more exciting. The intensity of the time we spent together was only matched by the secrecy surrounding those afternoons in her bedroom. We never discussed it with anyone else, not even to this day. I just knew that it was the one thing I looked forward to as I watched my seventh-period classroom's clock hover on 3:00 PM, and thought of how I would die if she ever stopped inviting me over to her house after school. My mother didn't know what was happening during those afternoons in Karen's bedroom, but she knew I was with her when I wasn't at home. "I think you're spending far too much time with Karen. It's unhealthy to be so attached to another girl," my mother said. Her face flashed a look of absolute disgust—the same one I saw three years earlier that day at the mall. And it was the same look of disgust I would see many years later after I came out to her—the look permanently burned on my brain whenever I think of that intensely uncomfortable, nakedly vulnerable visit. Her disapproval catalyzed a crippling, ominous filter in my mind that remained well into my adulthood. It caught daydreams that meandered to the surface before they could settle into the fabric of my thoughts. These daydreams and questions had lurked in the shadows of my mind for so long, but went no further.

'Til Death Do Us Part

I caught Eric's eye the summer following high school graduation while on vacation in Myrtle Beach. He was a Marine to his core. He loved being a Marine, was raised in a Southern family, and came from a long line of soldiers. He was driven by his need to protect those he loved, was proud of his chosen field, and was as loyal as anyone I've ever known.

We spent our first night together just talking, asking one another question after question about our hometowns, what our parents were like, pivotal life moments, and anything else we could uncover while exploring the possibility of a connection. I could see that there was so much pain underneath his bright and upbeat exterior. He spoke slowly and softly, proceeding as cautiously as a gravel truck during an ice storm, when he told me he had joined the Marines soon after his brother had taken his own life. Even though we shared so much of ourselves so quickly, I could tell that revealing this truth was not easy.

"I'm really never this open with anyone," he said, shaking his head in disbelief as though he was as much talking to himself as he was to me. "Ask any of my friends . . . family even. I'm usually the most guarded guy around, but something about you just makes me want to tell you everything, and I rarely tell anyone anything." This was the moment I chose to stay with him—this damaged person who was genuinely good, and deserved an amazing life full of happiness. He trusted me, and that felt like a gift. It felt like a changing of the guard. He was handing me his heart and now it was up to me to protect it. To keep it safe. Happy. Loved. I accepted his gift and committed myself to becoming everything that he needed me to be.

I was **eighteen** and Eric was barely twenty-one. Friends, family, and countless others said, "You two are way too young to be getting married. You need to slow down and do some growing up together." Naive and optimistic, we stood firm in our commitment to proving everyone wrong. The belief that we wouldn't make it was the catalyst that pushed us down the aisle. We were resolute in our commitment to proving to everyone that young, lasting love was possible.

Euphoria and elation carried both of us through the first six months, and by year's end, we were rolling through the drive-thru wedding chapel in Las Vegas, exchanging "I do's" with the same irreverence you might have ordering a #2 Value Meal at McDonald's. This seemed like a good idea at the time—romantic and exciting, even. A cynic might suggest, though, if you can't bring yourselves to get out of the car to declare your undying eternal love, you probably have no business saying "I do" in the first place.

So This Is Marriage . . .

I was completely content with Eric, and happy with our relationship. I was his everything. He was my comfort. Laughter was plentiful for him, as I never failed to deliver the perfectly timed punch line. I planned every trip we took with the precision and clarity that could only be matched by the most seasoned of cruise directors. I orchestrated the joyous moments of our life so he need only sit back and enjoy the ride.

He was a warm blanket in my life. He could talk me down off of my neurotic ledge when I was convinced our three golden retrievers would find a way to leap out of the back of our 4Runner and into oncoming traffic. He had the longest eyelashes of anyone I had ever seen—and was so secure in his own masculinity that he even let me apply my Clinique lash-lengthening mascara to them on one occasion. He indulged my gluttonous nature, too. Every Saturday morning, I knew I'd be awakened by the smell of cinnamon rolls, fresh out of the air-compressed Pillsbury canister.

Over the course of eleven years we experienced many things. We got our first dog together. We said tearful, gut-wrenching airport good-byes each time he left for yet another seven-month deployment; sealing our bond and pacifying the loneliness with countless letters, emails, and care packages. We bought and designed our first real home together—one that didn't have a plastic outdoor patio set standing in as a formal dining room table.

We became best friends over those years. We both knew that intimacy was an important piece of the equation—essential, actually—but we shoved it under the rug for a good while and tried not to dwell on it. We were so good everywhere else. Everywhere but the bedroom. I truly felt in my heart that a great friendship was enough to carry us to the very end. Perhaps I clung to this false conviction more than Eric did.

In the first years of our marriage, he was always the initiator of sex. The idea of it never excited me. I would have preferred to skip it altogether and fast-forward to cuddling. When he realized this, he pushed me on the issue. "Why is it that I'm always the one nudging us into the bedroom?" he asked flatly one afternoon. It was a Sunday afternoon—one without any obligations and perfect for a lazy afternoon of lovemaking. I could feel my face growing red with embarrassment, and my defenses rose. It was a fair question that deserved a thoughtful, truthful answer. But I couldn't give one.

"That's not true," I said. "I initiate."

"Name one time," he demanded. My mind was empty, and hurt by his accusation.

"I'm just not . . . "

He cut me off. "Not that sexual, I know! That's bullshit," he said.

From that point forward, I did my best to show my gratitude for his love—even invited him to the bedroom once each week—but he saw this as more of a chore for me, like sweeping the kitchen. And it was. He loved me so effortlessly and genuinely. I loved him the best I could, but loving someone and being in love are two different things.

The Search for Answers

Why didn't I want to make love to my husband? The answer was there, trying to peek out, but I still wasn't ready to discover it. I wanted so badly for things to fall into place, for the answers to come. But the courage wasn't there. Not yet.

During Eric's third deployment, I was confronted with an uncomfortable amount of alone time. I found myself spending countless hours researching message boards, online articles, and shopping the unlimited Internet marketplace for books on sexuality, thinking I'd find the answer once and for all and put this nagging lesbian suspicion away for good. The Internet became my most trusted confidant. It was there that I met a nameless, faceless lesbian, and engaged in a one-night stand of sorts, letting our keyboards take us in any direction we wanted. I came to life in a way I hadn't ever before with Eric. I felt parts of my body awaken for the first time. And what blew me away was that I could feel this way without even physically touching this woman. The sheer thought of being with her was stronger than anything I'd ever felt before in the presence of my own husband. It exhilarated me, and broke my heart all at once.

The day he returned from that deployment, I told him I had something to confess. He sat on the bed and looked up at me with his big, brown, kind eyes. "Tell me," he said as he gently grabbed my hands. There was a softness to his face that wrapped around me like a warm winter sweater and told me that somehow it would be okay. "I had cyber-sex one time while you were gone . . . with a woman." He stared at me as I stared back. I had spoken of Karen before, so this wasn't the first time he'd heard news of this nature. He decided not to push for details. Neither of us had the courage to address what we both knew was there. My secret was out on the table. Together, we reattached the lid to the box neither of us wanted to open.

Confronting Reality . . . Finally

Thirteen years into a military career, four reenlistments, and four deployments later, we found ourselves parked on the couch of a warm and friendly marriage counselor who coddled us in our admissions and cajoled us into reaching a compromise. Six sessions in I said, "I can't deal with the military and the endless separations anymore."

His reply? "I can't get out. I just can't do it."

I think in therapy this is what's called the "a-ha" moment. A heavy sadness blanketed us in that small room. We walked to the car together in silence. We sat down and clicked our seatbelts, and I stared at my lap while he turned the ignition. "Where do we go from here?" I asked, searching his face for an assurance that was no longer there.

His eyes slowly rose to meet mine as he said softly, "I don't know, Lib. I honestly don't know." We both knew in that moment that our shared vacation planning, days spent in the park with dogs, mornings opening Christmas presents together . . . everything that involved "us," was dangerously close to becoming a distant memory.

When Eric packed to leave that night for his fourth deployment, neither of us knew what to say or how to act. The relationship—or more accurately, the friendship—had dulled to a point unrecognizable to both of us. We were different people. We hadn't been living in the same house for almost a year due to the fact that he'd been relocated to California and I opted to stay in Phoenix. We no longer shared the end-of-day moments like most couples. I had friends he'd never met or even heard of. As I walked him into the airport, like I had so many times before, tears were not in my eyes, nor were they in his. We no longer felt like Eric and Libbie—the kids who met in Myrtle Beach more than a decade before. We were just two people who happened to share a stack of bills and a hefty mortgage.

There was a suffocating heaviness in both of our hearts, but not because he was leaving. It was because "we" were already gone.

"Be safe and call me when you get there," I said.

Five years earlier, in the same scenario, I would have demanded, between giant sobs, that he call me at every possible chance.

He nodded in assurance.

"Don't forget to feed the dogs when you get home," he said. It was my turn to nod.

Five years earlier he would have smiled at me and said he'd be thinking of me every second.

"I guess that's everything?" I said as he pulled down his last large sea bag.

Before, he would have held me in his arms and told me repeatedly that he loved me with all of his heart while he stroked my hair and I soaked his shirt with my tears.

"Yep," he said. For the first time we didn't know what to do. Do we kiss? Not wanting to force something that just wasn't there, he pulled me in and we hugged. It was the last hug we would ever share as husband and wife. We both knew it.

Soon after, there were scheduled phone calls and emails as there had been all those times before, but they were far less frequent and included the bare minimum of details. I shared with him that I had decided to take up playing guitar. He let me know that he was doing really well in his Fantasy Football League. We were skimming the surface of one another's lives.

With nothing but time, it's hard to continue to suppress everything you've refuted since you were young. I found myself thinking often of my high school days and the afternoons spent in Karen's bedroom. I retraced my virtual one-night stand repeatedly—reflecting on the words we used, the imagery we created as our bodies intertwined. I allowed myself some much-awaited latitude. I let my mind dwell on the feelings that created a barrier to a successful marriage with a good man. I entertained the thoughts I knew would be challenging for my friends and family to accept, especially my mother. I considered the emotions that seemed foreign to me but were stronger than anything I'd ever felt. My daydreams were daring—pressing on soft lips, meandering down the inviting curves of a faceless woman with a beautiful body.

"I get the feeling that something is up with you," Eric says over the phone with an undeniable tinge of concern in his voice, like he's bracing for something we both know but are afraid to confront.

I breathe in heavily, gathering every last bit of my courage. *So this is it. This is the moment that changes everything,* I think to myself before opening my mouth to say, "There's something that's been weighing heavily on me, for a very long time, longer than I can even remember." *Choose your words carefully, Libbie. Be delicate with his heart,* I remind myself. "I know saying this will affect the both of us in a way that is irreversible, which is why I've been hesitant to even think it, let alone say it," I say, buying time with awkward utterances as my voice quivers. I feel myself teetering over the edge of a cliff. My subconscious is screaming at me to *just say it already, woman!* as my conscious mind begins to pace around the sharp edges of the steep drop.

Silence ensues until he chimes in, "Are you there?" I run to the edge and take my leap of faith that's been patiently waiting in the wings for as long as I can remember.

"I . . . I think I'm attracted to women," I whisper. "I think I'm gay, Eric. Oh my god, I'm so sorry. I'm so very, very sorry." I feel my face grow hot instantly as tears begin to well up in the corners of my eyes. Silence. "Are you there?" I ask desperately. "Eric?"

"I'm here," he says. "There's no reason to be sorry," he says, choosing his next words with meticulous sensitivity. I sit down on the couch to steady my shaky legs. "Here's the deal . . . I just want you to be happy. Life is way too short to not live truthfully," he says.

His immediate acceptance is shocking.

"Are you surprised? Are you okay?!"

"I'm not surprised," he says. I reflect back to each and every Sunday night he went to bed while I slithered secretly into my *L Word* world; the confession I'd made to him one year prior; the story of Karen and me that I shared with him one night after two bottles of wine; the look on Karen's face when she first met Eric.

"We're going to be fine," he assures me.

"I love you," I say, and mean it.

"I love you, too," he says from the other end, thousands of miles away in the Iraqi desert. We hang up and I fall to the ground. It's done. Relief. I say it out loud for the very first time. "I'm a lesbian."

Awakenings: Navigating the Spaces between In and Out

Jeanette LeBlanc

Dear Abby,

Sometimes I fantasize about the girl down the hall in my dorm. Does that mean I'm gay?

Signed,

Confused in California

Dear Confused in California,

Fantasies are normal, a safe way of releasing and exploring our feelings. Having a same-sex fantasy does not mean you are a lesbian.

Signed,

Dear Abby

Whew. Relief. As long as "Dear Abby," or *Seventeen* magazine, or *Cosmo* said it was normal, then it was normal and I was okay.

In a college full of boys, he is a man. We leave the smoky bar, with its blaring dance music and beat-up pool tables, and go back to my room. We lie on opposite ends of my creaky little twin bed and talk all night long. By the light of a votive candle we explore hopes and dreams and wishes and fears. As the hours pass, we inch closer and closer together until I can feel his breath on my cheek.

Sometime near dawn the thick glass of the candleholder finally gets too hot, and it explodes with a loud snap that slices through the silence in the dark room. Somewhere around the same time, we kiss.

It is that kiss that makes me fall in love.

The year after college, I met Susan one night in a bar with my fiancé and his school friends. We connected over our shared history in dance. I was immediately entranced, but when I was with her, I might as well have been invisible. Boys stared, girls stared, and I became the loyal sidekick. She was beautiful back then, incredibly so. She had long hair, light brown with flecks of gold, and it spiraled around her face in corkscrew curls—a Pre-Raphaelite goddess.

I hadn't thought about her in years.

Walking through a parking lot I heard someone call my name and looked up to see an unfamiliar woman walking toward me.

"It's Susan . . . Susan Cookson."

I felt a rush of relief as time melted away and I recognized the girl I once knew in the face of the woman she has become. We filled a few moments with the awkward chitchat of once casual friends who were now all but strangers. Then, as she walked away, it all came rushing back.

I wanted to be close to her. I didn't fully understand it and was frightened by it, but I was drawn to her. I would have never dared give voice to these feelings outside of the darkest and safest corners of my soul, but I thought about her, dreamed about her, fantasized about her—illicit daydreams that stirred me in ways I was far too scared to fully contemplate.

She wasn't the first. She wouldn't be the last. In bed that night I remembered woman after woman. Different ages, different places, different feelings; all memories I had tucked away and never dared revisit. They filled me up and spilled over one another until I wanted to run, fast and hard and far, until my mind was quiet again.

I knew with utter certainty that no matter what happened, everything was going to change, and I was afraid.

Rebecca always had a power over me. I am aware of it, am wary of it. We are both masters of words, enjoy the power inherent in interactions that tantalize but never cross the line. I'm playing with fire, but pretend that I am safe.

One night we go out with a few friends. The food is sensual: crusty bread with savory brie, sweet fig and crisp green apples, organic greens with a tart vinaigrette, earthy red wine. We drink more at a nearby bar, fizzy peach drinks that dance in my mouth. We all go back to her place to swim. It's almost dawn, and the water is cool.

We swim, splash, float under the desert moon. After a hot day and a long night, it is bliss to slip through the water. Later we sit on the edge of the pool, she says something sarcastic, and I laugh, reach up, and briefly twine my fingers through the back of her long curtain of hair. I pull my hand away quickly. Something about this touch is too intimate and I know it.

A few days later at dinner she asks, bluntly. Is there an attraction?

I cling to my heterosexuality, use it as a shield. I want desperately for it to be the truth that will save me from all of this. I've never had much of a poker face, and as she holds my gaze from across the table, I see my truth and my panic mirrored in equal measure in her eyes.

We leave the restaurant and return to her office. We sit close to one another on the edge of the futon where her clients sit, and we talk in hushed voices. My head pounds with the magnitude of this night. I cannot focus on the words passing between us, but I know that our hands will eventually connect. This is dangerous, but I cannot seem to make myself walk away. Nothing more transpires between us, but the feeling of her thumb grazing my palm feels more erotic and more forbidden than any sexual encounter I have ever had.

The next day there is a harshly written email; she is withdrawing from my life. In my backyard, I lean back against the weathered wooden fence and sobs roll through my body.

Later that night in our bed, he holds me for hours as I cry. Without question or expectation, he cradles me in his arms and lets my grief and fear pour out of me until the pillow is soaked with my tears. And at the end of all that, so filled with love and gratitude for the man who is my husband, what choice do I have but to trust?

And so I tell him. Everything.

⌒⌒

Sean was leaving a local bar when the car pulled up. A young man got out of the car, the slur "faggot" flying from his mouth, an echo of the punch thrown by his hands. The fury behind that blow broke bones, and Sean flew back, fast and hard, against the pavement. The force of the impact caused his brain to ricochet inside his skull, separating from the brainstem. As Sean lay still on the pavement, the young man got back in his car and drove away.

Later, the assailant left a message for Sean's friend: "You tell your faggot friend that when he wakes up he owes me $500 for my broken hand."

Sean never got the message. He died.

My body is shaking. Bile rises in my throat and I feel dizzy, flushed, like I'm going to be sick. My eyes are stinging with trapped tears. I can't breathe, can't even see straight. The room blurs in a reaction so visceral and intense that it takes over my body and mind. I'm not prepared for it, don't know how to recover, so I sit there reeling as a new and heavy sort of knowledge settles over me.

I sat on my sofa, laptop in my lap, and read Sean's story, found by happenstance while browsing the Internet. Up until now, I had existed safely within the protective bubble of heterosexual privilege. It's wasn't the first time, of course, that I'd read a story like this. In the past I felt sadness, confusion, even outrage. But I felt it all from a distance, with a tacit understanding that that particular sort of hate was not reserved for people like me.

There was no distance now. I felt the hatred brand me, heard the words ringing in my ears, absorbed that sense of undesirable otherness into the deepest reaches of my soul.

And in that moment, Sean's story became a part of my own.

"Are you straight?"

I'm standing in line at the bathroom of a random bar. I don't know her, wasn't expecting anyone to talk to me here.

I pause for a second, raise my head, and look her in the eyes.

I reply, quietly and firmly, "No. No I'm not."

I can close my eyes and see her kneeling over me, looking down with intensity. Dark spiked hair, guarded blue eyes hiding years of hurt under a tough facade, freckled shoulders, multiple tattoos, pierced lip and tongue. Her hard edges and soft curves beckon me; make me want to know more. She is different from everything I have ever known.

I hear my heart pounding in my ears. Her small flat palm traces a slow, gentle path across my stomach, making me suck my breath deep into my core. My body is responding in ways I could not have imagined.

I don't think I breathed again until morning.

That night, under her hands, I meet my body for the first time. I know, in that first instant, that I will never be the same. For hours upon hours I become fiercely alive, exist in my skin in a way I have never before experienced. Every sensation is heightened to a level of such intensity that I react on a level beyond physical, beyond mental, beyond emotional. I am beyond.

Ani DiFranco is playing, on continuous repeat, through the speakers in the ceiling. The music becomes the soundtrack of my awakening; the rhythms knit themselves into my expanding soul.

come here
stand in front of the light
stand still
so I can see your silhouette
I hope
you have got all night
'cause I'm not done looking at you yet

I know that I will never hear that song again without being taken back to this night, to the sweat and the sounds, the twisting current and the sense of perfect clarity in the midst of total disorientation.

There is a rawness and urgency that would have been frightening if it were not so perfectly, instinctively natural. There is no hesitation, no nervousness. The energy flows through me as if it always has.

Everything in my life has spiraled to this exact point in time. Spiraled to a point as sharp as the blade of a sword that slices into my skin and leaves the thinnest line of blood-red desire.

There are no spaces between us. The universe is spinning faster and faster, and so is my head. I taste salt on her skin. No world exists outside this room and I am lost and I am found, over and over and over again. I am dizzy with the newness and exquisite familiarity. My soul has already been here, I understand that now, it has just been waiting for me to find my way back.

She is trouble. I know it from the first moment I see her. She is trouble and she wants me and I should run far and fast in the opposite direction.

I need this. I need this to not be gentle. I need to be reckless. I need to be off balance. I need. I need. I need.

In random moments it floods back without warning. Like a quick punch in the gut I remember all that I have done, all that has been lost. The pain is so fierce I question how much I can take. And I wonder, will I ever feel whole and complete again?

I already find it hard to remember so much. The last time I kissed my husband. The last time we made love. All the other seemingly inconsequential moments that usually pass by unnoticed.

What about the last time we took the kids to the park? The last time we put groceries in the same cart? What was the last movie we watched together? Where did we go the last time we rode together in the car? When did we last say, "I love you"? When did I last lay my head against his chest and feel peace?

I don't know the answer to any of these questions, and sometimes I want to scream.

I didn't mean for any of this to happen.

When did it end? Was there one specific final moment, or just a combination of lasts too numerous to count? If I had known that none of those things would happen again, how much longer would I have held on?

The psychic's twinkling eyes and lilting British accent keep me mesmerized as I tentatively give him my birth date and lay my hands, palms up, on the table between us.

"The key is forgiveness," he says. "You must forgive him for not being all that you need, and he must forgive you for not being all that he needs."

And when I express my fears that he had moved into this new relationship before truly dealing with the end of our marriage he replies, "Ah, but he's happy now. Isn't that enough?"

I think it has to be.

"What are your fantasies?"

We are lying nestled together in bed. We fit so perfectly that I forget she hasn't always been with me and doesn't already know the answers to all the questions. My mind is blank, and I am surprised to find myself without a response.

I pull my eyes away from hers and look down at our bodies, a tangle of limbs atop a white down duvet. My eyes run across the smooth expanse of her back, her strong shoulders, the curve of her breasts, that perfectly formed space between her ribs and her hips. I lift my gaze once again to her golden brown eyes, and as my hand traces a path along her arm I am in awe at the almost unreal softness of her skin. I interlace my fingers with hers and experience a wave of deep contentment and a rush of exhilaration so interconnected that they feel like a single emotion.

This breathtaking sweetness and lightness—this is exactly what I wanted for so many years. It's what I longed for, ached for, dreamed about, yearned to experience. Until recently I didn't even let myself imagine that I could possibly live this, that it could ever be real. But it is real—aside from the births of my children, it is the most true and honest thing I have ever done.

Lying here with this woman (who somehow found me despite the fact that I wasn't looking and was determined not to open myself to possibility)—

this goes far beyond anything I could have imagined or dreamed or hoped for.

"This. This is my fantasy."

And I lay my head against her shoulder, close my eyes, and breathe in the utter perfection of this moment.

I am on the floor of my bedroom closet. It is midnight and I keep the door closed so the sounds of my sobs will not be heard by anyone in the small two-bedroom apartment we now call home. Hot tears slide down my cheeks and emotions shake my body. I cry not just for tonight and tomorrow, but for all the countless moments of our lives when we will not be together. I cry for the reality that my daughters will forever be moving between two places, instead of resting securely in one. I cry for him and all that he has lost in the wake of my truth. I cry because the costs are so much higher than anyone could have possibly imagined. Self-pity, grief, and endless, all consuming guilt. It is a vicious combination.

It is Christmas Eve. Today I will say goodbye to my girls and send them back to the house that never had a chance to become my home. When I kiss them goodbye I'll know that I won't be the one to help them put out cookies and milk for Santa. I won't be there to remind them to include a carrot for the poor overworked reindeer. I won't tuck them into bed, and kiss them on the nose and recite from memory the familiar words of "'Twas the Night Before Christmas."

I won't be with them in the morning. I won't see them open the presents I bought to fill their stockings, or see their reactions when they tear into their gift from Santa. I won't hear their squeals of excitement or witness that gleam of magic in their eyes.

When the unraveling begins there is no way to predict where you'll end up when the vortex finally ceases. You know, of course, that there will be collateral damage, but even the most somber imaginings don't have the power to pull you from the necessity of just taking one more breath, one more step, of getting through just one more day.

If even the smallest of actions can alter the course of a lifetime, what of those that fracture a family? And what if you are the one who faced the truth, spoke the words, made the choice?

What then?

And so this is Christmas . . . and it won't ever be the same again. But within the changes, within the loss, within the grief, perhaps there is beauty to be found, gifts of a different kind, wholeness hiding amidst the broken pieces.

All I can do is hope.

"Was it worth it?" she asks.

I get emails like this on a fairly regular basis. Other women in circumstances like mine; struggling to navigate seemingly impossible situations; trying to minimize pain and hurt; fighting for wholeness in a world broken by our own actions.

Each of these is a treasure, evidence of the validity of my experience, a hand outstretched through the darkness, to say I've been there. I am there. I'm going there.

Some offer reassurance. Others desperately seek it. All of them say, in one way or another, I find my own experience within yours, and there is comfort—at least some small measure—in that. After all, what do we all want but to know that we do not stand alone?

Was it worth it?

I do not respond for almost a month, and when I do, I still don't have an answer.

How do I tell her I don't think there is any way to know for sure?

"What are you thinking?"

Scenes slide by outside the car window, blurring into one another. I see it all without taking any of it in.

She always knows almost instantaneously when I slip into that space where memories live.

I don't ever know how to answer her.

How can it feel for her, I wonder, when every adult memory I have involves us or includes him? She must notice how often my stories begin with "he did," or "we went," or "he always."

One-third of my life spent by his side. Sometimes it feels like those are the only memories I have.

It is midnight when it slams into me again, stealing me from sleep. I creep out of bed and go out into the living room, into the dark quiet where the tears flow freely.

I open my laptop. I need to look at our wedding photos, but the screen blurs within seconds. I can't remember what his arms felt like, can't recapture the essence of what we were together. I am struck by the thought that I won't know what his hand will feel like in mine when we're both eighty years old, and somehow—in the moment—this feels like the biggest tragedy of all.

There is a hole in my heart where he is supposed to be.

I always thought that regret was reserved for those who made mistakes. The rightness of this choice does not ease the ache in my heart tonight. I miss him, desperately so. I try to be quiet so she can sleep, but my grief overtakes me. The sobs rip through my body, until I am gasping, choking, the fierceness of this pain taking me by surprise even after all these months.

She opens the bedroom door and comes to the couch. Without a word, she leans my body forward and slips in behind me, pulling me back against her chest. She whispers in my ear, smoothes my hair.

"It's okay to cry. I have been in this place, and I know this pain. I will stay until you get to the other side."

She holds me and rocks me and I am amazed. It cannot be easy to comfort the woman you love now while she grieves the loss of the man she loved then.

"What was it like for you when you left? How did you feel? How did you cope? How many nights did you cry?"

Then I ask her the one question I most need answered—hoping that because she walked this path a full seven years before me that I will find solace and hope in her response.

"When will I feel whole again?"

She shifts her body to face mine. Through the pitch black of the room I can tell her eyes are locked on mine.

"It is my experience that you will never feel fully whole again."

Although it is not the answer I wanted, it is the first that has made sense. Perhaps it is in the acceptance of this truth that I will finally find some fragment of peace.

<hr />

We dance in the kitchen, our bare feet sticking to the floor where my daughter spilled a glass of orange juice this morning. The music is faint and we are surrounded by half-filled boxes, and open cupboards, and a life turned topsy-turvy upside down. We've been packing and lifting and moving for days and we're so aching and exhausted that we're giddy.

But still, we dance, and whisper, and kiss. She tilts her head back and smiles, that quirky half-smile that melts me every time. I look at her and realize something is different now; something has changed. Suddenly, I know what it is. I am here with her, fully present, in this reality. This now. This life.

Our life.

A few weeks ago I was struck with a powerful vision. It stayed with me long enough that I could record it in the battered black fabric journal that has held so much of this story.

I was holding something small, cradling it in the palm of my hand, and feeling filled with love and bittersweet nostalgia. The object was heavy and warm and egg-shaped, and I was wrapping it carefully and tenderly in something very soft. With all the gentleness in the world, I tucked it away in a very protected and private space. This thing would always ache, but I knew that I didn't need it anymore, that I could care for it without keeping it close.

Tonight I finally understand what the vision represented. The object that I tucked away with so much love was the part of my heart and soul that lived in the past. The part that belonged to him and us, and the life we had together. It is time to move on, to give myself a chance to live fully, to open my heart and to step into our future.

And so I smile back to her, burrow my head into the curve of her neck, and we keep on dancing.

⌒◇⌒

It's not a one-shot deal, this coming-out business. Extracting yourself from a cocoon takes time, fierce resolve, a willingness to be exquisitely vulnerable. It feels safer to stay in the space you're used to, cramped and dark but familiar. Everyone sees that inspiring transformation from caterpillar to butterfly, but did you know that the process of unfurling your wings hurts like hell?

You step out of your familiar, comfortable life into the vast, uncharted territory of another. You step with intention into that wide-open space, turn your face to the sky, throw your arms and your eyes and your heart wide open and just pray you've got enough grace to accept all that comes.

You just stand there, more exposed than you ever thought possible, and say, "This is my truth."

It has been the most liberating and the most shattering of experiences. I am free, soaring high, authentic and true, and I am broken, on my knees, sobbing tears that flow without end. I am both more than and less than I was before.

This Love Is Messy

Amanda V. Mead

I blame Angelina Jolie. If it weren't for her, I would have stayed blissfully oblivious. But she had those lips, the kind that send your blood rushing south at the thought of them pressed against your own. This was precisely the image that brought me to orgasm every time my fiancé's head was between my thighs. I thought it was perfectly normal then, and I would still agree that sexual fantasies of celebrities are normal—whether they are hetero- or homosexual. However, it occurred to me that I hadn't orgasmed without said image for years, if ever.

One afternoon when I was about twenty, I tried desperately not to think about Angelina Jolie, or her godforsaken lips. I tried to think of my partner, male celebrities, male coworkers, all to no avail. I could not come! I finally gave in to my fantasy and found sweet relief. As time went on, I questioned the fantasy. Was it about Angelina Jolie? Was it about the unattainable? Was it about taking sexual risks? Was it about being with a woman? I tried each hypothesis, gathering data in hopes of coming to a logical conclusion. I substituted other female celebrities, and it still worked.

Then I began to substitute the celebrities with women I knew, or strangers I saw in cafés or walking down the street. The common denominator was women. This scared the bejesus out of me. I asked myself the question I couldn't answer for another five years.

When I was a little girl I loved playing with dolls, dressing up, and dreamed of becoming an actress or a singer. I was also one tough cookie, with a few dust-ups under my belt to prove it. I swore like a sailor and was an honest-to-goodness born feminist. I stuck out like a sore thumb in my tiny town in northeastern Montana. I remember never feeling like I fit in. I wasn't cool enough, nerdy enough, athletic enough, or bad enough to fit into any of those particular groups. I was always one step behind when it came to trends, until I finally gave up and turned to baggy jeans and flannel shirts. I usually ended up injured whenever I attempted a sport. And even though I was considered smart, the only subject I really excelled at was English. I was often described as boy-crazy. I used to buy those magazines like *BOP* and *Teen* and paste the pictures of tween boys all over my room. I was also well-known for being loud and goofy, and completely unafraid. Behind the flamboyant façade was a girl traumatized by family dysfunction. This contradiction translated into intense anger during my teen years. I was a complete mess. However, I managed to keep myself together just enough to get by, because I had one solid thing to hold on to: my best friend.

Since third grade, Carol and I were inseparable. She was with me through my blackest days, and in return I was fiercely protective. She was sensitive and sweet, a vulnerable thing to be in adolescence, and I felt it my duty to keep her from harm. I recall one particular incident in junior high—a boy made fun of her for sitting in the front of math class. I was frantically searching my perpetually messy locker for homework when she came running toward me, bawling her eyes out. She tearfully explained the situation, which instantly sent me raging into the classroom. I grabbed that boy by the scruff of his neck and threatened to beat him within an inch of his life if he ever insulted her in that way again. Carol stood in the corner, still weepy, with the strangest expression on her face; it was somewhere between embarrassment, pride, and awe.

It should have been no surprise then that the other students began to whisper about us, especially me. Earlier in the year a new girl arrived at school, and I immediately befriended her. When Misty stayed the night at my house, I showed her the nudie mag I had lifted from my stepfather. I wouldn't normally have shared something like that with a girl I had just met, but I was inexplicably drawn to her. She was equally interested in the magazine. Initially, giggling fits ensued, but our reactions quickly morphed into intrigue. We turned the lights low, and spoke in whispers about the women and their bodies and what things must feel like. What I remember now is that I felt the strangest sensation when she touched me, and I didn't feel it again until I was twenty-two. The next week at school it seemed everyone knew what happened under the sheets that night, and it wasn't pretty. "DYKE!" was a common exclamation heard following me down the hallway. Misty was saved from the ridicule I endured. In her quest to become part of the "in" crowd, she had confessed to a very Christian and very popular girl that I had pressured her into doing these disgusting things. I was followed and taunted by groups of girls in the hallways between class periods, and on one occasion found myself cornered outside school, pushed into a brick wall, and told to repent my sins.

Carol knew that whatever happened between Misty and me wouldn't happen with her. My relationship with Carol was sacred, untouchable. She had once confided in me that sexual advances from girls made her uncomfortable. I took pride in being the one person she could always feel safe with, and I intended to keep it that way. Our friendship continued uninterrupted until our first year of high school. That was the year she met her first boyfriend. Initially there were some attempts at bonding, but eventually it became clear that he was not comfortable with me around. He asked her to sever our relationship, and when pressed for a reason, he told Carol that I was in love with her. She disputed his claim, but nevertheless followed through with the request. I have never felt as heartbroken as when I lost her. I sat with my acoustic guitar in the basement, wrote love songs, and ripped up all of our photos. I spent months crying my eyes out and punching pillows and walls.

Because my whole life revolved around Carol, I found myself utterly lost when our friendship fell apart. I spent the better part of a year completely numb. After the numbness, I tried some truly ridiculous ways of coping, like converting to Buddhism at age fifteen. What really enabled me to move on was witnessing how awful her relationship with her boyfriend was, and taking solace in her terrible decision. Eventually I found some new friends, and even fell in love with a boy. Evan and I had an extremely volatile relationship filled with heat and drama. My parents hated him. I suppose that was a large part of my attraction to him—and the fact that he was nothing like me. He was not terribly bright or ambitious; Evan's world consisted of three things: cars, drugs, and music. Teachers were positively dumbfounded to see us walking down the hallways holding hands, or pushed up against lockers intent on breaking the school's PDA rules. I could barely contain myself around him. We were so notorious for our inability to keep our hands off each other that a girl I had hardly spoken to "willed" us a bed at a local motel in the yearbook's senior send-off.

I enjoyed sex with Evan immensely. We stayed together much longer than necessary because of it. I finally broke it off with him a month before I left for college. I should have given myself some time to adjust to the changes happening in my life: moving away from home, beginning college, and tasting independence. Instead, I embarked on another serious relationship. Within two years, Reggie became my fiancé.

Reggie was, and still is, the ideal man. During one of our first conversations I mentioned how much I loved blueberry muffins because they reminded me of my Mamaw in Oklahoma. A few weekends later he woke me with fresh-made blueberry muffins in bed, along with a bagful that he made that I could take back with me to college. He was kind, thoughtful, ambitious, gracious, compassionate, loving, doting, smart, funny, attractive . . . the list really does go on. I could praise him for pages, and I doubt it would capture the gravity of his worth. So when the week of our wedding approached and I found myself absolutely panic-stricken, I was baffled. By that time we had been together for four years, lived together for two of those, and had a pain-free, easy relationship. We were both on track to finish school in the next year, our families loved us, our friends supported us, and we even saved enough money to pay for most of the wedding and a splendid honeymoon in Brazil.

I spent the week of the wedding running miles during the day, eating very little at dinner, and getting drunk at local bars. A few times I didn't come home until dawn. One infamous night I ate so many pot cookies that I forced myself to vomit just to come down. I was utterly terrified. The thought of getting married brought on waves of nausea. I even attempted to rekindle a love affair from high school with a man I had remained friends with over the years. It didn't make any sense. I knew I loved Reggie, that he loved me, and that our life together would be relatively bump-free. My logical brain needed to find (or make) a legitimate reason to support the haunting feeling in my chest. It couldn't. So on July 16, 2005, I married Reggie in an elegant but modest ceremony in my hometown.

The cracks were already there, I suppose, but they really began to show in the coming months. I'm not sure when I became consciously aware of my desire to figure out my sexuality, but suddenly it consumed me. A friend of mine found herself more active in the gay community on our university's campus after the demise of her relationship. She felt the need to fill her days and nights to get through the breakup, and I hesitantly joined her at some functions. I brought Reggie and friends along until I started to feel comfortable enough to go alone. Soon enough, I was spouting off about the injustices of inequality and writing poems about cute girls in my classes. I declared myself bisexual in embarrassing emails to friends. Nearly my entire circle of friends consisted of queer people. I belonged to this group. To Reggie, these changes seemed fairly benign. I did sense that he was apprehensive, but something otherworldly was pushing me to keep searching for answers.

All of the pontificating and proselytizing in the world on my part still didn't make me gay, and I knew it. I hadn't had a sexual or romantic experience with a woman since adolescence. I wanted to, but the perfect opportunity hadn't presented itself. I went to the potlucks, dances, and guerrilla gay bar nights, all coming to no fruition. Then one week my friend asked if I would join the Queer-Straight Alliance on a trip to a neighboring town for a dance party. It was an absolute blast. A fifteen-passenger van filled with social misfits is my kind of a good time. Secretly, I decided my goal for the weekend was to have a lesbian encounter. I envisioned being approached in a smoky room by a husky-voiced woman who would slide her arm around my waist, pull me in close, and kiss me savagely. A girl could dream.

I knew most of the people in the van, with the exception of a girl in the farthest seat with soft, milky skin, a rigid nose, and a distinct laugh. At the hotel room later, everyone was feverishly getting ready for the night out, and I was surprised by how pretty she was up close. She was intentionally boyish in looks, with her hair chopped short and styled into a faux-hawk, muscular arms, and a classic lesbian swagger. I was even more surprised when I saw how meticulous she was about makeup, clothes, and hair. Up to that point, the lesbians I had met fit into distinct butch or femme categories. I was making mental lists of why I could or could not be gay, based on what I saw. One glaring *no* for me was the butch/femme dichotomy. I wore my hair long, experimented with makeup, and liked fitted clothes, but I in no way felt that I was femme. I also practiced archery, worked as a security guard at concerts, and nearly always found myself in control of situations and relationships. I resented the idea that because I enjoyed some traditionally feminine things, I was excluded from being butch. Heather was clearly neither and both simultaneously.

At the dance that night I did not encounter my fantasy lesbian; nor does it seem to me now that she exists in any world other than *The L Word*. I felt pretty defeated after this realization, and was sulking at the bar when I noticed Heather standing alone at the edge of the room. A burst of adrenaline or drunken arrogance sent me sauntering over to her, and I asked for a dance. She followed me on the floor, and we awkwardly danced for a moment. Something came over me then, because I slid my arm around her waist, pulled her into me, and we moved as one rhythmic animal. My heart pounded, and I couldn't breathe. I placed my other hand behind her neck and brought her lips against mine. When her tongue slipped between my lips, memories flashed through my cortex and sent me spinning. This was it all along.

The next year seemed to come straight from a soap opera or torrid romance novel. Heather and I played merry-go-round three or four times, while Reggie tried to pick up the pieces and put me together again. Reggie knew about Heather to some extent, but I believe he was completely ill-equipped to handle the situation. He also couldn't stand to see me in pain, so he offered me the only gifts he could: love and support. My relationship with Heather was tumultuous, at times violent, and always painful. When I finally ended the nonsense that was our affair, I was nothing but a shell. I knew I had devastated Reggie—the only human being who ever truly loved me unconditionally. I hated myself. I was lost and delirious. As if things couldn't get any worse, my mom started to get an idea that something was going on with me. She stumbled upon my MySpace page, on which I listed myself as "bisexual." Not since adolescence had I even attempted a conversation about my sexuality, but her discovery sent us both reeling. She wrote a series of emails attacking me, Reggie, and our marriage. "Is this just another activity that's 'no big deal'? Something *you* consider 'normal,' like washing your hands? I'll never again be able to view you as the person I thought you were because now I know different. I'll always love you because you came from my body, but you're also a stranger . . . I hope your marriage survives."

Her reaction hurt me very deeply, and that was enough to send me scurrying back into the closet for a while. For two years I was in constant agony. I even contemplated suicide a few times. Slowly but surely, I began to sort out the real from the imagined. I unearthed memories that shed new light on my life, such as my junior high experiences. I recalled the demise of my friendship with Carol and the intensity of those feelings. I thought about every female friendship after Carol, and how they all seemed to end in disaster, usually because I had expectations that surpassed those of a normal friendship. Things began to come together, and they all added up to one revelation: I am gay.

Once I finally admitted it to myself, much of the work was done. What held me back from being fully out for much longer was the reality of what would happen next: losing everything. Obviously my relationship with Reggie would end if I officially declared myself homosexual. But I also knew I would lose my mom, and likely the rest of my family, and many of my friends who would feel betrayed by the news. My job and home security would be jeopardized, and everything else that comes with heterosexual privilege. When I finally came to terms with all of that, there was still one roadblock to overcome: I enjoyed being in a partnership with Reggie. I felt fulfilled in so many ways on a daily basis, and I was terrified that coming out would mean spending the rest of my days alone or unsatisfied. By that point I had met many lesbians, but none of them were partner quality. I feared settling for something less than what I already had with him. So I waited. I convinced myself that perhaps I could be satisfied with this life. After all, people had been doing it for hundreds of years. I am sure Reggie sensed I was settling, but he still loved me enough that he could live with that.

Then one summer everything changed. I was a devoted viewer of the show *Brothers & Sisters*, which featured a gay character named Kevin. One special Mother's Day episode, Kevin married his boyfriend, Scotty, in a touching ceremony surrounded and supported by his family. While watching the episode I contemplated the possibilities for my own future: coming out; getting married, or rather, not being able to legally marry again; and most painfully, I thought about losing my mother. The room began to spin, and I ran to the kitchen for water. Reggie came in to find me clutching the counter, doubled over and hyperventilating. He rushed to me and asked what the matter was, and suddenly all that had been consuming my mind for two years—the words I had never dared to speak out loud to him—came tumbling out of my mouth: "I think I am just gay." Instantly, I felt my stomach churning. I turned to the sink and vomited. He rubbed my back and told me the words I so desperately needed to hear: "I do not blame you, this isn't your fault, it just is." A week later, one of my dearest friends died after slipping in the shower. The grief of it all was too much, and I needed more time to be sure.

Thankfully, I had a great summer job working as a crew leader on a trail restoration crew to keep me looking forward. I was flown to Pittsburgh that June for job training and decided to try an experiment. I wanted to know what it would feel like to be known by complete strangers as a lesbian. I would not openly lie, but simply omit pieces of the truth. After my lesbian bunkmate, Jacqui, noted the rainbow-colored star tattoos on each of my hips, my colleagues assumed I was a single lesbian, and I didn't correct the assumption. It felt strange but exhilarating to take on that identity. Jacqui and I shared fun stories of ex-girlfriends and blind dates. I felt like a different person; there was no shame or guilt weighing me down.

On the last night in Pittsburgh we all decided to head to a local bar for a last hurrah before we embarked on trails around the country. A group of locals entered the bar, among them a statuesque woman with a definite lesbian swagger. After Jacqui and I remarked on how attractive she was, I joked with her that she should chat with the local girl. Jacqui said *I* should talk to her instead, then forcefully turned me around and pushed me into the girl. I did have a few drinks in me, and what did I have to lose? So the local lesbian and I chatted about Montana, the West, and my job. I was enamored of her within minutes. She was vivacious, strong, funny, intelligent, and absolutely full of life. When she laughed, she threw her head back and let the joy consume a room. In her presence, I felt more alive than I had in years. We spent the rest of the night talking, and kept on talking once I got back to Montana, oftentimes for two or more hours. When I was on the trails, we wrote letters, sometimes three a week. By the time the summer was over, I had come to terms with all of my fears, and what I knew needed to be done. The day after I arrived home, Reggie and I sat at the kitchen table and I ended our seven-year partnership.

I moved out of the home I shared with Reggie, and we were divorced by December. I came out to my family and friends, which resulted in exactly what I envisioned: my mom and I did not speak for nearly a year, and I lost some dear friends forever. However, I didn't lose Reggie. It was tentative at first, but we still have a strong relationship, based on honesty and a decade's worth of love. I also lost my teaching job. The town I worked in was a conservative small town in Montana, so I knew it was best if I kept my mouth shut about my sexuality. As is the case with most small towns though, secrets don't last long. Once again, whispers filled school hallways, and my sexuality was the topic of the week. Remember the girl from the bar in Pittsburgh? She moved to Montana that fall. Abbie and I were seen together all over town, and I quickly became a liability for the school district. Montana does not offer any discrimination protections for gays and lesbians, despite seventeen years of valiant efforts by local legislators. I was asked to resign, and I did so quietly and without argument.

Abbie and I have been together for almost two years, and we are still going strong. We moved to Washington and started over. Despite losing my home, two pets, a partner, a job I loved, friends, and much of my family, I am unreasonably happy. That isn't to say I have it easy. I feel the burden of inequality every day. Sometimes I miss being able to hold hands with my partner in public without stares, or sharing weekend stories with coworkers without worrying over pronouns. However, I make no efforts to hide my sexuality or my relationship. I have worked too hard to get here to let someone else's prejudices become my problem. I am working in the school system again, and I am teaching writing classes at the local LGBTQ youth center. Even my relationship with my mom has improved—she finally acknowledged my current relationship and has let go of my past marriage. Lately though, I am especially frustrated that I can't buy a ring, hop a plane to Vegas, and legally call Abbie my wife. But no one has it easy, and this is our cross to bear at the moment. What I do have now that I didn't have before is a guilt- and shame-free me. Authenticity is priceless.

Walking a Tightrope in High Heels

Michelle Renae

When my husband and I got married nearly thirteen years ago, I would have never dreamed that seven years later I would find myself in the process of coming out. Nor did I foresee during that process that I would still be married to him five years later as an out member of the GLBT community. You never know where love and a little honesty might take you.

My husband and I met at our small, liberal arts university, which also happened to be filled entirely with Evangelical Christians just bursting at the seams for Jesus. The school was located in isolated, bumblefuck Indiana, and was like a petri dish for growing the conservative, right-wing leaders of tomorrow. He and I were the leaders of the pack, as we were two of three students to have received the coveted Christian Scholarship; there were high hopes in our Jesus-filled tomorrows. To seal the deal even further, we were both pastors' kids: Christian full-breeds leading the charge. To say I was not well acquainted with the lesbian lifestyle would be a comical understatement.

In fact, growing up, I was really only aware of "gay" in reference to men. I knew it was wrong and such people did not go to heaven to receive their divine reward of spending eternity singing praises at God the Father's feet. Past that, I had no idea what these people were like. I could only remember meeting one gay person in my entire life, a man from San Francisco who had moved back to our small town to be with his family while he died of AIDS. My dad had "pastored" him through his last days and I had gone with my father on one such visit. This was the only interaction I had with a gay person until I was well into my twenties.

Nonetheless, I did know that I had always been different from the other girls. The "boy crazy" stage was entirely lost on me. I simply couldn't understand it. While I did feel some attraction to men, they more or less just didn't seem to hold my interest. I had no desire for a man to come in and save me. And despite my socialization, I did not daydream away the hours thinking of my wedding, and the babies Mr. Wonderful and I would make, nor did I practice writing my first name with his last name. I just couldn't see what all the fuss was about.

In hindsight, clues like this were everywhere. There was the little girl I had a crush on in kindergarten, then the little girl I had a crush on in grade school, then in college, and so on. I tossed all this in the pot of the unique relationship and warm feelings you have for your fellow sisters in Christ. But any gal with a short haircut and comfortable shoes could have recognized the signs a mile away.

On top of that, as I waded through the layers and layers of misogyny taught at my Christian university, I was bouncing back by becoming an "egalitarian." For those of you who don't speak Evangelical, that's a conservative Christian who holds all the usual beliefs of the group, except does not believe in male headship of the church and home. In other words, you believe that men and women are equal, a sort of radical feminism for the community I was in, and foreshadowing of my real self.

Yet during my junior year of college, I still fell head over heels in love with Jo, the man who would eventually become my husband. After being best friends for three years, we moved way out of the friend zone.

We were crazy about each other. We got engaged nine months after we started dating, and married about nine months after that—just two weeks after our college graduation, at the tender age of twenty-two. We were both virgins.

To say I was not well acquainted with my sexuality at this point would be yet another comical understatement. God literally knows that I had never masturbated. I understood the woman's sexual experience to be for the purpose of reproduction and to emotionally connect to her husband. I did not even realize that women could orgasm. Female sexual pleasure was a foreign concept to me. Fortunately, it was a priority to my husband. From the earliest stages of our relationship, it was important to him that I got off. Not only that, he wanted me to know my own body and be free to explore. Jo's openness to my sexuality was revolutionary when you consider the way we were raised.

Combine his high sex drive with my desire to explore, our love for each other with the fact that it all felt so damn good, and toss it with years of repression waiting to be released, and you get a pretty satisfying sex life during the early years of our marriage. We learned and figured it out together. He continued to champion the cause of my sexual awakening, buying educational books for me, as well as my first vibrator. I finally started having orgasms regularly when I began to masturbate about four years into our marriage. When you come from such repression, it takes a long time to learn how to let yourself go.

Running parallel with this sexual awakening was a spiritual one; I often find that the two go together. As we got to know ourselves better, our corset-like religious upbringings increasingly rubbed us the wrong way. We were living in Chicago's spiritual and artistic cornucopia. Being "good" started to be less important than being truly alive. We slowly and painstakingly tiptoed our way out of the church. It was not one single epiphany, but rather a thousand subtle moments that finally led us there. Leaving the church remains one of my greatest reliefs and most hidden sorrows. The relief of it stemmed from an obvious source: I was going to get myself back. As for the sorrow, the church had been my home—however abusive—for the first twenty-seven years of my life. You never quite get over the loss of your first love.

The city and its arts were like an intravenous drip line to our starved souls. As we interacted with the world without the barrier of the Evangelical Right, we began to see reflections of parts of ourselves that we had previously thought were either sinful or sadly unique to us. While this seems so basic, it was a shock to us to find characters in movies, musicals, and literature that were as sexually curious and complex as we were—or equally desperate to find their true voices. The realization that we were not alone in our desire to birth our real selves provided a new and deep source of courage. As I took in the world, and the parts of me I found there, my conscious attraction to women began to grow. At first it was subtle glances and musings as a woman walked by. But subtlety gave way to desire as things moved into the open.

Jo and I had always talked about our sexuality and needs. This was no new language to us. My desires for women, at first, seemed small and playful. I developed a crush on a woman I worked with. I told Jo and we laughed and talked about it often. Then there was the time when we were at a restaurant and joked about who we would want to sleep with most if given our pick; he and I chose the same woman. As my interest in women became more obvious, I began to gawk and turn my head when a lady caught my eye. Jo teased me, saying that I was such a novice, and I had to learn to be more subtle when checking gals out.

When I ask him about all this, he simply says that he has always deeply believed that when you encourage someone to truly be themselves, you end up getting more than if you try to make them be what you want them to be. Even so, to this day I do not totally understand why he didn't try to put the kibosh on it all right then and there. Sure, a fun little game, but clearly we were playing with fire—why not nip it in the bud and start discouraging this curiosity of mine? In some ways, it would have made life a lot easier. Instead, he began to encourage more serious discussions about it.

I, however, was starting to shut down. As I became aware of the deep desires I had for women, and started to put together the missing pieces in my personal story, I became totally overwhelmed. Talking about it felt like going through puberty with somebody watching. It was just too awkward for me to have an audience. I wanted to go off alone and figure this out very, very privately. On the other hand, Jo was my love and I did not want to shut him out. I settled into what would become a few years of therapy, as I tried to find a solid place to stand while unfolding myself.

Jo was less afraid of my orientation at this point than of my shutting down and pulling away. We had always been one of those tell-each-other-everything couples. This was entirely new ground for us and I was struggling to include him in my process. I wanted to be sensitive to his experience, yet some days I felt powerless to do so. Years of pent-up emotions and desires were flooding out of me at breakneck speed. Some days it just felt impossible to deal with anyone else's feelings. We both held on for dear life, some days to each other, other days simply to our history together, and hoped something good was on the other side.

Divorce was a thought, but never something either of us wanted to pursue. We were, in fact, happy together and wonderful partners. Ironically, our sex life was never a problem. It was broader than that. It was about who I was and my broader needs for sexual expression. At the time, we had no kids, so that wasn't a reason to stay together. It just seemed like such a waste to throw away a perfectly good marriage if there was a chance that it could expand enough to accommodate our natural growth.

I can't say it was an exciting, fun-filled journey. I generally felt terrified daily. As the months and hours of therapy passed, some degree of clarity began to form about who I was. Jo and I started to develop the skills and tools to interact with this. The idea that I was not heterosexual was becoming a more gentle reality as opposed to the slapping uncertainty that it was before. Yet, I had never had one single romantic or sexual encounter with a woman in my straight-arrow life . . . and I was dying to.

We discussed opening up our marriage for a good seven or eight months before actually doing it. The whole idea generally felt like trying to walk a tightrope in high heels. You might pull it off, but there was a bigger chance you would fall. There was still a chance, if ever so tiny, that you might make it to the other side.

Thank goodness my sexual awakening happened in the age of the Internet, since it was there that I was able to connect with other women, many of whom were in the same heterosexual marriage boat I was in. Jo and I were making every effort to keep him involved in the process as much as possible, yet it was a bit of a stretch at the time to saunter up to our local gay bar, hit on a gal, and then introduce him. Online it was easier for us to "meet" women together, and we felt much less intimidated by the whole thing. It took barely a New York minute for me to find a woman I hit it off with and was desperately attracted to.

Naturally, I will always remember my first time with a woman in sexual terms. It exceeded my high erotic expectations. But beyond that, I remember it as what it feels like to be myself. Me sleeping with a woman turned out to be about as natural as it is for fish to swim, and Jo really took such a legitimate unfolding of my true self as something to be celebrated. At the same time, there was also a big pill of reality for him to swallow in knowing that his wife had fully unleashed herself this way. In the context of our relationship, it felt like the peaceful silence that comes after someone has said something brutally honest. I will always remember my husband's response to that experience: he felt that it was more important for me to be myself than for him to feel secure. I had never felt more myself, nor more loved.

Yet now there was no denying it. It was no longer theoretical. The facts were these: my sexual orientation was toward women; I loved and enjoyed my husband; and he loved and enjoyed me. While we were both grappling with what this meant for us as individuals and as a couple, it was, in many ways, also a relief. While our relationship had been often foggy and bogged down during the bulk of this transition, there was now a sense of clarity and ease between us that was refreshing.

So began the long process of weaving together a marriage tailor-made to uniquely fit the above components. Our marriage remained open, as did our hearts toward one another. In time we slowly outlined the parameters that worked for us: what we were each comfortable with and so forth. For him, the insecurity that I will leave him for a woman has, naturally, taken many conversations to sort through, and is something we expect to always cycle through as we continue to dialogue about our needs. For me, coming to peace with the very real loss that I am not partnered with a woman has taken much time to accept. We are each choosing to sacrifice because we love being together. Is it complicated? Yes! But I believe that coming out and sexual rights are, at their core, about the right to freely be our full selves.

Some days my life is white-picket-fence heterosexual. I'm a writer, and a mother, and a wife . . . to a man. When my husband and I drop our little boy off at preschool together, the general assumption by the planet is that I'm hetero since I don't always think to wear my "Mixed orientation marriages can work" T-shirt on such occasions. Some days this all feels very natural to me, and like the kindest version of my life I could imagine. Other days, I feel pigeonholed and start wondering if anyone is selling an "I'm not straight" neon sign on eBay that I could somehow hang over my head. In terms of public perception, I constantly feel like a case of mistaken identity.

The interesting thing about this is that it makes me value my identity all the more. It keeps me aware of how important it is for all of us to have the room we need to freely be ourselves. And then, of course, there are times when it all seems pretty darn close to being in balance. As I was getting ready to go to the Pride Parade this year, my little boy looked at me and said, "Happy Pride, Mama." *Wow*, I thought, *how wonderful and complicated this all is*. Perhaps I can find a pocket of the world where all the pieces of myself co-exist in harmony. And perhaps it is true that you can give more to the people you love when being fully who you are.

For the most part, all of these choices have left me with a very clear sense of self. I know who I am and the realities of the life I have chosen. And while some of those realities put me in a tight spot sometimes, I accept them in exchange for the ways that they open up my life to live broadly and freely. In terms of labeling myself, I forever have an identity crisis. To say I am bisexual entirely overstates my relationship to men. I do not equally desire men and women. Yet, to say I am a lesbian cuts out the fact that I am still happily married to a man and enjoy sex with him. To paraphrase Virginia Woolf, who seemed to know a thing or two about this sort of situation, it's hard to fix labels on things in such a way as they don't fall off. So far, no label has seemed to stick comfortably to me. Everyone seems to have their own take on who I am, as well.

Many heterosexual married men refuse to take my orientation seriously. They need to believe that I am straight and just sort of playing with this whole thing. "But you're married to a man; that makes you straight!" they defensively exclaim. I can sniff out their fear that perhaps things don't always fit into nice, neat boxes.

The gay community, by and large, has been very accepting of me. Most people seem to realize that coming to terms with oneself and coming out take tremendous courage, no matter how you choose to live out your orientation.

On the downside, more than one lesbian has directly or indirectly shunned me. After all, I don't have to deal with the stares of holding your same-sex wife's hand as I walk down the street, or the biological or legal swirl around having a child. I can, and sometimes do, drink from the well of heterosexual privilege.

My knee-jerk first response is defense. I want to tell them that I too fight for gay rights. When I have extra bucks, I support my favorite GLBT groups. I want to explain that my husband and I are an interracial couple. While, thankfully, that is becoming less of an issue these days, fifteen years ago when we were dating in rural Indiana, it was a *huge* issue. I know what it's like to have angry, judging eyes staring you down for a little hand-holding. I've done the wedding where half your family won't show up because they disapprove. "Aha!" the protesters say, "but you *can* and *did* get married. See, you are not one of us!"

This brings me to my second response: They are right. No matter how much I protest, the fact remains that I am different. I get it. And if the tables were turned, I would struggle with understanding someone who was making the choices I have made. It would seem sort of, well, half-assed. A kind of have-your-cake-and-eat-it-too life built on a desire for convenience and social conformity. While this judgment from my peers makes me feel like a seven-year-old girl standing alone at the edge of the playground, I appreciate the sacrifices and journey of these other women too much to fault them.

It's not as if I haven't asked myself the very same questions. Am I taking the easy way out? Perhaps I am just the laziest lesbian on the planet, so wiped out I can't even be bothered to divorce my husband. At the end of the day I have to come back to my perspective on my life, and the reality of my experience. I chose to stay with my husband because I love him, and he loves me. Enough love, I might add, to make room in our life and marriage for all of who I am. The work it takes to sustain that kind of relationship is not the easy way out. I've sewn my life together as it is because such is the authentic reflection of who I am. My choices raise questions about what marriage is, what it is based on, and how it survives. Does love trump orientation? Most days I'm pretty sure it does. Some days I don't know. But either way, I believe in continuing to discover where love and a little honesty can take you.

A ~~Hushed Blue~~ Underworld

Lori Horvitz

Unlike other arty middle-class friends I made at the small state college I attended just north of Manhattan, Jessie came from a working-class background, a beneficiary of a federally funded program for disadvantaged students. For Jessie, college was a place to escape from the burden of family life, a reason to quit her full-time customer service job at JCPenney's, a ticket to a better life than her mother's. Although Jessie had no pretenses of being an artist, she fit right in with the spiky-haired dancers and hip film guys who wore thick black-framed glasses and knew all the lyrics to Elvis Costello songs. Jessie—pale-skinned with henna-red hair—had a tendency to barge into campus apartments of people she knew and scream, "You be fugly!" before slamming the door shut and running away.

Senior year of college, I lived in an apartment with a working phone line, even though no one ordered service. My roommates and friends took advantage of this complimentary line. My Ecuadorean roommate curled up in a chair and spent whole evenings talking to family in Quito, my roommate's boyfriend often phoned Finland, and Jessie spent hours on the phone chatting with her heroin-addict boyfriend and pregnant mother, both living in nearby Yonkers.

One day I showed Jessie my latest art project: sepia-toned transparencies of nude women in the school's locker-room shower. Jessie inspected each image with the eye of a jeweler. Before lifting her gaze off the last image, she inquired about Joseph, my boyfriend who attended a college three hours north. "How's the sex?"

I looked downward, felt my face turn red. "It's good."

Jessie lightly slapped my shoulder and cackled. "You're such a prude!"

Although she made me nervous—I stumbled over words and occasionally bumped into walls in her presence—I felt like a rock star around Jessie. She was my groupie. When I talked, she stared into my eyes and listened intently, whether it was about my family poodle that got mauled to death by a great dane at a Veteran's Day Parade, or my art history paper about Jackson Pollock. She told me about her mother, who had a bevy of children by different fathers. On weekends, she took the bus back to Yonkers to help out with the kids. The concept of someone my age having a mother who kept having kids was foreign to me. But Jessie made light of it, even laughed about it.

Now, focusing on the little birthmark just above her lip, I asked, "How good is the sex with you and *your* boyfriend?"

Jessie gathered the photos in a neat pile and handed them back to me. "It's all right," she mumbled, her eyes fixed on the top photo of a lean-bodied woman lathering her hair. "That's my favorite."

I showed Jessie more photos I'd taken of friends posing by the communal gym shower. Fascinated with the steel, space-age structure, I had attempted to demonstrate the contrast between the human form and modern technology. Underneath the rocket-like shower, I captured my subjects soaping their bodies, their arms extended, legs flexed, water swirling over flesh. In one image, the multi-headed shower appeared to be gushing out rays of sunlight onto the subjects; in another, the steamy haze made it difficult to tell where the edges of the imposing steel cylinder ended and the human body began.

Since I printed the photos on large sheets of see-through film, I could manipulate the setting. I highlighted certain sections of each image with silver paint and used aquamarine paper as a backdrop. Each rectangular image was now part of a hushed blue underworld of curves and steel and muscles and mist.

Jessie studied the photos of Liz, Belle, and Mandy washing their nude bodies. She looked straight at me. "If you want, I can pose for you too."

"Maybe," I said, keeping my eyes on the images in front of me. I ran into the kitchen to check on the pizza I was heating up. Jessie picked up the phone and called her boyfriend.

My shoulders stiffened. Was Jessie trying to come on to me? Why did she offer to pose? Did she think I was like *that*? Yet secretly, I liked that she liked me. In fact, I craved her presence; she made me feel desirable, attractive, and talented. On the other hand, part of me was repulsed by the idea that Jessie liked me. Later that afternoon, I typed a poem on my Olivetti manual typewriter:

> *I'm not that way, you're a good friend,*
> *I'm not that way, you're out of luck.*
> *I like you a lot, but the buck*
> *Stops there.*

A week later, I made plans to take more photos of two friends by the communal gym shower. I asked Jessie if she wanted to join them.

She lifted her legs onto the mustard-colored chair in my living room and held her knees. At first she agreed, but five minutes later, she looked out the window. With her back facing me, she asked, "How about I pose for you with my clothes on?"

The next day, in my living room, I set up lights and umbrellas and a black velvet backdrop. Jessie, wearing a red silk dress, placed her hands on her hips and puckered her lips. From behind my camera, I zoomed in on her elegant ears, her green eyes, her head-on gaze. Snap. I moved in closer, focusing on her angular profile.

Suddenly she broke out of her serious stance and laughed. "So, what do you think?" she asked.

I glanced out from behind the camera. "About what?"

Jessie looked out the window. "Do you think I'm sexy?"

I jerked my camera in front of my face and looked through the lens. "You look great in that dress." What kind of answer was she expecting? I could hardly turn the focusing ring on the camera.

Two days later, after printing an image of Jessie's profile, I highlighted her ear with silver paint; it looked like a conch shell.

That spring, Joseph visited more often. Jessie stayed part-time with her mother. The phone company got wind of the free line.

At the end of the school year, I graduated and moved to New York City with Joseph. Jessie graduated a year later and moved to New York City with her junkie boyfriend. Months later, I heard she had broken up with him and joined the army. Soon after, I broke up with Joseph, saved up money, sublet my apartment, and signed up for a month-long, dirt-cheap trip to Moscow and Peking on the Trans-Siberian Railway. I knew I'd get to see Red Square and the Great Wall of China. What I didn't know was that I'd meet Rita, a British woman from London. We shared a compartment on the train, and she talked of philosophy and feminism, had a mane of strawberry blond hair that she flipped back every now and then, and made me say to myself, over and over, *I'm not like that! Wouldn't I already know this by now?*

When the train stopped at tiny Siberian stations, we ran out to get cakes and Lenin pins, and I thought, *No way! I'm not a lesbian!* Back on the train, I played my crappy guitar and she sat by my side, and I sang Joni Mitchell songs and she touched my knee and said, "You're quite good." I felt my face blush, looked at the Siberian landscape, and thought, *Am I like that?*

Rita spoke about Simone de Beauvoir, a French feminist writer who had a life-long relationship with philosopher Jean-Paul Sartre. "But they never lived together," she said. "And they both took other lovers now and again."

"Sounds complicated," I said. Cleavage spilled from her tight burgundy sweater. I steered my eyes to the floor.

"It's the ideal situation," she said "Marriage is so bloody ridiculous. Imagine sleeping with the same person every night for the rest of your life. How boring!" She gripped the railing by the window until I could see the whites underneath her fingernails.

I never thought marriage was such a bad idea, but maybe Rita had a point.

Perhaps it was her gentle British voice, or the way she looked in my eyes when she spoke, or the way she flung her wrist in the air when speaking about marriage or how "bloody annoying" some of the other train passengers were; I wanted to spend all my time with her. I told her about Joseph's supposed left-wing, anarchist ideals. "But when it came to cleaning the apartment," I said, "he refused to lift a finger until it got too dirty for him."

"Bloody men," Rita said, rolling her eyes.

I let out a loud laugh. "That's right!" I said.

On the third day, Rita invited me to explore the train with her. "Don't you want to practice your Russian?" she asked.

It didn't matter that my knowledge of Russian was limited to basic greetings and single-digit numbers. Of course I wanted to explore with Rita. As we moved deeper into Siberia, I couldn't stop thinking of her, the way she caressed her hair when she talked to me, the way she touched my shoulder when making a point.

One night, while the rest of the group went to a dance performance, Rita and I swigged beer in her hotel room. She showed me her new acupuncture kit. "You could practice on me," I said. Rita demonstrated where each meridian point was on my hands and arms. When she touched me, my body tensed up. Goosebumps rose from my arm. She continued to touch my arms and show me meridian points. For a moment, we locked eyes. I told her I needed to use the bathroom. Afterward, I asked her how long she'd been with her ex-boyfriend.

"Two years," she said. "And you?"

"Too long," I said.

Now when I looked at her, all I could see were her sensual lips. All I could do was turn away and imagine my lips on hers.

But nothing happened.

A month after the trip ended, I visited Rita in London. Before long, I found myself on her bed, a little tipsy, both of us staring at the ceiling. We listened to Kraftwerk's *Trans-Europe Express*. I told her I hadn't spoken to Joseph, but learned that he missed me and loved me. He called friends and family to get my address. I didn't have an address. He wrote love letters and sent them to Crete, on the off chance I might have stayed at the youth hostel I stayed at three years before.

"Will you go back with him?" Rita asked.

"Probably not," I said. Before I could think about what I was doing, I moved my body next to hers and wrapped my arm around her waist. She turned toward me and held me. We kissed. Kraftwerk's album played over and over and over again as we felt each other's bodies, our arms and legs intertwined, our hands moving, gliding up and down, and finally, I felt at ease, in a foreign land, with a foreign woman. For hours, but not long enough, we kissed and touched, until the doorbell rang. Rita jumped up and ran out of the room to greet her friend Martin. The three of us went for dinner, two of us with flushed cheeks. "We took a nap," Rita told Martin.

"A very nice nap," I said.

When I arrived home, Joseph begged me to come back. I agreed, with the stipulation that we could see "others." Others including Rita. But my long-distance affair ended a year later, after Rita invited me to the Black Sea. On the day of departure, I learned she also invited a boyfriend.

Then I met Amy. I kept our affair a secret from mutual friends, from Joseph. It smelled of commitment—commitment to my sexuality. And that felt scary. But she gave me an ultimatum: "You either make a go of this or I'm out of here."

And so we made a go of it for over three years. I continued to be closeted. On the streets of New York City, I would pull my hand away from hers. "We'll get killed. Gay-bashed," I'd say.

For the next ten years, I continued to date women, and continued to keep an illusion in my head. *Maybe one day I'll meet a man and get married and have kids and be normal after all.* But that never happened. And following the demise of yet another relationship with a woman, I attempted to date men again. After one man tried to kiss me on the lips, but only got my cheek, I ran out of his car and washed my face with rubbing alcohol.

And washed the illusion out of my mind. *I'm a friggin' lesbian!* I told myself. *I like women and that's okay!*

Just recently, on Facebook, I've reconnected with a friend from college. I told her that I'd been involved with women for years.

"That's cool," she wrote. "You know, we used to sit around the suite and talk about how you'd make a good lesbian. I'm glad you finally figured it out."

⌒⌒

Four years after I'd last seen her, Jessie phoned me from an army base in Biloxi, Mississippi. She had gotten my number from a mutual friend. In the background, her three-month-old baby screamed. She laughed about the kids. "Yeah, one's four and one's new. What a trip being a mother." Her husband, also in the army, was away on active duty. "I was thinking about you," she said, followed by a nervous laugh. Her familiar voice transported me right back to my college apartment, the tension that I now understood.

I told her about my job as a freelance designer, and how every year since graduation, I saved up money and sublet my apartment and traveled Europe for months at a time. And then, out of the blue, she asked if I'd ever been with a woman.

"Yes," I said. "My first was with a British woman. We had a long-distance affair for over a year. What about you?"

"No, never. But I wanted to . . . with someone."

"With who?" I asked, already knowing the answer.

"With you. I had a big crush on you, didn't you know that?"

"Really?" Gratified to hear Jessie acknowledge that tense, scary, exciting feeling, I responded, "I guess I had a crush on you too."

"You guess?" she asked.

"I didn't know it at the time. I just knew I loved hanging out with you."

"This is like having phone sex," Jessie said, despite the fact that there wasn't any talk of sex, just a sexy tension. How erotic can a conversation be with a baby screaming in the background?

Eventually she needed to tend to her infant. We promised we'd keep in touch. I wrote her name and address in my phone book with a permanent marker. That year we exchanged Christmas cards.

After I hung up the phone, I remembered Jessie in my college apartment, curled up in a boxy, wooden chair with mustard-colored pillows, speaking in hushed tones to her boyfriend. I walk past, smile, and look away, keeping that mysterious pang at the edge of my heart under wraps.

Beyond Sexuality

Holly Edwards

I have always had a problem with the notion of sexuality being a major lifestyle choice. It annoyed me when people suggested that being gay was somehow a personality trait to be considered above all others, when in fact I felt it was akin to, or less important than, the color of one's hair. But of course, my gay friends told me, I *would* think that. I was straight, and I spoke with the full force of heterosexual privilege behind me.

When Leo told me of his fear that he might be gay (and fear is the best word for it; white-knuckled, pant-wetting fear of being forced to live a life he didn't want), I told him to chill out. Why worry? Just keep on trucking. If you get to the next stop and realize that you prefer boys, that's just fine. Who cares, as long as you're happy? I couldn't understand his frustration. He had a support network, he had his family behind him, so what did it matter which side of his bread he buttered?

But it mattered to Leo. He couldn't stand not knowing. The indecision was killing him and he found my advice unhelpful. I didn't know what he was going through, he protested. I'd never questioned my sexuality. Not knowing whether he preferred girls or boys, he said, was to inhabit a limbo where you can never be truly happy. He was stuck on the fence, desperate to pick a side, but paralyzed by the fear of choosing wrong. As far as he was concerned, the choice was a one-way ticket.

And he was right, I didn't understand. I'd never had any trouble working out who I fancied; it was as easy as putting on my shoes. I liked boys, and I always had. In fact, at this moment in my life, I liked one boy in particular, loved him in fact, ached for him, yearned for him, dreamed about him. It was my own private misfortune that the object of my affections was the poor, tortured Leo, and the more he wept on my shoulder for his own miseries, the more I loved him.

We limped along together for some months, nursing our own torments: his, the uncertainty of who to love; and mine, the terrible certainty of who I did love. One night it came to a head. Lying in bed together (we often shared a bed, but he never laid a finger on me, the swine) he confessed that his dream was to meet the perfect woman and settle down. The gay lifestyle was not for him. He wanted a family, a stable relationship, a *normal* life; he silenced my protests that this was an unachievable goal for gay or straight alike. He told me that if only he could silence the gay demon on his shoulder, he would marry his perfect woman. He told me her name.

It wasn't me.

I dug my nails into my palms so tightly I drew blood to prevent myself from shrieking "What about ME? Why not ME!?" I knew then that I needed some distance.

My parting advice to him, when I left town the following week to travel and try to get over him, was not to take life so seriously. Sexuality is not the be-all and end-all—lighten up! He shook his head, as if to say, "Thank god you'll never know what it's like."

I kept on the move. While I loved Leo, I knew I had to keep going. To stay in one place too long would be to fester and mope. So it was then that I found myself climbing down from a Greyhound at nine in morning, blinking in the desert sunshine, and shaking hands with a man named Ian, who was to be my new boss.

Sixteen hours on a bus from Brisbane—to a young British girl it felt like I was flying to the moon. I come from a small island; if you're not careful, a sixteen-hour bus ride could end up in the sea. The town of Barcaldine felt like the quintessential middle of nowhere.

In Barcaldine, I felt good about myself for the first time in a long time. When I woke up each day, thoughts of Leo were not the first thing that came to mind. Over the past couple of months I'd obeyed some very strict rules: I only allowed myself to look at his picture once a week, and then only for five minutes. I was to keep telephone conversations to a minimum, which wasn't easy because he called me every day to update me on his state of mind. After I hung up, to stop myself from brooding, I had to immediately occupy myself with some task, preferably slightly unpleasant, like cleaning the toilet, or picking up the dog turds in the garden of the house I was staying in. And if I found myself thinking about him, I would sing, as loud as I could, anything as long as it made me feel better. "Applejack" by Dolly Parton was a favorite, or "Coward of the County" by Kenny Rogers (I avoided anything by Donna Summer, as I used to listen to her with Leo, who was, unsurprisingly, a big fan). This therapy was worth the funny looks I got.

Barcaldine is well served by pubs; there are six of them all in a row along the main road in town, which equates to roughly one per family. I worked as a barmaid in the Commercial Hotel, and found that I enjoyed country living. My tastes in music were suddenly not as esoteric as I had thought, and it amused me to be in a community where a man's worth was measured by the number of kangaroos he'd shot. I settled in quickly, and even found myself a boyfriend, a wide-eyed lad called Noah who drove a utility truck, wore a Stetson, and had never been to the city. For the first time in months, I stopped thinking about Leo with longing. Life was good.

Everything changed when Terry came to town. She was Ian's daughter—his pride and joy—and had been riding in her car to Alice

Springs when it hit a horse. The driver was in a coma. Terry had emerged bruised and cut to pieces, but otherwise fine. She was, however, utterly shaken, and so had decided to come to the country to recover with her family around her. I sometimes ponder the hand that fate played in this. If Terry's car had not been coming 'round the bend at that exact time, if the horse hadn't been there, would life just have continued along as normal, with me never knowing what might have been? Or would fate have contrived some other way to interfere?

There was something about Terry that appealed to me. I found myself trying to impress her, telling jokes and tall tales to make her laugh. I was jealous of people in her company; I wanted her all to myself. When we worked together behind the bar, I resented the boys who flirted with her, and gave them half measures of rum out of spite. When she confided in me that she preferred women, I felt a thrill of something like delight, although at the time I couldn't place it; it was in the background, like a half-teaspoon of cinnamon in a chili con carne. My palate wasn't sophisticated enough to discern it.

One night Noah took us to a party in the village. He brought his friend Ned, and later confided that he thought Ned liked Terry. I was horrified by the idea, and poorly concealed my distaste. Noah took offense, insulted that I didn't think his friend good enough for mine. I stood my ground, but was confused: what did it matter to me? When Terry drunkenly proclaimed that she would go home with Ned, I counseled against it. I told her she'd regret it in the morning, that she was far too good for a country boy like him. She decided to take my advice, and Noah, furious with me for showing him up, insisted we all go home.

I was in disgrace on the walk back, and the boys stormed off up ahead. I felt nothing but relief that I had prevented Terry from making a terrible mistake, but when she asked me why I cared so much, I couldn't tell her. The answer hid in my subconscious, like a particularly hard *Where's Waldo* cartoon. I kept thinking I had it, but when I looked again it turned out to be a girl in a stripy sweater, or an old man in a red bobble hat.

Terry knew, though. She was teasing me. I think she'd known from the first day we met, when I tried to hold her attention with outrageous stories, like a child diving into a pool for the first time: "Look at me!" Walking back that night, she admitted that she didn't really want to sleep with Ned. She stopped and held my gaze.

"It's you I want."

Were there fireworks overhead? Did all the streetlights come on, and did I imagine the Hallelujah Chorus singing behind me? The answer was clear as day, and I almost slapped my head at my stupidity, but until that moment it had never even occurred to me that my possessiveness toward Terry had been because I had a crush on her.

My relationship with Noah fizzled out after that, but I barely noticed. I was too busy embarking on the first affair of my life that could be termed "steamy." It was a tabloid headline writer's dream: HORSE CRASH VICTIM AND BRIT BACKPACKER IN LESBIAN SEX ROMP. It was intense; all thoughts of Leo evaporated, and my every waking thought was Terry. As if this weren't exciting enough, our relationship had to continue in secret: we were both living in the rooms above the Commercial Hotel, separated by the thinnest of walls from Ian and Maxine, Terry's mother, both of whom were unaware of their favorite daughter's deviance.

Leo, when I told him, was aghast. Where was my crippling indecision, where was the specter of doubt over my head? How had I escaped the sleepless nights, lying awake staring at the ceiling, tortured by uncertainty? But it seemed I had taken my own advice: I didn't stop to question what I was feeling, I simply went with it. *So I'm into girls now, am I?* my subconscious mused. *Cool.*

Early on, in the white heat of first love, it wasn't girls I was into, per se, just Terry. After all, I reasoned, why would I ever need to look at anyone again, male or female? I had Terry. It was only when things between us turned sour that I realized that people expected me to make a choice, and it was only then that I encountered the indecision that Leo referred to.

I had entered a strange realm where people appeared sexless. I was attracted and repulsed by everyone in equal measure. I could no more decide on which particular sex to pursue than I could proclaim to only be interested in people if they were exactly 5'4". This didn't stop constant speculation around me. How could I simply have changed? Did I not love boys as I always had? Was I a *lesbian* now? I recoiled at the label, but could not pretend to be straight; and as the dust settled over my feelings for Terry, I started to notice other women. Women had been so much white noise before Terry, interference that I largely ignored, but it now felt like someone had changed the focus on my lens. Now it was men who were blurry and featureless and women who were crystal clear.

I began another affair, but I wasn't ready. It felt emotionless and stale. I liked the girl, and she seemed to like me, but there was none of the heart-breaking passion that I had had with Terry. Another affair fizzled and died in the wake of the first. It appeared that I was no longer able to treat relationships as lightly as I had before I met Terry. It could be that I simply held women in a higher regard than I had men, but I suspect it was more to do with being hungover from first love. My relationship with Terry may have ended, like it began, with a car crash—albeit a metaphorical one—but it had given me my first brief taste of what being in love could feel like, and after that, settling for anything less was like eating a baked potato plain, knowing how much better it would taste smothered in hot, melting butter.

Love, however, is hard to come by, and while I waited for it, I was plagued by an existential crisis: was I still a lesbian if I wasn't presently attracted to anybody? Despite my brief forays into lesbian romance, Terry remained the only woman I had properly fancied. I was annoyed when people automatically assumed I was straight, but felt like a fraud saying I was anything else. I felt like I had to prove my lesbian credentials if I was to be accepted. I cut my hair and tried to dress more butch, thinking that would help, but it only served to make me feel even more uncomfortable and less like myself.

It took a long time for me to work through this and find my identity again, and I realized that until I did, love would have to wait. I remembered the advice I had given to Leo all that time ago and realized that I would do well to take it to heart myself. *Who cares, as long as you're happy?* Leo was now happily cohabiting with his boyfriend, whom he called the love of his life, so it seems my words of wisdom hadn't been so unhelpful after all.

⌖

As the years went by, I started to meet new people who had never known the heterosexual me, and as her ghost faded it became easier not to fret about my sexuality. I stopped expecting people to laugh out loud in disbelief when I told them I was gay, although I did start to dread the inevitable questions that straight people feel it's okay to ask: "How long have you known?" "Have you *ever* been with a man?" I missed the immunity from these questions that heterosexuality affords, but as time went on I was more prepared to meet them head-on.

As I became more comfortable with my new sexuality, I started to feel more comfortable in gay spaces. I no longer expected to be stopped at the door, to be denounced as an impostor the moment I crossed the threshold; rather, I felt a sense of inclusion. After a while I was delighted to discover that in my circle of friends, nobody seemed to give a toss whether I was gay or straight. I felt like I had earned my stripes.

Lo and behold, as if to prove a point, it was at this time that I met Cassie, the love of my life. I was finally comfortable with myself and my sexuality; and because of this our relationship fell into place like the conclusion of an Agatha Christie novel. All the clues suddenly made sense, and the culprit was unmasked at last. We've been together for three and a half years now, and I've never been happier. At this point, I cannot imagine how my life would have been had Terry's car not hit that horse, but I equally cannot imagine not falling in love with Cassie if I met her in another life.

I think now that Leo was both right and wrong. Sexuality is an important part of who one is, and it can be unsettling to feel unresolved about it. But it *shouldn't* matter; it's only the perception of others that makes these decisions difficult. The biggest adjustment for me was the realization that if I weren't straight, people around me would always demand an explanation; they would never allow me to be uncertain. It was only by shutting out their voices that I was able to find myself in a place beyond male and female, beyond gay and straight, beyond sexuality.

Love and Freedom

Aprille Cochrane

I spent the first thirty or so years of my life as a heterosexual female. I thought women were beautiful, but I rarely thought of them in a sexually gratifying way. I thought the only thing another woman could do for me would be to join me in a drunken, unexpected threesome and leave immediately afterward. I admired Pam Grier for her strength and sex appeal. I thought Halle Berry had beautiful skin and the most radiant smile ever. I appreciated Vanessa Williams's exotic blue and green eyes, but I never saw myself falling in love with women.

I grew up in an attractive family with high standards. There were no traumatic events that made me form a negative opinion of males, females, or sexuality. From an early age, I embraced alternative views. I took a white boy to my first Sadie Hawkins junior high dance, and defended my interracial relationship against slurs. I thought nothing of fighting for my right to do as I pleased with whomever I pleased. Back then, I didn't consider it controversial or defiant. I was just being me.

I married a man I thought I would be with forever. He was nice to me. He worked hard. I believe he was faithful. We had mutual friends.

He rubbed my feet, was well endowed, and was a generous lover. He was nice to his mother. He was handsome and intelligent, educated, and street smart.

But he was a stranger to emotions outside of love and hate. He thought working harder could solve our issues. He thought money defined his identity as a man. I believe he became resentful of my education and success. We stopped talking. We stopped supporting each other. We stopped making love. We stopped sharing space and ideas. We distrusted each other. We turned to other people for our emotional stability. At least, I did.

I went on a much-needed vacation with a few of my best girlfriends. Toward the end of the trip, one of my girlfriends began flirting with me. This was a friend I was very close to, felt safe with, and who was aware of some of the marital issues my husband and I were experiencing. She was extremely attractive. Initially, I didn't know how to interpret her attention, because this was the first time our platonic friendship boundary had been challenged. Steamy texts and the thrilling threat of being caught made the idea irresistible.

Before I seriously entertained the idea of opening myself up to her, I examined myself. How would I know if this was right? How did I feel about carrying on with a woman in this way? What would my friends and family say? What was my opinion of the gay world? Would this be just a fling and then we would go back to being platonic friends? How did I feel about cheating, *if* I considered this cheating? Would I be able to look myself in the mirror? Would this change my spiritual views? My answer was simple: Listen to your body.

I challenged myself: if you're really this free-loving, liberal, and conscious person, open yourself up to receiving this experience. After she put her hand on my thigh, my body and soul electrified somewhere around the back of my neck. A prisoner of the flesh I may be, but it felt like no other touch I had ever experienced before. And it was just a touch! This moment could have been attributed to the thrill of seduction, the bad girl concept, or even a seed planted during a pornographic movie.

It could have been subliminal media and video messages, or plain old curiosity. Either way, I consciously and willingly surrendered to it. I took my marriage vows very seriously, but I had always felt that honoring the Universe and its potential were important too. I knew, in that one instant, my life and views had changed.

My life had not changed so dramatically because I had cheated, but because I was privy to new facets of my sexuality and emotions. I felt lucky, like I was being included in a secret that had been hidden in plain view. Colors seemed to blink neon. I swore I could hear in new ranges. My creativity shot though the roof. Instead of seeing women, I *noticed* them now. I noticed their walks. I could read their confidence. I valued them more, family members included. I had understood intimacy as a concept, but I could count the number of times I experienced it up to this point. I now knew intimacy had layers, and sex wasn't the prerequisite or the climax. Intimacy could be expressed as sitting at a table, lying in the bed, cooking, watching a movie together, or a special supportive touch. It could be a tone understood in a conversation, a compromise, a special trinket, or a simple text. It could be taking a bath, caring for each other's pets, or confiding a secret. I couldn't go back to acting as if seeing the basic colors was the most I deserved in life. I was adding new dimensions to my life, and I wanted to honor the place these new emotions stemmed from, without losing my husband—or myself—in the process. That didn't mean I could.

My husband and I struggled to make love well before she laid her hand on my thigh. I felt lost in my marriage well before she made me feel at home in her house. My husband and I lived separate lives well before she supported me through literary and emotional endeavors. He and I separated emotionally well before I moved out physically. I lost my happiness well before the Prozac. I would hate to admit she fulfilled the emotional gap he could not, but she satisfied a place in me no one even knew existed before. She became an emotional and physical refuge. She was a safe place to fall. I struggled knowing that I had vowed to make my husband that safe place, but I no longer felt I could be vulnerable enough with him to do anything other than stand up straight.

It was stressful to feel cut off from my husband while I remained vulnerable with a woman. I became resentful that he wasn't her. I became jealous that she was out and had freedom. In trying to please them both, I lost myself. Becoming comfortable with deceiving my husband changed me at my core. During the end of my marriage, I became a liar and a cheat. I am not proud of that. I learned to disguise my shame and guilt with him. I was never, ever able to let down my guard completely with her. I was always aware of my surroundings and who could see me. I wanted to be as comfortable with her as she was with me, but the truth is, I was scared to death. I felt transparent. I tried to cover my tracks. I wanted to be true to the moments with her, yet I was scared of situations that could get back to my husband before I could explain. I wasn't ready to confront the consequences of my actions yet. I couldn't return affection as naturally as she could. I made excuses to him about why I was late. I pushed limits with both. I became mean, stressed out, irrational, needy, immature, and depressed. I pride myself on being true to myself, and I put myself in a situation where I couldn't be true to anyone.

Losing my freedom to explore who I was becoming was detrimental to my health. I wasn't comfortable living life in the shadows. My obligation to my marriage and fear of hurting my husband were strangling my soul.

One thing is clear. I didn't leave him *for* her. I left him for my *sanity*. Yes, I continued to explore myself with her, but these two things happened concurrently, not sequentially.

I knew I had shifted from being a straight girl. Where along the continuum I landed, I wasn't sure yet. There was no confusion about what I liked about her. One of the things I enjoyed was her body. I liked her hips, thick thighs, breasts, and softness. Men generally weren't built like that. I considered lifestyle as part of being a lesbian, and since I was still married and living with my husband, I didn't consider myself a lesbian; although I was clearly doing lesbian things and attending lesbian-inspired events. Did I consider myself bisexual? If I had to pin down a label, I guess so. I think "open" is more accurate. I enjoyed having a physical outlet with her that wasn't male-centered. Her time and mine weren't measured by orgasm. We both enjoyed being women. No one was trying to be the man. As I mentioned, my husband was a generous lover, but things were just different with her. I wasn't confused by both experiences; I was stressed out by the lack of freedom to express them both.

⌒⌒

After a lengthy and dramatic fallout, my friend and I are still in each other's lives; in fact, we are best friends. We scraped and clawed our way back to each other and we are proud of what we have reestablished. We created comfortable boundaries and we see each other often and talk many times a day. I have moments of confusion when I look at her romantically, but those pop-ups are few and far between. The depth and satisfaction of our current friendship is worth more than any fling we could have that might threaten it. I still feel a different kind of intimacy with her than I do with my other friends. My other friends and I are very close, intimate, and affectionate, but I have never crossed the romantic line with any of them.

On the outside, not much changed. I didn't make any drastic physical changes. I locked my hair, but I had been working toward that for years. I was still most comfortable in sweats, jeans, and T-shirts. I was no stranger to heels and a short skirt either. Strappy heels and new wedges still excited me just as new tennis shoes did. I looked forward to the latest makeup colors. I coordinated my purses with my mood. I wore makeup as needed and rarely went without lipstick and earrings.

Inside, a part of me still wavered about whether my changing sexuality was sparked because of who she was, as my friend, or because she was a woman. I do still desire women and I am open to them romantically. I am just as choosy with women as I am with men. The integrity of whom I choose to date is still just as high. If there's no chemistry, there's no match. And if I'm not treated well, they won't last long. Dissecting the dynamics of my sexual spark has become less important to me over time. I am comfortable with where I am now.

An opportunity presented itself recently for me to open up to my friend Dianne about dating women. Up to this point, she had said that people needed to mind their own business when it came to other people's love interests. She didn't believe in judging gays or lesbians, although it wasn't her preference and she didn't understand it. I felt safe and the timing seemed appropriate. I wanted her to know that my choices weren't a reflection of her. I hadn't planned to, but I felt I needed to honor the moment. I took a deep breath. I was so nervous. My voice was shaking— and then I did it.

I told her I had started dating women since my separation from my husband. In the moment, she asked a few questions, and generally seemed to accept it. She said she wasn't too surprised because of how often she'd seen my "friend" and me together. She commented that it wasn't that far of a stretch for me, because I hadn't ever really been very mainstream. She said that I was a good person, with many accomplishments, and that she didn't love me any less. Those comments made me feel accepted, and I felt emotionally lighter knowing I had been honest.

A few hours later, it seemed her opinion changed. She wanted to know why it was such a big secret, and thought I could be emotionally unsettled— since I had much going on. I said that there wasn't much to tell up to that point. I confided that I was afraid of disappointing her, and that was why I hadn't said anything until then. I was fearful of her rejection and judgment. I don't fear many people's opinions, but honestly, I valued hers.

Later, I felt like a fool for bragging that I came out and that she was so cool about it. I didn't know if she was initially only saying what she thought I wanted to hear or if this new opinion was the reflection of a conversation with a third party. This person had always been the kind who was up-front, so I was truly baffled and devastated at the change of heart. I realize I must honor other people's process, but I was still shocked and hurt.

After I told her, we didn't talk for three weeks. Normally, we connect at least once a week. During this time apart, I felt rejected and sad. A few days ago, we were able to smoothly resume some normal activity. I am thankful for this little bit of progress and feel we haven't missed much of a beat. Her reaction opened my eyes, though. I had planned to tell other people because I didn't see it as a big deal. I would hate for them to hear rumors from someone else and not feel free to speak with me about it. I am not ashamed of my choice to date women, but after this reaction, I decided that whom I had an intimate relationship with was nobody's business. I wasn't getting married to anybody anytime soon, and it was my private choice. However, if an opportunity presents itself with someone else, I will most definitely honor it.

I am still open to dating men, but I am more excited about dating women. There may be men out there with all of the emotional nuances that are quite comparable to the characteristics I like in a woman. If I find one, then maybe I'll keep him. Until then, I'm open to what comes my way.

I opened up about my experiences to free myself and partly in defiance of the stereotypical myths. I am including women in my private life *not* because I was molested, am a man-hater, didn't have my dad in my life, secretly wanted to be a man, was promiscuous, was confused, was raped, loved rainbows, didn't receive enough hugs, am a feminist, had short hair, coached, preferred pants over skirts, liked sports, didn't attend enough church, am running out of options, don't have children, or because I am now over thirty-five. I welcome women now because my horizons have expanded. Women are beautiful. I listen to my spirit.

Memoirs of a Wanton Prude

Sheila Smith

*L*aughter, feasting, talking until midnight. I invited guests from my Unitarian Universalist congregation, my writing group, my dog club, my neighborhood, and my family to my seventieth birthday bash. My new love threw the party for me. Nothing unusual except at age sixty-nine, I'd fallen in love with a woman.

Sick! Immoral! Perverted! That's what the psychiatric and religious authorities proclaimed homosexuals to be back when I was a teenager in the McCarthy years. Gays and lesbians were persecuted along with Communists and considered just as subversive. Since homosexuality was outside the range of my experience, I absorbed the experts' attitudes. I expected to live a conventional life of marriage and children. Having a career outside the home was the most radical thing I could envision for myself.

Mother taught me that women need men to survive. That seemed logical. In those days, no one questioned women being paid less than men for the same job. It was perfectly legal to ban unescorted women from bars and restaurants. Personally, I wanted to be able to live well and have access to public accommodations.

My journey away from the prevailing '50s views began at a girls' high school. I fell in love with biology and I adored my female biology teacher. I hung around the lab looking for opportunities to wash glassware. One day I was railing to her about Mother's efforts to turn me into a girly-girl. According to Mother, acting stupid and helpless was the way to capture the necessary man.

"You can be a girl and a scientist," my teacher said, taking my hand. I still remember the warmth and acceptance it conveyed.

Girls' high school meant little association with boys. Unlike my classmates, I wasn't boy-crazy. I didn't even socialize with boys. The one exception was when Mother persuaded her friend's son to escort me to the prom. What would I say to Hughie? Turned out he didn't know what to say either. That one endless, awkward evening of sweaty-handed dancing composed my high school dating experience.

My emotional life centered on other girls. My best friend, Margaret, wrote in my senior yearbook, "You know how I feel." I felt the same about her; we spent a lot of time together and had a deep emotional connection. However, I had no sexual feelings for Margaret and we had no physical contact.

After high school, I worked as a counselor at a girls' camp. I remember two of the counselors spending all their time together, which seemed altogether natural and right to me. I never speculated on what they did inside their tent. Looking back, maybe they were more than friends.

At college, I found myself a man. I expressed my rebellious nature by choosing one with a beard. After we married, I continued my love affair with biology by working in a fruit fly lab.

Although I enjoyed our physical relationship, the marriage lacked emotional intimacy. I sought close emotional relationships with other women. When I was a young mother in the early '60s, I had a best friend I saw nearly every day. I could confide anything to Sarah. I loved her so much. I wished I could give her sexual pleasure, but at that time I believed only men could do that for women. I was so naïve I didn't realize that heterosexual women don't think such thoughts. In retrospect, I realize I was in love with Sarah.

We talked about living together when we were old ladies, although I had no frame of reference for women forming lasting partnerships with each other. The only all-woman household I knew of was that of my unmarried aunt who shared a home with my grandmother. After Sarah followed her husband to another state, she stopped writing or phoning. I grieved for years.

In 1961, there were anti-sodomy laws on the books in every state. Sometime during that decade, my husband's department hired its first woman professor. She wouldn't accept the job unless her woman friend was offered an administrative position in the department. There was talk that May and Liz were lesbians. I protested. How could such gracious women be lesbians? Looking back, I think they must have been life partners, and very brave women as well.

Ten years and one son later, my husband and I separated because he fell in love with his graduate student. Perhaps he was seeking emotional intimacy; I know I was. I still missed Sarah. Was there another woman with whom I could be close? That summer, 1972, I was working in a greenhouse as a lab tech. I met a coworker twelve years younger than me. Caroline and I hit it off—we talked and talked. Our friendship grew intense. I cared for her as much as I had for Sarah.

One day, Caroline confessed she was gay. I was surprised, but I'd heard of gay people by then. I could accept whatever Caroline was, although I told her I was straight. Our relationship heated up as the sun poured through the glass roof of the greenhouse and sent the inside temperatures to steaming. We talked for hours, went for long car rides after work, and wrote poetry to one another. Soon she told me she was in love with me, and therefore wanted to go to bed with me. Aghast, I turned her down. I was a girl from the '50s, a time when love didn't automatically lead to sex. Caroline protested my edict, but we continued to see a lot of each other.

Late one evening, we were lying on big pillows on my living room floor, listening to a Joan Baez record. The beauty and yearning in Joan's voice kindled a similar feeling between us. Caroline drew me to her and kissed me; I kissed her back. I wanted to go further but I wouldn't. I was still married and I reasoned that I would be committing adultery, just like my husband. Although Caroline gave up trying to bed me and moved to San Francisco, I was a changed woman. My relationship with her, truncated though it was, had opened a door, but I wasn't quite ready to go through it.

The following year, the American Psychiatric Association removed homosexuality from its list of mental disorders, but my upbringing held sway. It was bad enough raising my son in a one-parent family, but saddling him with a lesbian mother? No way! I could lose custody of him if my ex found me out, even though Oregon's anti-sodomy laws were off the books by then. I had to take the cure. I found a man to have sex with, responded, convinced myself I was "normal," and married in haste—possibly to stave off those "bad" feelings about women.

Over the next fifteen years, I realized that in an overpopulated world, sex was meant to cement relationships, not to reproduce. So it didn't matter which sex you did it with as long as it wasn't with someone else's partner. Also, in the '90s, the customs, the psychologists, and the law no longer pushed same-sex love into the shadows. By the time I reached fifty, I admitted to myself I was a lesbian, at least in theory.

But I was living fairly happily with a nice man. In coming-out stories I've read, the narrator leaves the opposite-sex partner in order to live a more authentic life. But for me it was more true to who I was to keep commitments. I didn't believe it was right to break up just because I wanted to seek greener pastures, any more than it would be if he left me to chase twenty-year-old bimbos. So I stayed with him. I lived the life vicariously by reading lesbian books, and I kept my feelings about women under wraps.

A few years later the marriage foundered because of too many disagreements over money. About then I met Dora. We were somewhat attracted to one another, but I sensed we wouldn't be right together. Also, the timing was all wrong. I needed to learn to live alone so that I would enter a new relationship out of want, not need.

I used my hiatus between relationships to explore lesbian culture. I went to potluck dinners, book discussion groups, women's music concerts, gatherings in restaurants. My new lesbian friends seemed like independent, kind, fun, loving, generally fine women. At first, going out with a bunch of lesbians was pretty scary. *What would the serving staff think? What if I saw someone I knew?*

In 2003, the U.S. Supreme Court overturned all state laws against same-sex relations. I'd been having coffee and lunch dates with a variety of gay women, but I didn't click with any of them except Bonnie. We talked for hours. She confided so many intimate things to me that I thought she wanted to progress to physical intimacy. When I confessed I had feelings for her, she told me she was a committed celibate. Rejected, I wailed "Greensleeves": "Alas, my love, you do me wrong . . . "

Over the next few years, I learned to savor solitude. I had interests, activities, a part-time job, and friends. Although the romantic aspect of my life was on the back burner, I was content, if not ecstatic. On Christmas Day of 2007, when my son and his family were scheduled to visit his father out of town, I spent the day happily alone. I'd made it! I expected to stay single for the rest of my days.

The following year at a gay fundraising event, I met a self-assured woman about my age with dark, knowing eyes. We introduced ourselves and chatted a few minutes about upcoming movies. I asked if she planned to see *Milk* when it came to town. She nodded. "I'm gay," Diana said. "You, too?"

"Sort of," I said. After all, I hadn't really ever done enough to earn my lesbian stripes.

We made a date for coffee. At Starbucks, we bonded over our love for movies, and animals, and our twisted senses of humor. We'd grown up on opposite coasts, but we had similar values. Diana had even begun attending my Unitarian Universalist church about a month earlier. She seemed to be what I was searching for: smart, kind, generous, emotionally open, attractive. The kind of woman I could live with the rest of my life.

Yet I didn't trust myself. After all, I'd made mistakes before. I needed another set of eyes and ears. I invited her out with a couple of trusted lesbian friends to see what they thought. "She's a keeper," my friends said. "You go, girl!"

"Am I being vetted?" Diana asked. Yep, she was sharp.

Still, before my mind became clouded by passion, I had to get to know her better. We had coffee, lunch, and dinner dates for a couple of months. Diana told me it wasn't so much she wanted to go to bed with me; it was that she wanted to wake up with me. Was this woman handing me a line? Diana added, "Lesbians are about intimacy." Intimacy was what I'd been seeking all my life. With a woman I could have emotional and physical intimacy in the same package. I let down my guard.

More worries arose. It was all very well and good being a theoretical lesbian, but going to bed with a real live woman who might have needs I couldn't fulfill? Who might want me to do things I wasn't comfortable with? I wouldn't be able to refer to my books in the heat of passion. Finally I screwed up my courage and told Diana I'd like to be more than friends.

The next step, one that many gay people accomplish in their teens or twenties, was coming out. A sandwich board proclaiming, "I'm Gay!" wasn't necessary, but I wanted to share this significant development with the important people in my life. My annual Christmas letter let me come out to my long-distance friends. In town, it went over better when I said I'd fallen in love with a particular person who happens to be a woman, rather than baldly stating that I'd become a lesbian.

Folks you expect to be tolerant aren't; folks you expect to be disapproving aren't. A friend with whom I'd been having dinner every Friday night for ten years made excuses to cancel our standing date. One of the women in my writing group attends a conservative church that disapproves of gay marriage. I took her out to lunch, told her of my new love. Not only was she not shocked; the first thing she asked was, "How did you meet Diana?"

The most significant coming-out hurdle was my son and his family because they had the power to keep my grandchildren away from me. Rather than tell them "Your mother is a lesbian!" I sent them a copy of my Advance Directive, which gives Diana the authority to pull the plug if I'm near death. They figured out that she's the most important person in my life and are happy I have someone who cares for me.

In contrast to many people of faith, coming out to my Unitarian Universalist congregation was effortless. In every Sunday's "Order of Service" these words are printed: "This Unitarian Universalist community welcomes and celebrates the presence and participation of transgender, gay, lesbian, heterosexual, and bisexual people." Diana and I always sat with each other, acted like a couple, and soon people recognized us as such. It's a blessing to be open.

Recently, we attended a gay choir concert at our church. Diana sat beside me, our thighs touching. I opened my eyes to see friends from town in front of me. I turned around to glimpse friends from the church community behind me. I sent out a prayer of gratitude for finding love in the winter of my life.

I Knew What I Was Giving Up

Sara C. Rauch

I left my boyfriend of three and a half years for a woman whose name I didn't know.

All I knew was that when I saw her, when she took my order for coffee and handed me back my change, our exchanges were more intense, more vivid, more real than the life I came home to every day.

And it was a good life: a beautiful apartment, part-time work I enjoyed, an attractive, intelligent, hard-working boyfriend my family loved. Everyone assumed we would get married, buy a house, have kids—and I did not disabuse them of this notion. If anything, I encouraged it. To everyone concerned, I was happy and I was lucky. Those two words were like a noose around my neck, because I was neither, and I was suffocating.

I knew I wanted to be with women; I'd known for years, had even indulged in college when I was far enough from home to keep it secret. But to my family, and to my new friends, and my coworkers, and every stranger on the streets of Northampton (ironic, if not self-torture, that I would choose a lesbian mecca to call home), I was straight. No one doubted my sexuality, no one questioned my choice of boyfriends, no women ever hit on me. I was very good at keeping my longings secret.

Until she appeared.

One June morning, on our way into town for the farmers' market, there she was, talking to customers in the coffee shop where she worked, and when I saw her—short brown curling hair, tattooed arms and legs, toothy smile, and these unthinkably large eyes that stared right down into me—I knew I was in trouble. My heart started pounding so hard I could barely say I wanted a small coffee, to go. My boyfriend, clueless as ever, didn't even notice the strain in my voice, didn't notice how quickly I walked away from the counter, grabbed my coffee, and left. I was embarrassed and exposed. Not to anyone else, but to myself. The part of me that I wanted so desperately to be hidden had just emerged. It felt like an unruly monster, something I had to avoid at all costs, lest I disturb my life's delicate balance.

But it was too late. I couldn't keep myself away from the coffee shop, hoping she would be there behind the counter, for the little electric shock that I got when she smiled at me, or just the pleasure of seeing her behind the counter making drinks. I started dreaming about her, and would wake up happy, only to realize I was still in my real life—still finding my boyfriend in his study, still sitting down at my own desk to write (more and more often about her, pieces I could not show anyone, that I kept in a separate folder, pieces I loved as truth, but was also completely afraid of), still showering and going to work, holding my breath, wishing I could go back to sleep. My (already tiny) sex drive collapsed, and terrible fights ensued, where I told my boyfriend to go find someone else to sleep with— what I wanted for myself—and he told me he never would. I struggled and pushed and he wouldn't let me go. I began hating him for trying to make our relationship work, thinking if only he would end it, he would be to blame. I wanted to not feel so guilty, so indecent, so wrong.

I felt like I couldn't say a word, not even a peep to my best friend, about what was happening. When I finally let it slip in a poem I gave to a friend to workshop, she said, "You need to leave him." But I couldn't, or thought I couldn't, because there was a lease, and shared furniture, and cats I didn't want to give up. I didn't have the money to pay first, last, and security on another apartment, I couldn't tell my family I was unhappy and needed their help. I was scared they wouldn't help me if they knew what was truly going on.

I had spent three and a half years in a relationship that sucked up all my energy and gave me nothing in return—isolated and lonely and faking a happiness that no one could see through. Honestly, I had spent my whole life there, so afraid of how I felt that I couldn't even admit it to myself. I was so envious of the women I saw every day who were living their lives the way they wanted to. I was fascinated by women who could never "pass," the way I did, as straight. After I left my boyfriend, it took me months and months to forgive myself. Forgive myself for suffocation by my own hand, forgive myself for holding myself hostage with an idea of perfection (straightness) that was my own creation. Looking back, I still have a hard time understanding why I was so driven to make myself fit into the lifestyle that I thought was expected of me. Despite my youth, my progressive education, my liberal upbringing, I still wanted to turn away from the truth: I liked women.

<hr />

When I confessed to my mother that I was unhappy, that my relationship was failing, that I wanted to move out, but needed to borrow money, she said, "Of course. How much do you need?" An offer of help. No questions asked. A life raft in the vast ocean of my difficult decision. She came to look at new apartments with me, took me to lunch, asked no questions.

And so I moved out. It wasn't the first apartment where I'd lived alone, but this one was a new start. It was my first ever expression of independence. A third-floor attic apartment with steep, pointed ceilings and skylights and carpeted stairs.

I scrubbed every inch of it, vacuumed, and with the help of my brother, brought the furniture up the twisting stairs. I was in a great mood the day I moved; I had a set of keys in my pocket; I could breathe for the first time in years. I brought both cats over, and we were immediately at home.

I left my false life behind me, and confessed to my friends and coworkers and family why I was leaving. One of my friends said, "It's about time." My coworkers asked for updates: Had the girl in the coffee shop smiled at me? Spoken to me? Would I introduce myself? My family said they only wanted me to be happy.

My best friend put it bluntly, "I knew you weren't happy. I haven't seen you smile in years."

Of course, after the commotion of moving settled, and the last box was broken down, I was left with myself and my strange longings. No more distractions or shackles. I wasn't really sure what to do besides introduce myself, via coffee cup with a note on it, to the woman whose very presence behind the counter of a coffee shop had provided the impetus for me to find happiness. As it turned out, she was already taken, but she was kind to me and acted flattered by my awkward attention, and always stood ready with a smile and wink when I went in for coffee. Without even knowing it, she saved me from something akin to death—not physical, but mental, emotional, and spiritual, all before she'd ever introduced herself.

It took time, and some stumbling, to figure out what I was doing. I kept looking around at all the women I saw, and I soon began understanding their fear, their insecurity, their lives, just as complex and difficult as my own. I tiptoed slowly into a community of women who like women, making little connections here and there, trying to gauge the learning curve, which was steep. It was strange to me, and a lot less safe than the straight world of lies I knew how to navigate so well.

I had spent my whole life being straight—the stories, games, books, movies, role models: all straight. That is not to say that loving someone, truly loving someone, differs from one gender to another. Love remains essentially the same. But the social world of things, the terminology, the flirtations, the kissing, the who-calls-who, that was all different. Being the kind of woman who had always been pursued by men, I wasn't prepared for taking on the role of pursuer. I still went out with my straight friends, and I still got hit on by men (it was life-changing, learning to say when pushed, "No, thank you, I'm gay"), but women didn't come near me. It was frustrating, and lonely. There were a few times when I called up a friend and said, "You know, I'm not sure I'm cut out for being a lesbian. Maybe I'll go back to dating men." And quickly that friend would remind me of all I had told her, how miserable I had been, how I hated the mask I'd been wearing my whole life, how I needed to be brave, and how brave I'd been so far.

A friend suggested I look at the personal ads on craigslist. She found one that read "Seeking low-maintenance, high femme," and said it was perfect for me.

I said, "But I'm not a high femme."

She said, "Yes, you are."

"No, I'm not girly at all."

"Sara, you paint your nails, you wear dresses and lacy underwear, you put on eye makeup, and you like pink. If that's not femme, I don't know what is."

"But I fix my own toilet when it breaks, and I drive a standard, and I know the difference between a Phillips and a flathead screw driver. I keep my nails short!"

"Yes, that's the low-maintenance part."

We both laughed. She was right, and so was I. But that word—femme—doesn't come close to defining me. It is a label that perhaps suits my appearance (on the days I choose to wear a miniskirt, or paint my nails hot pink), but doesn't suit my attitude. "Butch" and "femme" are desperately inadequate terms, and yet they are so ingrained in the common culture that I don't think they'll ever disappear. And I am no more drawn to one type of woman over another; if anything it is women who resist any kind of categorization that are most appealing to me. There is beauty all along the spectrum, and now that I am free enough to admit it, I see that beauty everywhere.

Since others see me as femme, despite my resistance to the word, I am given some reprieve in a world that still, despite all the progress made, likes women to look a certain way. Standing alone at a busy intersection, I can almost guarantee no one would identify me as gay. And I can't change that, so maybe what bothers me most is that I still "pass." It both amuses and annoys me when I tell someone I've just met that I'm gay, or mention my partner. The look on their face gives them away. I was seeing a specialist recently, and after a short exam, he sat down to write out a prescription, saying, "So, tell me about yourself—Are you married? Single?" When I replied, "Well, neither, but my partner and I just bought a house," he actually stopped writing, looked up at me, and said, "You're gay?" I nodded my head, not knowing whether I should be angry or if I should laugh at him. "Well, congratulations on your new house," he said, trying to cover his embarrassment.

<hr />

I met my partner at a dinner party one early November evening—cold enough to wear boots and sweaters, the beginning of another New England winter. She was sitting at the kitchen table when I walked in, and when she looked at me and smiled, I was so embarrassed that I tried to hide behind the friend I had come in with. We made introductions, and I spent the whole night, and much of a month after, wondering if she was flirting with me. She had touched my arm, did that mean something? She had followed me into the room where I was putting on my jacket to leave; certainly that meant she liked me. Or at least wanted to talk to me. Over and over, these questions, asking my friends, what did they think? I wanted to see her again, but I didn't know how. I tried wishful thinking; I tried hinting to the host of the dinner party; I hoped I would run into her on the street. Nothing. So, I tracked her down on MySpace. A friend of a friend of a friend. I felt silly, I felt like a stalker, but I woke up one morning and realized that if I didn't see her again, if I didn't express some interest, I would regret it. As I pressed the friend request button I thought, if she's not interested, at least I tried.

Over the computer, she said we should have coffee sometime, but when I messaged my phone number, she messaged hers back. My coworkers said, "You have to call her. She wants you to make the move." But hadn't I made the first move, finding her on MySpace? "Yes," they said, "but she wants to know you are truly interested, she wants to know you're sincere." I was way out on the limb of discomfort already, and had to go even further.

I wanted so badly to be swept off my feet without having to do any work, because that's the straight relationship myth, propagated in every fairy tale, movie, and storybook romance. I wanted to be found. It felt so strange to pick up the phone to call her and leave a message saying that maybe we could get coffee in the next couple of days. When she called back a half hour later, I saw her number on the caller ID and almost let it go to voicemail. My heart was beating so hard I thought I wouldn't be able to say hello. But I answered—and it was so natural—as we talked about our cats and our holiday plans and made a date for two nights later. She called back an hour later and said, "I was thinking, would you like to come with me to my work holiday party tomorrow night?"

"It's a friend's birthday," I told her. "I'm supposed to have a drink with her. Let me see when that's happening, can I call you back?" I was stalling. I wanted to say yes immediately, but then, I didn't want to look desperate, and I didn't want to break plans with a friend on her birthday.

When I called, my friend said, "Of course you are going with her. If it isn't going well, you can use me as an excuse to leave. If it does go well, we'll get together some other time."

That first night together was a revelation. Just sitting next to her on the couch, in a house filled with a hundred of her coworkers, it was as if we were the only people in the room. And later, back at her apartment in the quiet, kissing her for hours, barely being able to stand up to leave at 2:00 AM.

She swept me off my feet, and I reveled in our long nights together, our long looks and longer kisses. Every inch of me responded to her, my whole body, my insides; when she looked at me, when she touched me, it felt like every feeling, every emotion that I'd stored up for so many years, was surfacing. It was overwhelming, it was exhilarating, I was turned on, inside out. Within days I knew I was madly in love with her. Walking together in the snowy woods, surrounded by a mighty quiet, felt like a blessing bestowed: within two weeks I agreed to meet her in Paris a month later for a whirlwind tour of the city where she fluently spoke the language and love is magnified in every old building, every narrow street, every tiny, darkly lit restaurant.

Not to say there wasn't doubt, worry, anxiety, reality impinging on our blissed-out state. Those things were there in the background, bringing up questions about my intentions, my past. More than once, she asked if I was sure I wanted to be with women. What if I didn't like it? I could only tell her that I was certain. It had been a very long, careful decision to leave my previous relationship, and I had had several months of being single and considering my choice. I knew where my attraction lay, I knew I would always be unhappy and faking it if I were in a straight relationship. I was more certain of my decision than I was of anything else. I knew what I was giving up. I knew that despite the little bubble of Northampton, there would be (and always will be) the possibility of disapproval, or hate, or silent condemnation. I knew I was giving up my right to always hold someone's hand in public, because in Northampton it is okay, but it isn't okay in Boca Raton, or Houston, or Peoria. I knew I would have to use my intuition and keep my mouth shut in places where being a lesbian might make me unsafe. I knew that I might meet people who judged me and my lifestyle, people who would think there was something wrong with me. I knew not everyone would accept my life and love with the grace and equanimity that my friends and family do. I knew I was giving up the heterosexual privilege I had enjoyed my whole life.

I also knew, and still know, I made the right choice.

The Claim

Crystal Hooper

I was a stable, married, twenty-nine-year-old mother when I fell in love with a coworker . . . a *female* coworker. There was no tangible affair to speak of, yet my heart became more emotionally attached to Zoe (not her real name) than it had ever been to my husband of six years. Songwriting became my outlet. I expressed my frustrations and confusion about my personal hell in my lyrics. Since I kept my feelings a secret, this escape granted me the release I needed. Words poured out of me as the beginning of yet another song.

I've been driving myself crazy trying not to go insane. I foresee the complications but I can't deny the claim.

I loved my husband dearly. He was sensitive and sweet. Complicated and temperamental. And he was known to some of our friends as the "girl" in our relationship—a label he willingly accepted with humor. We were best friends who could share everything. I believed I had chosen the right companion, and would have never married if I thought otherwise. So I lived out my perfect suburban life with my husband, while I fell in love with Zoe in silence.

In college, I had never "experimented" with women, although I had wanted to. The opportunity just didn't present itself. I began dating guys in seventh grade. It didn't feel unnatural, though I could not relate to the term "boy crazy."

I graduated high school still a virgin. But don't get me wrong, everything that *wasn't* intercourse was fair game as far as I was concerned. I racked up my fair share of rural, backwoods parking with my high school boyfriends. It was always very mechanical. I cared for my boyfriends as friends, but fooling around was never an extension of my affection for them. It wasn't personal. Sexual experimentation is a basic part of growing up. And damn, it just felt good.

Ever since I was eight years old, I have known that my uncle was gay. I was raised to believe homosexuality was perfectly acceptable, and would get defensive if anyone stated otherwise. Before falling for Zoe, I had only dated guys and my attraction to girls was limited to hoping just to kiss one some day. So the thought never crossed my mind that I might be a lesbian. I thought my same-sex attraction was more a curiosity than a lifestyle. If it happened, the experience would be strictly experimental, and would not lead to a relationship.

I was drawn to girls who walked with confidence and wore tattoos as a mark of independence and nonconformity. Someone like that could overpower my shyness, and I would have no choice but to submit to her advances (as if succumbing to an aggressive admirer would exempt me from claiming any responsibility).

But I did get married without having ever kissed a girl. As a wife, I wasn't the jealous type so it never bothered me if my husband said another woman was sexy or beautiful. In fact, sometimes I would agree (or disagree) with his opinions, and I spoke freely about different women that I found attractive. He thought he had the coolest wife ever, and we both thought our relationship was the pinnacle of bonds. We could tell each other anything. We always said that nothing and no one could ever come between us if we didn't let it. It was up to us. I couldn't imagine spending the rest of my life with anyone else.

Then along came Zoe.

All my life I knew I belonged in Nashville. When I arrived as a teenager to attend Belmont University, it felt like home. And the music industry was the central reason for that feeling. I wanted to be a songwriter, and I knew this was the place to make it happen. But for seven years, the Music Row inner circle had been playing a most fierce game of Red Rover with me—I was never allowed to come over no matter how hard I tried. I knew some reputable contacts, recorded several demos at legitimate studios, and had the opportunity to meet with ASCAP and multiple publishing houses about my songs; but something just never clicked. So I spent my days collecting a pitiful hourly wage doing administrative work at a music publishing company. I took the job to get my foot in the door, and hoped it would lead to something more.

The company needed to hire someone, and I was given the task of interviewing candidates. Zoe was one of them. She showed up for the appointment dressed in dark slacks and a white button-down shirt. Her long wavy brown hair was parted down the middle and suggested she was low-maintenance, yet stylish. She smiled easily and radiated calm. During the interview, I assessed her personality. Laid back. Cool. Unpretentious. Slight sarcasm. Little did I know that this stranger, barely in her twenties, would soon rock the foundations of my personal world.

Zoe got the job, and we immediately struck up a friendship. She and I mirrored each other on a wide range of topics, including our humor, musical tastes, favorite foods, and a love of the same obscure television shows. Sometimes at work we would just look at each other and crack up, knowing we were thinking the exact same thing. About a month into our friendship, she revealed that she was gay.

I was shocked and secretly excited at her revelation. Shocked not because she was gay, but because I had never known someone who *looked* like her who was gay. To know that this beautiful, feminine woman was into other women was . . . sexy. *Really* sexy.

She was so much like me, *and* she liked girls. That was almost too much for me to handle. My platonic affection for her shifted into a mild infatuation at that point. If only I could have looked ahead to see where I would be two years later. I would have celebrated that day—or cursed it—as the first in a series of days that were consumed with a confusing, enchanting, passionate, pure, deeply rooted obsession for another woman. I wanted to know more about this side of her. I had never heard her speak of any romantic relationships, so my curiosity ran wild. Did she have a girlfriend? Had she ever had a girlfriend? Did she ever have a boyfriend? Ever kissed a guy? Ever kissed a girl? Had she had sex with a man? Did she have sex with girls . . . and if so, how? I was getting visuals. I was intrigued by her and wanted to know all the details, but I restrained myself from overwhelming her with questions and settled for tidbits when she offered.

I soon learned she had never had a girlfriend. Never felt the touch of a woman. *Just like me.* She longed for this connection and I wanted to fill that void. I found myself yearning to be the person who got to kiss her . . . hold her . . . touch her. I wanted to guide her through her first physical and emotional experiences. And in turn, she could guide me. I knew it was wrong, but I wanted to be that person. The first way I admitted the attraction to myself was when I thought that if I had met Zoe before I met my husband, I could have fallen for her. And the thought of being with her slowly began to take over my mind.

After several months, these pleasurable, entertaining thoughts began to dominate my consciousness. It became difficult to function on a daily basis. She was a permanent resident of my mind. No matter the task—brushing my teeth, feeding my daughter, driving to work, watching TV, hanging out with my husband—I was always thinking of her.

On the surface, I appeared to be living the perfect life as a happy, young, married woman raising my first child. Yet, on the inside, my frustrations mounted daily and I felt unsettled. While grappling with my dilemma, I came to the conclusion that the key was control. There was no denying that I loved Zoe. And those were feelings that I could not shake.

So I focused on what I could control, and that was how I chose to handle the situation. I chose at that point to remain committed to my husband. I did love him very much. He was my best friend and the father of my daughter, and we had seven years together. Hurting him was something I would strive to avoid at all costs, which meant not revealing my feelings to Zoe even though the stress of not telling her was taking its toll inside me.

One night I had the most amazing dream. In this dream, the room was quiet. The bed was soft. The colors were very pale and dream-like. And she and I were lying on that soft bed next to each other. Together. Cheek to cheek, looking up. And the only thing I felt was an overwhelming peace.

My morning alarm abruptly stole me from my oasis. But I woke up with a smile on my face. And after I turned the alarm off, that feeling of peace was very real. It lingered for several minutes. The sensation faded as I started my daily routine, but as always, the thought of her followed me.

When I left the music industry for a new opportunity, I grieved the loss of not seeing Zoe every day. She was one of my closest friends, and above all else, I didn't want our friendship to change or lessen because of it.

On my last day working with Zoe, I promised to go with her sometime to a local gay bar so she wouldn't have to go alone. She was beginning to get frustrated with her love life, or lack thereof. I was excited to accompany her to a gay bar, even if it was only to scope out potential girlfriends for her. Lipstick Lounge was considered to be the hot spot. And after our first night out at Lipstick, we liked it so much we made it a weekly ritual.

At first, Lipstick Thursdays were an excuse to see Zoe. It was a guaranteed, once-a-week fix for my addiction. But it quickly became much more. I began to need Lipstick Thursdays just as much as I wanted Zoe. My feelings were beginning to expand beyond her. I started to think that maybe even if I couldn't have her, I could possibly be with another woman. I could have a *relationship* with another woman. It was the first time in my life that I considered that notion.

At Lipstick Thursday, I was free to be myself, without the pressure of fitting into a mold. It had a very welcoming, non-clique atmosphere that I absorbed like fresh air. Each week, I went home after work, spent some quality time with the family, and put my daughter to bed. After that, I put on fresh makeup and did my hair as my husband settled in for the night, rocking away in his chair and zoning out to his favorite music. My nights out were also his quality nights alone. He enjoyed solitude, and began to look forward to Lipstick Thursdays just as much as I did. And since I was going to a lesbian bar, there was no fear of me getting hit on by other guys. He did not anticipate that the downfall of our relationship would be my attraction to women. It was during that brief four-month run of Lipstick Thursdays that my two separate lives pulled me in opposite directions.

Zoe soon found a girlfriend, which affected me deeply. I was happy for Zoe, but found myself almost paralyzed from the pain of realizing I would never have a chance to be with her. Thoughts of her distracted me at work, leaving me to regroup in the bathroom so I could focus on the tasks of the day. This made me feel weak—and pissed me off beyond belief. I was stronger than this. I was committed to my husband and planned to be with him to the end, but I couldn't stop thinking of Zoe. It was completely frustrating that she had such a hold on me. I had no power over my emotions.

I knew being with Zoe was not right. As much as I wanted to believe she felt for me even a fraction of what I felt for her, I was pretty sure she thought of me as a friend and no more. I was, after all, married with a child. I wanted so desperately to forget about her, and forget the knowledge that my love for her exceeded the emotional threshold of my marriage. But Zoe was in me. Meeting her introduced me to love in a way that I hadn't experienced with my husband or other guys. And if this raw emotion existed, I knew there were greater emotions that he and I were not providing to each other. He could sense a change in me, and the tension in our house was evident to both of us.

I needed help sorting everything out. I invited Zoe and her girlfriend (who was now my friend as well) out to dinner in order to discuss, in general terms, the burden of my same-sex attraction. I listened to their coming-out stories, and their stories of discovering true identity. I related to their stories of grieving over the ideal of a traditional family, and the ability to create a new life easily with your partner. I analyzed every aspect. So far, I had stayed with my husband, and it wasn't working. It never resolved anything within me. My feelings had continued to intensify and I could barely function. Something had to give.

As we talked, I realized the limits of our relationship were fair to neither me nor my husband, but I needed to weigh what I would be giving up against what I would gain. I had more than just myself to consider. My decisions would severely impact the lives of my husband and my daughter, the two most important people in my life. Was it selfish of me to consider other options? Would I finally be accepting who I always was, or was this a recent shift? Was it just the fabled marital seven-year itch?

There was no easy way out. When I asked Zoe and her girlfriend what they thought I should do, they kept saying the same thing.

"I think you know what you need to do."

And deep down I did, though I wasn't sure if I was ready to admit it.

When I got home that night, my husband was already several bottles into his case of beer. He stayed up in the bonus room as I got into bed alone. Wide awake, I looked up at the shadows on the ceiling. I remembered that dream I had of Zoe and me, beside each other. And that feeling of peace returned. All the tension in my body released and gave way to a pure calm. I knew what I had to do and I was comfortable with my decision. If he hadn't been drinking, I would have had the conversation with him then. But that wouldn't have been fair to him. I had to wait until the next day after work.

My night of sleep did not change my mind. I woke up with a mission. I went to work, my mind whirling. Before walking into the office, I found solace in a coworker when I confided my secrets to her in my car. Tears poured down my face as I asked, "What would you think if I told you I was gay?" She said she would not be surprised at all if I was. It was one thing to admit it to Zoe and her girlfriend, another to confess it to a straight coworker. Although it was a simple answer, it played a large part in giving me the courage to go through with my plan.

That night I told my husband, "I think I might be gay." He was the first to say the word "divorce," and immediately called his parents to give them the news before allowing us the space to fully digest what had been set into motion. I stood silently and watched as my husband collapsed and sobbed on the floor. There was nothing I could say or do to ease his pain. I was the cause of his suffering, and knowing that tortured me.

It was an intense night, but I could see the bigger picture. I knew there would be some messy times in the near future, but they wouldn't last. I had faith that my husband and I would find our way back to being positive forces in each other's lives. We would always be family, even if we weren't married to each other.

And I was right.

It took nearly a year, but our relationship transformed into a beautiful friendship. There were times when his healing emotions became erratic, and I absorbed the blame. We struggled to find consistency for us, and our daughter, in our new reality of separate households. We continued to support each other emotionally, and I encouraged his excitement in realizing that new relationship doors would be opening for him as well. In those first few months of transition, I met KJ, the girl I now consider to be my wife. I believe if my life had gone according to plan, I would have never settled for that office job in the music industry and had the eye-opening experiences that led me to KJ.

My husband taught me about unconditional love. Even after we divorced, his love for me as a person remains; as does mine for him. All along he loved me for who I am, even if I was changing and evolving into a person that needed to be with someone other than him. He and my daughter are true constants.

My transformation has been the product of love. Zoe introduced me to raw emotion. No matter how hard I tried, I couldn't make myself not love her. It was only after my separation and months of processing my emotions that I decided it was the right time to tell her, to let go, and free my heart up to give and receive love. We got together for dinner one night, and I asked her to join me afterward in my car for a private conversation. She was aware that my issues started when I fell in love with a particular girl, but I took a deep breath and revealed to her that she was that girl. I broke down and cried while she listened, genuinely unaware of the impact she had on my life. There was some noticeable tension in the car, but neither of us would allow the drama to overshadow the reality of our friendship. Finally liberating myself from that emotional baggage gave me the closure I needed to move on, putting Zoe behind me and focusing on my budding relationship with KJ.

I met KJ on a Lipstick Thursday, two months after I separated from my husband. Our relationship took a fast course and I found myself in a committed relationship much sooner than I would have anticipated. We are complete opposites, but we balance each other in a way that complements us perfectly. With her, I am able to experience a deeper level of being. And I know that completely sounds like I made it up, but if I didn't experience it myself, I would be just as skeptical. With her, life is more vivid. I can actually *feel* our love.

I remember the moment I fell for her. She laid her head on my chest and in one fantastic moment, my heart absorbed all I would feel for her in my lifetime. I could see her face aging with the years in my mind, and I knew . . . KJ was "the one."

If I died without ever knowing that feeling, I would have been cheated. I have no doubt I made the right decision to leave my husband.

It took over two years of processing to get here, but I am now safely on the other side: where my family includes my daughter, KJ, my ex-husband, my ex in-laws, and my new in-laws. The support I received from family and friends has been humbling. I can only hope I would've provided that same positive support if this had happened to someone else I knew. But it happened to me. And if this can happen to me, it can happen to anyone. I was stable. Focused. Responsible. And this thing hit me like a brick wall. But I recovered. And I am proud of my resilience. You could say that I am gay. But all I really know for sure is that I am in love.

Wedding Gown Closet

Katherine A. Briccetti

The summer I was fifteen, my mother pulled her ivory wedding gown from the closet. She placed the oversize white box onto her dressing table and pulled back tissue paper before lifting out the satiny gown. I took it from her and, holding it in front of me, studied my reflection in the floor-length mirror. My braids flopped across its bust, and dirty sneakers poked out from below its hem, but it looked as if it might fit. Posing in the mirror, I imagined wearing it on my own wedding day. I loved the idea of tradition, a mother's wedding dress becoming her daughter's.

Fifteen years later, in 1987—the era of the Moral Majority—my lover Pam and I climbed our favorite trail in Point Lobos State Reserve near Monterey. On that fogless morning in May, cotton ball clouds hovered over the horizon, the sun so bright it made the ocean glitter. Resting at a lookout, we gazed at the boulders below sprinkled with cormorants and dozing sea lions. The water swirled and waves battered the boulders, sending spray up almost as high as our perch.

At that time, lesbian and gay couples were just beginning to celebrate unions in churches and temples, but it wasn't common practice yet. Representative Barney Frank had just come out publicly. Matthew Shepard's murder was still a decade in the future. To our families, we were only roommates. Pam and I had left our friends behind in the Bay Area, opting instead for a private commitment ceremony; our only witnesses that day were the terns sweeping past overhead. Next to the ocean, we inhaled the warm scent of the Monterey pine trees, the cool, briny breeze, and the baked mulch of the path.

Wearing jeans, sweatshirts, and hiking shoes, and with the whoosh of the ocean as background music, Pam and I exchanged gold and black jade rings. I caressed her cheek with the backs of my fingers, still surprised at its softness, so different from my whiskered lovers of the past. After scanning to make sure the trail was free of hikers, I leaned over and we kissed.

Pam and I met at the public school where we both worked and quickly became friends over lunchtime chats about books. On visits to her cozy Berkeley house, I perused the tall bookcases filled with novels and poetry. At lunch, though, our interests turned to Shirley MacLaine's reincarnation memoirs, Jane Robert's *Seth* books on psychic channeling and ESP, and anything we could find about past lives, astral projection, and communicating through dreams—phenomena we called "woo-woo." We were not gullible, we reminded each other, rolling our eyes to show we hadn't been truly converted. But we were still fascinated, something drawing us both into the past, to the possibility that we had lived before.

After my fiancé and I broke up for the final time, and I moved out, Pam and I met at the movies, for dinner, and once even braved a psychic fair in Berkeley. I began to feel like a high school girl around Pam, restless and eager for our next meeting, when we could embrace in greeting and parting. When she brushed my arm in conversation, a warm blush traveled across my skin. Some mornings, she left a miniature bouquet of pink Cecil Bruner roses tied with a rubber band on my desk before I got to work. We exchanged Hallmark friendship cards and talked on the phone late at night, drunk with sleepiness and promise. "Good night, sweet friend," she said, and inside my chest something shifted. But even in my journal I was afraid of admitting my feelings. "We're just friends," I wrote.

Growing up in Indianapolis, I had known only one openly gay person, a florist who rented the apartment above our garage, sharing it with his woolly mammoth–like St. Bernard and an occasional boyfriend. I don't remember conversations about homosexuality in our house, but the unspoken message had been that our tenant was a good person, a welcome addition to our social circle.

When I was in college in Indiana, Anita Bryant had begun her "Save Our Children" campaign to fight an anti-discrimination ordinance in Florida. I don't remember boycotting orange juice, but I knew she was a bigot and I enjoyed seeing her get a pie in the face on television. When my Grandma Rose heard I was moving to San Francisco, though, she cited a news magazine article referring to the city as the "Sodom of America." I had to look up the word "Sodom," and although I didn't understand all of its connotations, I took her words as a grim warning.

When I moved to San Francisco at age twenty, the owner of the downtown office supply store where I first worked was an older gay man, and the manager was a lesbian. I hadn't known any lesbians before, and she both intrigued and frightened me. Once, when she reached in front of me to collect extra bills from the cash register, her bare arm brushed against mine, and I recoiled, stepping back so we wouldn't touch again.

Except for one other straight woman, the sales clerks were young gay men who wore creased khakis and Izod sports shirts over their muscular chests and biceps. In certain sections of town, gay men walked with their hands in their boyfriends' pockets, an intimacy that had surprised me. When they kissed in public, I was both fascinated and appalled. Some of them flaunted it, precisely because people like me were trying to send them back into the closet with our moth-eaten morality, and—a novel realization for me—because they were not ashamed. San Francisco had been a brave new world for me when I arrived. I wore a beige London Fog raincoat with its belt tightly cinched and rode on the outside of the cable car, my waist-length, blond hair blowing behind me. I was so straight, so naive.

Almost ten years after moving to California, and a few weeks after the psychic fair in Berkeley, Pam and I met after work for dinner at the 4th Street Bar and Grill, a seafood restaurant near the Marina. The young trees outside the restaurant sparkled with white lights wound around their winter-bared branches. Inside, warm scents of spices and colognes intermingled. Seated at one of the tables next to the windows, we smiled at each other, as if it were impossible to stop.

"This is nice," she said, her curls shimmering in the candlelight. I tuned out the people on either side of us as we talked, gradually aware of the flip-flopping, tingling sensations in my stomach and rushing heat connecting my face, gut, and groin—something I'd felt only with men before.

"Hey, let's send a message in our dreams tonight," I said. "Just one image or one word. Want to?" There was an even stronger charge between us that night, and I was sure we could communicate this way, too.

"I'll send it," she said, her stare boring into my eyes, "and you concentrate on receiving it."

"And tomorrow at work I'll tell you what word or image I get." I met her intense gaze, and felt giddy. I was eager to get to bed, to carry out our experiment, so I could be with her in my sleep, too.

When we parted outside the restaurant three hours later, we held our embrace longer and tighter than I had with other female friends. This was different from friendship; I didn't want the evening to end, didn't want to say goodnight to her. But I didn't know what I meant to her, or whether she behaved this way with all her straight, female friends. Even though she had lived with another woman for many years, and someone at work had spelled it out for me, I even began to question whether she was gay. Lesbians had boyish haircuts, wore clunky boots, and didn't shave their legs. She didn't fit the stereotype.

At home, I fantasized about kissing her and tried to imagine what it would be like to make love with a woman, how it would work, how it would feel. But this was not in my life plan, and I didn't know how to understand my feelings. Was I enjoying a temporary diversion? Was I experimenting, resisting expectations? I had always believed I would marry a man and have babies. I didn't want a relationship I'd have to keep secret. Time was running short, I was almost thirty, and I needed to find my life's mate. I wanted those babies. This, falling in love with a woman, was not supposed to happen.

At seven o'clock the next morning, Pam's 1970 VW Bug buzzed to a stop in front of my San Leandro apartment. She had never dropped in like this; my apartment was not even on her way to work.

"Did you get my dream message?" she asked when I opened the door and saw her standing there next to a spray of calla lilies. Tiny wings inside my chest fluttered. I'd gone to sleep the night before desperate to receive her words, but it wasn't words that had appeared to me. Instead, I'd dreamed about swimming, finding her underwater and kissing her, the two of us hidden from the rest of the world beneath the mirror-like ceiling above us.

"No, I didn't get it," I said. "I really tried. What did you send?"

She smiled, shook her head slightly. "You try sending me something tonight, okay?" Pacing my tiny kitchen while I sliced tomatoes for my lunch, she said nothing for several moments. "What's happening here, with us, I mean?" she said finally, smiling with her mouth and frowning with her eyes.

"I have no idea."

"I wasn't looking for this—falling in love with you."

My stomach flipped over. "Me neither."

I placed the paring knife in the sink and wiped my hands on a kitchen towel, trying to steady my hands. As she passed me, I reached out and rested a hand on her shoulder. She spun to face me, and I leaned down to kiss her, shocking myself with my audacity. It was a gentle kiss; we joined tentatively at first, then more passionately, releasing the tension built over the weeks. The softness of her lips amazed me.

"Wow!" she whispered after we stepped apart.

I clasped my hands behind my back to keep them from trembling. "What are we going to do now?"

She shook her head, kissed me softly again, and left for work.

"I'm not attracted to women," I wrote to my friend Nancy in Indiana; the friend who in high school had known me as boy crazy, who had taken me to get a pregnancy test in college. She was married now, pregnant for the first time. "But I'm falling in love with this person," I wrote. Instead of mailing the letter, though, I hid it in my journal.

Over the next months, I was torn. On weekends, Pam and I walked our dogs together on the Berkeley campus, ate dinner in town, and held hands in the dark watching art films at the UC Theater. We sat kissing in one of our cars before parting for the night.

The excitement, novelty, and temptation to act out, to radically part with what was expected of me fought with my need to keep things unencumbered and safe. "I just want a normal, happy home life and family," I wrote in my journal. Normal. But normal was changing. I'd become friends with the gay men at the stationery store, had been called a fag hag one night outside a disco by a carload of boys cruising by. I was no longer afraid of a lesbian brushing against me, but I still couldn't share this with my family and friends. My Indiana friends and family did not openly disdain gays and lesbians, but I think we had shared an unacknowledged sense of superiority, even relief, that we were not *that way*.

As my friendship with Pam deepened, I wanted to believe—*needed* to believe—that my parents thought life was more interesting, more harmonious, when differences were embraced rather than dodged. But it was one thing to rent an apartment to a gay florist, another to learn your daughter was kissing another woman and contemplating making love with her.

Even after kissing Pam, I didn't feel "gay," and I didn't think being gay happened like this, so immediately. Everything I'd read suggested that people suspected they were gay at least by adolescence, and that was not my experience. I couldn't explain what was happening to me. I also couldn't understand what was wrong with something that felt this good, this right. How could it be wrong to love someone? Eventually, I even began to feel slightly *superior* to heterosexuals. *Look what I'm experiencing,* I thought, *I bet you aren't as enlightened as I am.* But I was still confused, and sad that I couldn't share what was happening to me with anyone.

After several weeks' titillation, kissing, and tentative touching, one evening I took Pam's hand and led her to my bedroom. Clothed, we lay next to each other on my bed, and with fingers, lips, and tongues, explored skin hidden under shirts and slowly unzipped jeans.

I stopped dating men. Every Friday evening, I loaded my laundry basket and my dog into my Nissan Sentra and drove the ten miles to Pam's house for the weekend. We were in what we called Phase One of our relationship: in love and hot for each other.

At work, we behaved with collegial reserve. We feared that telling the truth could have caused us irreparable harm. Although it was hard to imagine, I believed my family might disown me, and I'd read about gay teachers being fired, even in the late '80s, even in California. When people at work asked about my love life, I shrugged and laughed. Sometimes I invented boyfriends, conjuring up men I'd dated in the past. While I was more in love than I'd ever been and wanted nothing more than to be with Pam seven days a week instead of two, inside I was a mess. I had a huge secret, and I hated keeping it. I asked my mother to call me on Thursday evenings instead of Saturdays, making up something about a ceramics class so I wouldn't have to tell her why I wasn't home on the weekends.

On Sunday evenings, I reluctantly packed up my clean laundry, led my dog to the car, and returned to my apartment. I had many friends, a strong sense of community in my adopted state, but this secret disconnected me from my circle. I began to grind my teeth in my sleep, and I shouldn't have been surprised by the return of the dream that had chased me since college.

In the dream, I can't find my way back to the dormitory after classes. I wander outside, my breath quickening; I can't locate the right building. Then I'm inside a dorm, roaming its halls looking for my room. The building is usually a tower, often the halls are circular, and I trudge around and around looking for a door that looks familiar. I climb the stairs to try another floor, but I never find my room.

Months after our private oceanside ceremony, Pam and I were still giving each other monthly anniversary cards, calling each other "Sweet Love," and spending hours in bed exploring each other's bodies. Falling in love with her had fulfilled me, excited me. And it still confused me. I was still unsettled by the way my life had strayed off my carefully plotted course: *love, marriage, baby carriage*. As a teenager, I'd had crushes on boys in school and infatuations with male rock stars and movie stars. I'd covered my bedroom walls with magazine posters of long-haired, smooth-faced boys with sharp jaws and baby-blue eyes. I loved Shaun Cassidy, Bobby Sherman, Davy Jones.

I read everything I could find in the library about how sexual orientation develops, and most anecdotal evidence was consistent: From a young age, gay men and lesbians had some inkling of being different. For most, falling in love with someone from the same gender did not come as a surprise, but felt as if something finally fit.

Not me. As a child, I sat on my bedroom rug orchestrating elaborate weddings for my Barbie doll, staging my own future ceremony, directing the action, and dressing her in glimmering gowns and those ubiquitous spiky heels; my brother's G.I. Joe doll waiting for her at the end of the aisle.

Even after I moved in with Pam, slept curled around her, loved only her, I still had sexual fantasies about men, had pleasurable memories of sex with men, and when I looked at women, most didn't turn me on. The exception was an occasional butch lesbian with a boy haircut, a female version of the boys and men to whom I'd always been attracted.

Because of my unrest, I found a support group at the Pacific Center in Berkeley, just south of the university and housed in a restored Victorian painted two shades of purple. I believed if I went to a coming-out group, it would speed up the process, and I could begin to acknowledge my "inner lesbian," understand my heretofore-denied sexual orientation, and finally accept it.

During one of the first meetings at the Pacific Center, I introduced myself and told my story. "I don't feel gay," I said. "I just fell in love with this person."

Several of the women in the group smiled. "We call women like you 'dykelings,'" someone said. She fit the stereotype: a short boy's haircut, a man's shirt, baggy jeans, and boots that might have weighed ten pounds each. Others nodded, as if they'd been there. Dykeling. I liked the term; it was clever and irreverent and it might explain what was happening to me: maybe I just hadn't evolved into a full-fledged dyke yet.

Over the years, I have contemplated my attraction to Pam, the timing of my finding her, my decision to commit to her and raise kids with her. Now, I think sexual orientation is probably biologically determined, and in ten or twenty years scientists will locate the gene or combination of genetic markers that influence sexual attraction. Someone will prove that those heat-seeking pheromones can be hetero-, homo-, and bisexual and that they fluctuate over time. Perhaps some of us take detours off our genetic map. That could explain why I've been attracted to men over the years, and more so again around fifty. I call it midlife hormonal regression to heterosexuality for last-chance perpetuation of the species.

Or maybe I'm a straight woman who has simply lived for over twenty years with the person she loved the most. Because I still feel different from some of my lesbian friends, I feel as if I've never been a legitimate member of the Lesbian Club; that I've been pretending to be someone I'm not, my internal voice chanting, *imposter, imposter.*

Now that the club is sometimes broadened to GLBTQ, the Q for questioning—usually referring to youth or those in the process of coming out—I wonder if someone can spend decades of her life questioning her orientation.

Maybe someday I'll learn how it is that I spent thirty years on the heterosexual side of the seesaw and then switched sides. Or the better image might be me standing in the middle of the seesaw, straddling the center bolt, moving my weight back and forth. While the bisexual character in the movie *Torch Song Trilogy* alternated between genders on a monthly or yearly basis, maybe I'm one who spends decades on each side.

What some call a choice—whether to follow the heterosexual or homosexual or bisexual path—didn't feel like a choice for me, nor did it feel like I was following biological inclinations. It did seem like a predetermined path, though, a spiritual blueprint. I might have convinced myself that I needed to have that Barbie-doll wedding to a man, slip on my mother's dress, dance at my reception, and open stacks of gift boxes wrapped in silver paper. But of course I didn't. The pull toward bliss was too great.

Clarity

Rachel Smith

K. and I went on a "non-date," since I was married and she was in a relationship with someone we both worked with (though her relationship was on its last legs). It was supposed to be a night out—yes, at a lesbian bar—with some of her friends, a couple of drinks, and lots of laughs. In the weeks leading up to the "non-date," we flirted a lot, through texts and emails. In one email, I confessed that I had a secret crush on someone without naming names. That someone was K.

At the bar that night, I expected to feel very nervous and awkward. But spending time with K. was easy and comfortable. She was easy to talk to: attentive, interested in my opinions, *fun.* And toward the end of the night, after a couple of beers for liquid courage, I kissed her. Afterward, we both sat there stunned and surprised. I had not planned to kiss her (although I did have a crush on her, and had for years). After all, this was supposed to be a "non-date" where two soon-to-be friends go out drinking to get to know each other.

My life was never the same after that kiss.

We tried it again, just to see if it was all about the "surprise" aspect the first time, but the second kiss was even better. We even tried it a third time, just to make sure it wasn't the alcohol, and the results were the same.

So, after a couple of weeks of making out, flirting, talking, and spending time together, I had a sudden and uncontrollable urge to completely change my life. I had to come out to someone. I wanted to move out of my house and away from my husband. There was no shame attached to these feelings. In fact, I felt like I was shedding my skin—coming into the true me, at least a truer me than before.

I've always known that I've had attractions toward other women. I've had crushes and admired others, usually from afar. But, I've also known that my friends and family wouldn't have been able to accept it.

This time was different. I wanted to declare my feelings for K. from every rooftop. Instead, I called my best friend M., who lived halfway across the country. M. encouraged my attraction, explaining that she knew me well enough to know that I have been searching for something most of my life and that my previous relationships never quite quenched that desire I had for a real connection with someone. That day, she also informed a mutual friend of my situation, and that friend replied, "It's about time she came out! She's the only one who didn't know that she's gay!" Seriously? I was on a high, feeling accepted and loved. And I got brave (or foolhardy) and called my mother to come out to her. The response I got was not nearly as warm and fuzzy:

- She wondered if it was a hormonal imbalance that made me feel this way.
- Maybe I should see a shrink who could prescribe something for me to level my emotions out.
- It couldn't possibly be real—lesbians don't look or act like me. I'm too feminine.
- They don't have children, or if they do, they leave them behind to live a wild and decadent life of orgies and one-night stands.
- How could I be attracted to another woman when my husband was so good-looking?

- Just go away for the weekend or for date night and have tons of wild sex.
- Why leave a good man for someone else to snap up?

I thought I would faint right there holding on to the phone. How could this supposedly open-minded woman say such things to her only child? Her princess? She was the very same woman who taught me to be accepting, to educate myself about other cultures and ethnicities, not to discriminate. She encouraged me to pick my friends based on the content of their character and not for any other superficial reasons. But all of this flew out the window when I came out to her. She even questioned my priorities as a mother, and implied I was putting the happiness of others before my own children's well-being. I couldn't believe it. Needless to say, I was devastated.

After crying a great deal, I picked myself up off the floor and agreed to see a therapist. My goal was to coordinate the chaos in my head. I also agreed to start a journal so that I could make more sense of what was going on. I needed to mull things over, but doing so over the phone with unpredictable people was not the safest way to go about it.

I scoured every bookstore I could find, looking for books about women in similar situations. The few books I found were several years old, and related personal stories. Many of the women sacrificed a lot, lost connections with friends and families, and underwent years of self-loathing and guilt. Some turned to drugs, alcohol, and other destructive behaviors. Many of the relationships didn't survive. But I did (believe it or not) locate a positive side in all of this. I was not alone in my struggle. I wasn't some unnatural oddity. I was merely someone who finally had an answer to some of my unspoken questions.

I was ravenous for information about the gay community, potential support groups, anything related to my circumstances, and LGBTQ websites and blogs were another source of comfort and information for me. I found solace in the postings from women from all walks of life who were also searching for answers. Many sought someone or something to guide them through this tumultuous time. They wanted not just validation, but a game plan or a checklist—instructions that told them what to do. And they weren't finding it. There are very few resources focused on married women in our situation. I tried to reserve Lisa Diamond's *Sexual Fluidity* from my local public library and have waited for months. It's still checked out with no end in sight!

I found that I truly had to learn to trust myself, have faith in my decisions, and do the best I could. Becoming self-reliant was the biggest lesson I learned from all of my research. No one was going to come rescue me. I had to rescue myself.

In the meantime, K. and I continued to talk and text daily, even though she was on a two-week vacation in Europe. And my worst fear came true. My husband, suspicious that she and I were in such constant contact, found an incriminating, romantic text message from her. Days of crying and apologizing followed. My husband raged, and I feared for my physical safety. Completely and utterly exhausted, he and I agreed not to make any rash decisions until we both saw therapists and figured things out.

I had tried to describe my struggle to him in the past, but it didn't go very far. He was too threatened by the thought of me being attracted to anyone else—male or female. His insecurities didn't allow us to have open and honest dialogue about many different issues within our marriage, including my sexuality. Until now, I hadn't believed that I would meet a woman I would want to have a relationship with. It had never happened in the past. I had only experienced physical attractions, without positive results. I never got to know the women, or had meaningful and interesting conversations with them. They were purely physical responses, and I was ashamed of them. But K. was different. And different from me.

I'm very feminine, a girly-girl even. I love pedicures, lipstick, and dresses. K. is an athlete—very tomboyish, and lives in khakis and polo shirts. I am opinionated about politics (local and national), and she couldn't care less. I'm from an urban environment and she's from a small town. I think that's part of the attraction.

There are some things about K. that are soft and feminine: her long, gorgeous hair, her ever-changing green eyes. But she's no princess. She's the perfect blend of masculine and feminine. Added to that, she's courteous—almost chivalrous. She opens doors, pays the check, and is very considerate. When I ask my girl why she does these things, she says it's because she thinks that I'm worth the extra efforts she makes; she wants to show me how special I am to her.

When we first got together, it was surprising to me how much I didn't know. I assumed that because we are both women, we would intuitively know how to physically please each other. We have similar body parts, so we should know everything there is to know about sex with another woman, right? Very wrong. My girl was terrific, kind and generous, eager to make sure that my first time was special and memorable and worthy of remembrance—not some sleazy roll in the hay. But, I (being a very type A, eager-to-please person myself) researched and studied and found that I didn't have the foggiest idea what sex with a woman actually involved. I had been to sex toy stores and watched porn movies, but it blew my mind. I felt like such a novice. I had so many questions, so much curiosity and fear. I'm older than K. by almost ten years, and I had this idea that I was supposed to be more of a teacher and she the student, and yet in this circumstance, the roles were reversed.

I've spent a great deal of time since that first kiss trying to determine how to define myself and my sexuality. How should I label myself? Should I even do so? What I've come to is this: I don't have to. The person I sleep with, fall in love with, am attracted to, is my business. Lesbian, bisexual, straight—none of these labels feel comfortable to me. There is no doubt in my mind that visibility matters and that the labels are an important component in efforts toward equality, but they do not serve me and my journey. I choose to let my personal be my political. Living a healthy, happy, joyful life is what I'm striving for. My girl likes to compare herself to a can on a grocer's shelf that doesn't have a label, which I like. And that's what I go by. At least for now.

I feel like people spend far too much time trying to define themselves—compressing their essence to fit within some narrow margin. It's more important for me to focus on the relationship rather than on labels. I also came to the realization that my roles as mother/daughter/friend are far more integral to my identity than a label that's strictly related to my sexuality. I take my role as a mother seriously. Nothing else in the world is more important to me than ensuring that my children are healthy and happy and whole.

Which leads me to one of my biggest concerns: How can I live my life for myself and balance the needs of my children? How would I explain what was happening and why our living arrangements were going to change? My son is ten and my daughter is almost three, so they have very different levels of understanding. Most of the experts I read said that children are primarily concerned with how any kind of change will affect them. Following one of the books I read, I tried to have a conversation with my son, and made a great effort to be age-appropriate, but honest. It was a disaster. We both ended up crying. I think the entire situation, especially the thought of potentially losing daily access to his father figure, frightened him. I needed to approach this conversation in a different way.

K. and I took the kids to the park, to the library, to pizza night at her house. We just spent *time* together. Both children found that they liked her, and soon they looked forward to seeing her on a regular basis. They are actually disappointed if she isn't in my car when I pick them up from school. I learned a valuable lesson: Discussing the subject in an abstract way didn't do anyone any favors. My children needed to see love in action.

At this point, I am still legally married. My role as a wife has changed dramatically, due to the fact that I'm in a relationship with K. Additionally, I have accepted something about myself: I'm not cut out to be a wife, at least not a traditional one. There are so many expectations that society places on heterosexual wives, including the one that requires a wife to surrender a large part of herself and sacrifice her dreams for the greater good of the marriage. That was the case in my marriage. My husband, who by and large is a good man, was raised in a very traditional home where his mother's entire purpose in life was to cater to her husband and children.

She was expected to put her needs and wants on the back burner, and her traditional Korean upbringing reinforced this belief.

I, on the other hand, was raised by a single mother who championed education, independence, and self-reliance. Culturally, as an African American, I was taught that my load would be heavier, but that I should have the fortitude to bear it. It's interesting to note that while my mother stressed these attributes, she also strongly encouraged me to immerse myself in my marriage, and depend heavily on my husband for stability and support.

My husband was stable, traditional, and faithful. I tried everything I could to be the kind of wife that he wanted—to be a suburban soccer mom (not even close to my personality), to be the supermom who handled the home (cleaning, shopping, bill paying, cooking), and a super stepmom to his daughter. I worked a full-time job while obtaining an advanced degree, wore Victoria's Secret thongs and heels, and gave in to sex on demand. At the same time, I was exhausted, resentful, angry, and cold. I tried the "fake it till you make it" thing but I never quite got there. I seldom enjoyed sex because it seemed like one more thing I *had* to do. And that wasn't my husband's fault; it was mine. I rarely said no to anything or anyone. I was over-extended. I didn't put my foot down and say, "Wait a minute—we are a partnership. Start acting like it!" I allowed things to continue like this until it was too late to salvage anything.

When we got married, I think we both just accepted the concept that the wife generally bears the brunt of the responsibilities. Many times, we made jokes about the "Honey-Do" lists that I left for him to accomplish on his days off from work, how as the "scrimper and saver," I had a better handle on the finances than my "spender" husband. It shouldn't have been so one-sided—we both should have been doing the hard work. Looking back, he acknowledges that he should have made more effort.

Many people step outside of their marriage when their needs aren't being met within their marriage. I doubt that I would have felt the need to explore my feelings for K. if my marriage had been on firmer ground. I do believe that we would have been friends and would have gotten to know each other. But, I don't think that either of us would have explored more than a friendship.

I would like to think that I've come to a realization about myself: that I've lived in fear and shame for too long and that my relationship with K. is the catalyst for me to live a more honest, authentic life. I would like to think that I can offer her "forever," but one of the lessons that I'm taking away from this situation is that I'm not sure that I can offer that to anyone. It's far more important for me to focus on the day-to-day relationship than to make a long-range plan for the future. Life happens.

My husband and I have been forced to educate ourselves about different marital options, and come to a compromise, even if it's temporary. It's not financially feasible for either of us to dissolve our marriage at this time. We can't sell our home due to the current economic conditions, so we have made the difficult decision to leave it and live under different roofs. We are slowly untangling ourselves from this marriage, one step at a time. It's all about keeping the peace right now.

I know that relatively soon, my marriage will end. It will end for a number of reasons. I will be forced to start over, create a new identity for myself, and undergo a number of changes and adjustments within my relationships as I come out to more and more people in my circle. Leaving a marriage to a man for a woman is not "just a phase." It's a tremendously difficult situation. But, it happens to be necessary to be true to this woman's soul.

Credit in the Un-Straight World

Trish Bendix

I've always felt like I was somewhat of a fraud in the gay community. It took me a while to feel as if I were actually a part of it, like I had to do something to earn my lesbian credentials other than date a woman, or simply have feelings for one.

I didn't come out until I was twenty, and that's because I really had no idea I was queer until then. When I look back on it now, I can see some signs. There had been times I'd thought, *I could probably be with a girl—no problem,* as if it were a dare or something I'd be willing to do at gunpoint.

Growing up, I don't recall having any crushes on girls—and I played sports. (I guess I quit softball too soon.) I attended schools in two different cities in Michigan throughout my adolescence. One was a diverse college town where I lived until I was fifteen, and the other was a small town that had a history with the KKK. I wasn't finding my soul mate in either one. In both places, I was adamant that I'd be getting out of the state when it came time for college. That's where I'd meet the one who was destined to be my match, someone who had interests in film and music, rather than pigskins and pickup trucks.

I'd always assumed this "one" would be a guy, although any semblance of a relationship I had in high school ended in heartache, and my last real boyfriend now dances on cruise ships. Looks like we were a match made in Gay Heaven. It's no wonder we didn't like making out.

Thinking of myself, my education, and my career made me feel empowered, like my peers just didn't have it together like I did. They'd be on the fast track to marriage, babies, and boredom, while I was in Chicago drinking coffee and having intelligent conversations, working on novels, networking, and feeling well-connected. Eventually this dream would involve a partner, and someday, I'd meet him when the time was right.

But by age nineteen, I hadn't met him. I had met several "dudes," who were fun to kiss while drunk at parties, but I usually followed that up with frenching my friends. And when my friends schemed about how to go home with said dudes, I was slipping out the door to catch the train home. My subconscious had no plans to bed a man. My conscious mind said *I'm just not that kind of girl.*

The thing is, I'm totally *that kind of girl.* I'm just that kind of girl for a girl.

The summer before my junior year, I applied for a position at my college newspaper. The first interview went well, so I was called in for a second. I walked into the office and took a chair by the front door, waiting for my turn to talk to the two editors of the paper. Then a girl came walking by me, and I recognized her face from her column in the paper. She had what I thought was a totally gay face, or maybe it was just her dykey haircut. Nonetheless, she was a lesbian, and I was now seeing her in the flesh.

"Hey, how's it going?" she addressed me nervously, walking out the door toward the bathroom. I barely had time to say, "Good," and process that her presence had made me feel a little excited. In one split second, the sight of this person, this girl, had made me a little shy. I could have been blushing.

She ended up being the editor I'd be working under. Needless to say, I got the job.

Working together made it all the more apparent that I had feelings for this person, this girl. She was smart and a great writer, she liked the same kind of music I did, and also liked consuming lots of caffeine. She had a girlfriend whom she lived with, but ended up breaking it off because she had the same kind of feelings for me that I had for her. She was even willing to put up with going out with "a straight girl."

She was my first everything, and I had to grapple with the feelings that I assumed I should have felt much sooner in life. *How can I be gay?* I thought, instantly feeling bad that I questioned it. Some of my best friends were gay, but they'd known it forever. My friend Kevin has a videotape of himself at age four answering that his favorite Christmas gift was his sister's curling iron. Where was my gay history?

Now knowing that I'm a femme, through and through, I can't take my cues from fashions and bad haircuts. I've always preferred dresses, skirts, makeup, and dyeing my hair to jeans and T's. I also quite enjoyed "girly" things like fashion and boy bands and anything else that safely falls under the category of "Things Straight Girls Are Prone to Like."

Maybe, I thought, I'm bisexual. That would make sense, and make me less fraudulent. I could count some girls that I possibly had crushes on but never really acknowledged the feelings for: the hot singer of a band I skipped my high school prom to see; the girl with a lip ring whom I desperately wanted to befriend in a music class my freshman year; the one I wanted to get high and play Truth or Dare with all the time in hopes we'd get dared to make out.

Okay, getting a little gayer.

I tried to put things in perspective, which was possibly made easier by the fact that I was taking two women's studies courses at the time, and sexuality was part of our weekly discourse. It's also possible I was even more confused. But my feelings didn't lie—I liked a girl. I kissed her. I didn't die. I felt breasts, and I was into it. It felt awesome, in fact.

While in high school, I had taken my gay best bud to prom with me. I had argued passionately in speech class that gay marriage should be legal.

But I'm a Cheerleader was one of my favorite films. And I did sometimes grab my friends' asses, just for fun.

The hardest part about coming out in college is that it made me feel a bit cliché. It's considerably easy for friends and family to think it's a phase or some sort of liberal college social science experiment. But I would not have frivolously chosen something like that for myself if I knew it'd cause my mom to ask, "But what am I supposed to say when people ask me if you have a boyfriend?"

Maybe if I had known I was a lesbian at age twelve I could have been prepared for this answer a little better. But I think I did pretty well in saying, "I'm sorry, Mom. I forgot this was all about you."

Also, I never had a boyfriend to speak of, really, so it shouldn't be much of a change for her to say, "No." She could feel free to answer, "She has a girlfriend," but at the time, saying that seemed like it might push her over the edge. Eventually, she'd come to introduce my girlfriend as "my other half," and that was good enough for me. Baby steps.

In my first real relationship, I was with a woman for four and a half years. We did everything I'd hoped to do with a partner, and even though it didn't work out, it wasn't because she was a she. And in being with her, I realized that being bisexual was sort of out of the question. My attraction to men was (and is) non-existent. Somehow my sexuality was just not tapped into until I met the first person that I was really and truly attracted to, mentally and physically. And since then, that has happened several other times. (All female. It's true—I'm official.)

One of the things I came to accept was that I came out at the perfect time for me. I had crushes on boys because they were closer to my type than the femme girls I palled around with. My type is an andro-butchy one, and I did not go to school with any of those kind of girls, unfortunately. Had that happened, this would likely be a completely different story.

Maybe coming out at twelve or thirteen would have given me a different coming-of-age story, but it could have also made my experience much harder. I would have embraced it, sure, but it's easier said than done. I have many friends whose realizations came along with gay bashings, being called "dyke" in the hall at their all-girls' school, or sleeping with a lot of guys because they thought they'd need to "get used to it."

Luckily, that never occurred to me as a good idea. To quote from *But I'm a Cheerleader*, "It's easy to be a prude when you're a homosexual."

I have finally found myself, and my coming-out experience has been instrumental in my authenticity and my happiness. After coming out, I wanted to write about life as a lesbian, or about lesbians doing cool things that are otherwise invisible to the straight world. I've actually become a "professional lesbian" of sorts, as my day job is to make sure every facet of queer female-dom is written about and analyzed by as many people as possible.

I actually feel like I'm a better person as a lesbian. I think the only time I wasn't being myself was when I was clueless about my sexuality. I have never once been closeted in any situation since coming out. In fact, I think I'm probably considerably annoying to some people because I talk about my girlfriend all the time. I like to give lectures on lesbian sexuality to people who ask, "How do you guys do it?" or "Who is the boy in the relationship?" I'm really proud to be gay, and never having the gay shame that some people I know grew up with, I am trying not to feel like I missed out on an imperative experience. Everyone's experience is different, which is something I learned after reading an eighty-year-old woman's coming-out story in *Newsweek* a few years back.

My mom, despite her momentary freak-out, is supportive. My dad has always said that whatever makes me happy, makes him happy. My sister and I love to joke about our family of diversity, as I'm the lesbian and she's in an interracial marriage and mother to a mixed-race baby. Our parents are happy with us, the way we are, and that's something I couldn't feel better about.

I still like to hear other lesbians' coming-out stories. I want to know when they knew, who their first crush was, when their first kiss was, and I love to see their scowls and eye rolls when they describe a failed attempt at a sexual experience with a man. It might be the only thing I have going for myself in the official lesbian department: I'm a gold star. Now where's my card?

First Date with Ann

Meredith Maran

April 27, 1984

I'm barely awake when the clenched fist in my abdomen sends me an unmistakable two-word message: bladder infection. "Fuck!" I swear aloud, naming at once my reaction, the cause of my condition, and the activity I'm afraid this condition will preclude.

I planned to become a lesbian today, and while I'm pretty sure lesbians don't call what they—we—do "fucking," it's what I've always called sex, and will, until someone teaches me something better. Which is what I was hoping a semi-stranger named Ann would do, about five hours from now.

Sitting on the toilet dribbling pee and wincing at the all-too-familiar searing sensation that follows, I curse my ill-fated decision to give sex with Richard one last try. Was it two nights ago, or three? I can't remember . . . as usual. Which is one good reason that my ten-year, two-child, one-mortgage, two-car, one-checkbook marriage is ending. I'm counting on Ann to give me another one (good reason, not marriage—that fantasy will come later).

"Not bloody likely," I fret, noting the bright drops of blood in the toilet. Is that a smidgen of relief I feel at the thought that a medical restriction might come between me and my long-anticipated new sexual identity? I grab the bottle of sulfa pills out of the medicine cabinet, promising myself, as I've done each morning since my husband left our home six weeks ago, to scrub out the razor hairs and dried-on shaving cream blobs once and for all.

Before I can set off for my rendezvous with destiny, I've got to get the kids to nursery school. Tying their sneakers is so painful I'm wondering how I can possibly pull off a tryst. I explain to their teacher that Peter and Jesse's dad will be picking them up tonight, limp stiff-legged out to my car, and struggle to stand up straight—so to speak—long enough to pump a tank full of gas.

So far, I admit to myself as I head north out of San Jose, the big day isn't going terribly well.

By the time the San Francisco skyline comes into view, the drugs have kicked in. So has the high anxiety. Ending a marriage is one thing. People do that every day. Becoming a lesbian is another. People only do that every day on *Donahue*.

I barely know this woman. We spent three days together, along with twenty thousand other people at a publishing convention in Dallas, eleven months and one marital separation ago. I thought she was a boy until I saw her name on the book she was at the convention to promote: *One Teenager in Ten: Writings by Gay and Lesbian Youth*. She thought I was a married straight woman until she caught the lusty look in my eye. Until she read the poem I sent her as soon as she got home to Boston and I got home to San Jose—ambiguous in intention, but undeniably horny in inspiration. We exchanged equally ambiguous letters and phone calls throughout the next year. When Ann called to say she was coming to visit her brother in California, we began a series of awkward negotiations to determine the nature of our impending liaison.

"I'll stay with my friends in San Francisco. You and I could meet for lunch . . . if you have time," she offered.

"You could stay with Richard and me; we could all hang out together," I countered.

"I could just come meet the kids," Ann responded, beating a hasty retreat around the bush.

And then, six weeks before Ann's scheduled arrival, four years' worth of marriage counseling came to an end and Richard moved out. Days after his departure I called my one lesbian friend, a therapist, and asked her where someone would go if someone wanted to have an affair with someone of the same gender who was coming for a visit from an unnamed East Coast city. And someone's house wasn't a possibility because it was where someone's husband would stay with someone's children while someone went off for the weekend to have sex with someone she'd never had sex with before (who happened to be a woman).

"It's about time," applauded my adviser, who'd had not-entirely-covert designs on me herself. "Go to a gay resort on the Russian River. Try Fife's or The Woods. And tell someone I hope everything . . . everyone comes out great." She was still chuckling as I hung up the phone.

I called Fife's. "I'd like to reserve a room for two . . . " So far, so good. I was pretty sure the guy on the other end couldn't tell I wasn't really gay. Yet. " . . . with twin beds."

Long silence. "Twin beds?" he repeated, incredulously. Clearly, this wasn't a request he got often. "All we've got are queens," he'd answered imperiously, sounding very much like one, even to my uninitiated ears.

"Well, it's for me and a friend," I stammered, "and we don't really want to sleep in one bed . . . "

"Hold a sec," my tormentor snapped. I heard his muffled voice, then another man's. Then laughter.

"Turns out we have a couple of twins we can roll into a cabin," he said. I hoped fleetingly that he meant twin beds, and that I wouldn't be charged extra for a menage-a-twins. This was going to be enough of a challenge with just Ann and me in the room.

"I'll take it. Thanks," I said, and promptly broke into a full body sweat.

But all that was weeks ago. Before I'd prepared my still-husband, my best friend, my uncomprehending two- and three-year-old sons, and my journal for my upcoming journey to The Other Side. And before I'd managed to get this goddamn bladder infection.

And now, bladder infection and last-minute terrors notwithstanding, I'm on my way. Slowly. I'm having to stop every few minutes to pee, and the truth is, heterosexual marriage—especially the kind I had, in which sexual encounters were easily prevented by bladder infections, nonspecific apathy, or imperceptible shifts in the atmospheric pressure—is looking pretty appealing. I'm not sure what's less appealing right now: the thought of letting the seam of my jeans, let alone a new lover, touch my lower chakra—or the thought of embarking on yet another new phase of my thirty-four-year-old life.

I pull up in front of the house where I'm to meet Ann, and practice my Lamaze breathing. It doesn't do a bit more for me now than it did when I was screaming for mercy in labor. I knock on the door, and the woman I've imagined myself in bed with for the past eleven months answers it.

She's very small. She's smiling. I think of a photo of herself she'd sent me, ten years old, with braids down to her waist. I wish she still had those braids. I wish I had those braids. We hug, stiffly, unembracingly. I realize she is exactly the same size as I am. My bladder aches, my heart pounds, my brain's taken the last train out of town. "Hi," we both say. "So you were really there all that time," I say. She nods and smiles again. When she's not touching me, she seems so small.

Ann slings her knapsack over her shoulder and we get in the car. "I've never been to the Russian River," she says. Having spent seventeen years as a heterosexual woman grappling with the ethics and feasibility of faking orgasms, I am faced—and so early in my career as a lesbian—with deciding whether or not to fake previous homosexual experience. "Me neither," I say.

Fortunately, Ann initiates small talk as we head across San Francisco. I, meanwhile, have been overcome by acute respiratory distress. My lungs seem to have collapsed, and I'm desperately trying to suck some air without making my condition—this new condition—apparent to my unsuspecting suitor . . . suitress?

The next words I speak are to an Alhambra Water delivery truck driver, twenty minutes later, when I finally get enough oxygen to my brain to realize that somehow the car I'm driving is heading south—back to San Jose, and away from the Russian River.

"How do I get to the Golden Gate Bridge?" I manage to squeak out. The truck driver glances at my license plates; he seems surprised to see that the car isn't a rental. "Do you have a map?" he asks. I glance at Ann to see if the weekend is over yet. She seems quite unconcerned. I realize then that she and I are very much unalike. By this time, I would've asked, snidely, just how long she'd lived in the Bay Area (twenty years, in my case). I would've asked, ever-so-patiently, if she wanted me to drive. I would've told her to let me off at the nearest lesbian bar so I could find myself some competent, real lesbian worth spending a weekend with.

"I'm getting to see more of the city than I'd thought I would," Ann says, with no detectable sarcasm. I apologize, she shakes her head and smiles, and we fall silent. Once we've left the city and are zooming up the right freeway in the right direction, I steal a surreptitious peek at her chest. Pay dirt! Her pale blue button-down shirt is gapped between the middle two buttons, providing me a clear view of her bra-less, petite, but undeniably female breasts. I allow myself a moment of disappointment—they're not quite the voluptuous kind I'd dreamed of—before acknowledging that, like her body, her breasts are about the same size as mine.

We arrive at Fife's. I park the car. Together, silently, we approach the registration desk. It is not just my heart and bladder that are pounding now. My fingernails are pounding. My eyelashes are pounding. I say my name to the man behind the desk.

"Ah, yes!" he exclaims loudly enough for all the real gay people in the fifty-acre resort to hear. "The ladies with the twin beds!"

Without looking at Ann, I snatch the keys from his hand and slink back to the car.

"I just thought . . . " I mutter in Ann's direction as we approach Cabin 7. "It's okay, Meredith," she says, her smile a bit stretched now. "Whatever you want to do is fine."

What I want to do, I realize as we let ourselves into Cabin 7, is lie down. With Ann. I don't care about the food I've left to spoil in the car or what my husband will think or all the years I've spent longing for sex with a woman, or even the resounding pain in my bladder. I don't know what I want to do, once we're lying down together. I just want to do it. Just like I wanted to with John Melnikoff in fourth grade. Just like I wanted to with Paul when I first saw him hawking his underground newspapers outside our high school. Just like I wanted to, at one time, with my clearly soon-to-be-ex-husband.

The most unexpected thing about this feeling is that it's so utterly familiar. I always thought lust would feel different when it wasn't heterosexual.

I really do want to have sex with this person, I realize to my own great surprise. *I really do want to have sex with this woman.*

But not just yet. Before I can cross the line that I have approached and avoided for thirty years or so, I must avoid it a while longer. I say I need a nap. Ann says she'll go for a walk. I declare that I'm not really tired. I jump up and suggest a walk together. Ann and I walk along the narrow sandy path to the river, and there, on the rocky river bank, I am overwhelmed again by the magnetic pull of gravity, or lust. So I do. Lie down. On my back, with my too-small breasts and my fantasies pointed at the sky. Because I simply cannot stand up when I am this close to Ann, this close to my dream.

She stands with her left foot brushing my right thigh, skipping flat rocks across the slow-moving, muddy river. She places three sun-warmed stones carefully on my stomach. She might as well have reached down and caressed my clit. I'm sure she can hear the gathering and dripping of juices between my legs. I wonder if this is lesbian flirting. If she feels what I feel. If she would believe that I feel what she feels.

We go to a restaurant for dinner. She eats a burger; I toy with my tortellini. "I thought most lesbians were vegetarians," I comment. She winces but says patiently, "I'm not."

It's getting dark out. Ann orders a beer. "Are you an alcoholic?" I ask. (I restrain myself from confiding that I'd read that many gay people are.) She asks why I'm asking. I ask how old she was when her father died. She asks if I'm nervous about going back to our cabin, about going to bed. I nod. She says, again, "Meredith, we don't have to do anything you don't want to do." We go to the cabin. What do I want to do?

I unpack the nightgown I've purchased for this occasion—a flannel one, to prove my intimate knowledge of lesbians' affinity for flannel. I go into the bathroom to put it on, peeling the sopping, sticky underpants off my inflamed genitals. When I come out Ann is in one of the twin beds, wearing a white cotton T-shirt. I wonder if that means I won't get any points for the flannel. I wonder what else, if anything, she's wearing.

I climb into the empty twin bed. I'm shaking; my teeth are chattering. I think of my husband, my children. I close my eyes and see a movie of me getting up, getting into bed with Ann, her arms folding around me, her fingers doing things between my legs no man could ever know to do, my hands squeezing her breasts, her nipples against my nipples. If I ever had a bladder infection, I can't remember it now. If I ever thought I was kidding about this lesbian thing, I was wrong.

I kick the blanket off my legs, leap up, and slide into bed with Ann. She puts her arms around me and breathes deeply. I am quaking inside and outside. She says, even now, "It's okay, Meredith. We can just hold each other."

My body has a need that's burning a hole through the mattress. My brain is hanging on for dear life to what remains of my heterosexuality. Ann strokes my arms with her soft, small, hairless hands. I think of the night, just a few short weeks ago, when Richard and I told our sons we were separating. I think of how Peter asks every day when Daddy and I are going to live together again. Ann's hand brushes past my breast. My cunt clutches. I pull away slightly.

Eventually Ann falls asleep. I listen to her kitty snores and think of the nights I've spent kicking Richard so he'll stop snoring, snores that shook the bed and made sleeping together intolerable and finally impossible. Snores that made me wake up angrier even than when I'd fallen asleep.

Ann's digital watch beeps on the hour. After the fourth beep I slip out from between her arms, pull on my clothes, and walk into the dark night. The air is scented with jasmine, like the jasmine Richard planted along the fence of our home in San Jose. There's a phone booth outside the hotel office, with a night light that guides me to it. I dial my home number, where my husband and children sleep.

Before it rings, I hang up. What will I say? "This is your last chance to save me from this," I imagine myself saying to Richard. "Please . . . save me from this."

I know he can't. I know I can't. I know that lesbian isn't really the right word, that my need to separate my life from Richard's and my need to feel Ann's hands and mouth on me are two different needs with two different sources. I know that I have lusted after men, and that I now lust after a woman who sleeps just a few yards from where I stand. I go to where she is.

Living the Authentic Life

Micki Grimland

My daughter Haley came in half-undressed from ice hockey practice. She was sobbing, a very rare experience, as she is my stoic child. I would have expected my daughters Taylor or Cami to come in crying about all kinds of things, but not Haley.

"Honey, what in the world is wrong?" I asked.

Between tears streaming down her face and sobs she said, "Mom, I just found out my two ice hockey coaches are lesbians, and they are a couple!"

This was something I had known but had never uttered to anyone because they coached kids. We lived in the very white, very Republican, very conservative Bible Belt suburbs of Houston, a place where too many people think "gay" is synonymous with "child molester."

"Oh, honey," I said.

She replied, "I'm not crying because they're gay, Mom. I am totally okay with that. I am crying because they are living a lie."

A thunderbolt of lightning raced through my body. My world stood still. My heart pounded and blood began pulsating through my system. She caught it in my eyes.

"What's wrong, Mommy?"

"Haley, I struggle with the same thing that your coaches do."

She immediately stopped crying.

"Are you coming out to me, Mom?"

I said, "Haley, you've teased me for years about being a lesbian." At that moment, Taylor walked in.

"Mom's coming out to me," Haley said. "I need some therapy."

Because I am a therapist, this was a common joke between the kids when something heavy needed some lightness. Taylor's eyes flew wide open.

"What?"

"Haley's hockey coaches are closeted lesbians, and I struggle with the same thing they do." At the time, I had been married for twenty-three years to my college sweetheart, the son of a very conservative Southern Baptist family.

"Mom, it is one thing for *us* to tell *you* that you're a lesbian. It's a completely other thing for you to tell us!"

Once, doing a homework assignment, we were unable to get onto Taylor's Internet account, so we used my account. She said, "I know your password; it's 'lesbian.'"

I said, "Why would you say that? That's not my password."

She pulled me eyeball to eyeball and said, "Because if it weren't for Haley and Cami and I, you would be a lesbian."

Many comments similar to this were uttered over the years before I came out.

To step into the authenticity of who you are when you are a closeted gay woman—a mother to three girls whom you worship—married to a man you love and respect (and have great sex with), is a complicated web of paradoxes.

Carl Jung said it best: "Soul is made in the tension of a paradox." I held that tension secretly for years. In college, I was acutely aware of being attracted to a friend of mine, but I chalked it up to her making me nervous because she was so beautiful. Then, as a young professional, I was at a conference on marital therapy in New Orleans. Late one night, some friends and I went to a nightclub. Walking behind my friends, my eyes fixed on this beautiful woman in white pants. I was transfixed. Her boyfriend leaned down and whispered, "What are you, a lesbian, or what?" His words still sting in my ears. It was my first awareness that I didn't look at women the way my other girlfriends did.

On my fortieth birthday, my husband threw me a surprise party. As the night went on, a friend pointed out, "You are *so* connected to your women friends. You're the most like a lesbian without being a lesbian of anyone I've ever known."

My good friend Sarah had been openly gay since she was a teenager. She and I began spending more and more time together. I was intrigued by her—mesmerized by her, in fact. I told myself it was her spirituality and interest in in-depth psychology that drew me to her. As a therapist who had done a lot of my own interpersonal work, I was not prepared for the lessons my unconscious was preparing to teach me.

One day on the phone, Sarah said to me: "You know, Micki, you are the most touchy-feely person I know. You touch everyone: people you love, acquaintances, even strangers. But you *never* touch me!" I began to shake and sweat. I said, "That's not true!" She was right, I hug everyone. I was totally unaware that I had never touched or hugged her.

She said, "I'm coming over tonight and you're going to give me a hug." I laughed it off, but became very nervous and my heart began to palpitate. She did come over that night. Being the control freak that I am, I turned her around to hug her from behind so that I could be in charge of the hug. She turned to hug me face-to-face, and to my shock and surprise, I kissed her. When I did, something deep inside me shifted with an almost audible click . . . as if I'd found that one puzzle piece that had been lost under the sofa for years . . . the one that completes the picture. After that kiss, my world began to shake and quiver. An emotional earthquake was imminent.

I fell deeply in love with her. I call her "the pathmaker of my becoming." As a Southern Baptist, deeply devoted mother, and believer in the vows of marriage, I also fell into a deep depression. I was totally split. To quote my analyst: "What kept me alive the first half of my life was keeping me from living the second half of my life."

I was forty years old, married to a man who I didn't want to hurt, and I was mama bear to three children. I believed that my calling in life was to protect them from pain. *And* I was madly in love with a woman. In her depth of love for me in return, Sarah moved out of state because the split was killing me. I was living a total lie. I lost twenty pounds, my hair was falling out, and I was taking antidepressants. My analyst, whose devoted compass kept me afloat during this time, kept telling me he didn't think I was gay. He thought I was breaking free from the "good girl, adult-child-of-an-alcoholic-home, driven-to-perfection, OCD, control freak paradigm" from which I operated. I convinced myself that he was right, put Sarah in a sacred locked box in my heart, cut off all contact with her, and tried to squeeze back into my old self. However, nothing felt right anymore.

I lost interest in sex with my husband, poured myself into the girls, and tried not to be gay, convincing myself it was just Sarah. I did pretty well until two years later, when I went to my daughter's ice hockey tournament in Canada and was smitten by a woman there. She said to me at one point, "You've been with a woman, haven't you?"

"Only one," I declared, "and I'm not going down that path again—I'm married."

We became email buddies and she would periodically ask, "Are you single, yet?"

I began open discussions with my husband, who would say, "You're not gay, Micki. You're just ecumenical. Your mind is open—you just can wrap your arms around more things than most people." However, I began to think about it, and came to the conclusion that we have sex based on our identity. If we're crazy, we have crazy sex. If we're passionate in life, we're passionate in bed. If we're shut down inside, we're usually shut down sexually. If we're gay, we're most fulfilled in same-sex relationships. Being gay is about identity more than sexuality. Sexuality is a by-product of your identity. I began to accept my identity as a gay woman. It wasn't Sarah, it was me.

Talking to the kids and going through the divorce was a deeply emotional, painful process. We were able to get a "collaborative divorce" with no battle. Even though that made it very civil, it was still very hard for all of us. The deep hurt my sexuality has caused my ex-husband and his family and my kids is my only regret. To walk into the fire of this transformation is hard, but holding steady to the truth makes it doable. Like the coal burning the diamond into freedom, so is the coming-out practice.

Today, I am happier, more fulfilled, more complete than I could have ever imagined. Sarah and I remain friends and I treasure her deep gift to my becoming. I have been married to a woman, Sharon, for three years now. I never could have imagined a relationship this intimate, this honest, this deep, this fun, in all my days. She is my rock, my resting place, my exhale, my lover, and my best friend. I shall age and die with this woman by my side. We married in a chapel in Texas in front of 250 guests.

I am now fifty-two; my children are twenty-two, twenty, and fifteen. They are happily adjusted and love my partner. We recently had the joy of telling our story on *Oprah*. It is our desire to help people see us as their neighbors, their friends, and to see that our sexuality and identity are nothing to fear. We are spiritual, we are mothers and fathers, workers, shoppers, devoted family members, much more similar to heterosexuals than different. We're not here to destroy families, seduce straight people, or scare anyone. We are here to live our lives and love the people we love. One of the unfortunate aspects of being gay in our culture is that while I had so many rights as a married straight woman, I do not have the same rights as a married gay woman. I still pay taxes and support my country in many ways. It is unfortunate that my rights are not equal because of my sexuality. We are here to be Americans, to claim the truth of "All people are created equal," and to receive equal access to the constitutional pursuit of our happiness. It will be a beautiful day when that happiness— alongside our rights—will be recognized for all Americans.

A Door Opening Out

Susan Grier

"**I**magine a door in your mind," Ray instructs, our pens poised to begin the first exercise of the morning. My graduate writing workshop is gathered around a picnic table on the back deck of a sprawling stone mansion, home to our program's ten-day summer residency.

"Describe the door," he continues. "Then imagine walking through the door and describe what is on the other side. Now imagine that someone approaches you. Describe the encounter you have with this person."

The words flow from my hand—an old, rustic door opening out to a lush, exotic garden that draws me into its shelter; the gentle rustling of someone approaching to tell me I have entered a new dimension of my life; the awe I feel at the beauty and richness of this place; the sense of peace enveloping me as the door closes forever behind me.

Afterward, when we share our responses, Ray has a comment about mine. "Hmmm," he muses. "I don't think I've ever had anyone write about a door opening to the outside."

The scene I'd conjured intrigued me on that warm July morning, but the residency's packed schedule left little time to ponder its meaning. At age fifty, maternal obligations fulfilled, I had gathered my courage and applied to the program to find out what I was made of as a writer. The work infused me with excitement and possibility, a certainty that I was doing the thing I was meant to do, finally, and it was taking me—the me who had crouched, insignificant, in the shadows of my own life—to a place I'd never been before, a place that felt good and right.

Months later, back at home in Maryland and well into my third-semester work and teaching, I returned to Ray's comment with a mix of disbelief and amazement, seeing in my words a truth I couldn't have fathomed before summer turned to fall, before seemingly random forces and events fell into place.

That fall, as I will always think of it, the chair of the English department asked me, via last-minute email, to mentor a new adjunct. I'd met Trish briefly at the pre-semester faculty meeting, taking her in with one glance. In contrast to my summery outfit of striped capri pants and matching sandals, she wore thick jeans and brown lug-soled shoes in a way that read butch, a look and manner that usually set off a vague internal alarm—*careful, watch yourself, not too close*—even as it fascinated me. But the yellow of her shirt brought out the softness of her blond cropped hair and the pink of her cheeks, and her eyes held a kind of earnestness, an unexpected vulnerability that drew me in. When she sat down beside me, I felt a secret thrill.

"Of course," I replied to the English Department chair.

Trish and I overlapped in the faculty lounge on Tuesdays and Thursdays, twenty minutes between the end of my class and the beginning of hers. It was a natural time to check in, see how things were going, make easy conversation. She was reserved, in the way people are who take care to be polite. She was also kind, smart, funny, and I wanted to know more of her.

I still remember the day I admitted to myself how attracted I felt to her. She stood near the copy machine, I on the other side of the conference table across from her. Our eyes met across the table, hers gray-green, clear and shining with a light that seemed to pierce me deep in my gut, and it was as if she could see what was hidden there—or maybe it was I who could see it and know it for what it was. Something in my chest caught, like the creak of a door hinge the moment before it opens.

That fall, I had been married seventeen years to my second husband. The marriage wasn't going well—had not gone well for most of its duration—but I'd stayed for the usual reasons women stay: the illusion of security, the status and privilege marriage conveys, a comfortable lifestyle, a reluctance to admit failure, the dread of upheaval and going it alone, the thinking that things will magically get better if only I persevere, the voice that rationalized, *it's not that bad, it could be so much worse.*

When we got together, my two children were small, and I believed that by marrying again I could knit my little family back together. More than anything, I wanted to be a good mother, to create a nurturing, harmonious home for my children. But there were problems: step–parent problems, relationship problems, financial problems. Seven years in, I had almost left, and from that point on the marriage had felt like an endurance test. *I have got to get out of this marriage,* I would tell myself, *when the kids are older, when I earn more money, when I feel stronger.*

We lived in a two-story brick colonial on a winding lane, a small neighborhood of gently rolling lots and open spaces. I loved my house, its sunny kitchen, the way the rooms flowed one to the next, the perennial beds and herb garden I had cultivated outside. Over the years, I had poured myself into making the house a home—paint, wallpaper, window treatments, furniture—bit by bit, piece by piece, the selection of each detail slow and painstaking, as if something huge hung in the balance of each decision, as if the composition of tastefully appointed rooms could hold the marriage together.

At one point, we remodeled the master bathroom, enlarging the space to include a separate vanity for me, whirlpool tub, multi-sprayer shower, and private toilet stall. The room felt airy, serene, indulgent. Sometimes in the middle of the night when I'd get up to use the bathroom, I'd sit there in the dark and think, *How can I give up this bathroom that makes me so happy?*

Though it had not been a conscious intention, pursuing a master's degree proved a step away from the marriage, taking me far from home twice a year for on-site residencies, directing my energy and focus into a whole new world that was mine alone, allowing me a kind of separateness I hadn't known in a very long time. The distance, both physical and psychological, gave me the clarity to see how miserable I was in the marriage, how much it damaged my spirit to stay, how I was compromising myself, tolerating conditions that should have been unacceptable. With each completed semester, I could feel the strength in me churning, mounting, and I began to picture a different kind of life for myself.

I fantasized about finding a cottage on the river or in the woods and fixing it up to suit me, painting all the walls pink if I wanted to. I didn't care if it was small or run-down. I could feel the relief of living alone, the space all mine, female, peaceful and serene. I couldn't imagine wanting to be with another man for a long time, if ever. Yet I wanted to believe that somewhere out there was the kind of love I'd always longed for, a deep connection that was passionate, profound, soul-stirring.

At times during the marriage, I had told my husband outright that if things didn't improve, I would leave him one day. Now, as I began to envision my escape, I kept quiet. I feared his anger, the verbal and emotional abuse that would rain down on me once he learned I was leaving for sure. If I didn't maintain the status quo, I risked losing control of the process that would see me through the successful completion of graduate school before the chaos of splitting up began. I was not going to let this man ruin the best thing I had done for myself in years.

※

That fall, I was reading Carolyn Heilbrun. Her 1988 book, *Writing a Woman's Life*, resonated so deeply it had become the backbone of my third-semester critical thesis. She talked of patriarchy, its continued hold on women's lives despite two decades of radical feminism, the subtle ways it still silenced us, forbade our most authentic emotions, isolated us from one another. She talked of the bonds between women, our ability to give each other something men could not. She talked of the power of autobiographical writing to transform women's lives, to free us from "the stories and houses of men."

Born and raised Southern, I knew about patriarchy, knew first-hand the power of male privilege. I called myself a feminist. Yet my upbringing had been one of such privilege, such seductive beauty and grace, that I still lingered under its influence, still acquiesced to its unwritten codes, so deeply internalized I wasn't even aware of them. In response to an essay I'd written the previous winter about my father buying me, at age fifty, a Lexus, my very liberal male professor had exclaimed in disgust, "Where is the rage?" and I hadn't understood. Reading Heilbrun's book, I finally felt in my emotional gut the depth and breadth of what patriarchy had stolen from me. It was a loss of self, my female spirit denied the opportunity to explore its own bounds, flex its own muscles, discover its own voice. Instead, I had been groomed to dress, speak, and behave in ways that would win the approval of men in exchange for the promise of protection, security, status—even a luxury car.

"Women come to writing simultaneously with self-creation," was one of Heilbrun's lines I kept returning to, ignited by the thought of my work, my writing, leading me further into the undiscovered self I could sense there, ready to emerge. My critical thesis may have focused on other women's lives and works, but the inquiry was ultimately about me, about breaking free from a way of being that had held me prisoner from the moment I was born.

That fall, I decided to ditch one of the two medications I took for depression. My doctor had added Lexapro for anxiety several years before, after my older son left for college and the younger one totaled my car. I had been fragile and shaky then, had lost too much weight. But now I felt strong, on top of things—teaching three composition classes, taking yoga twice a week, stimulated by the work of my critical thesis.

I wanted a different relationship with my body: more accepting of its limitations and weaknesses, more compassionate and respectful. Surely there were other ways to achieve at least some of what antidepressants did for me—more yoga, meditation, time outdoors, exercise. Maybe I needed one antidepressant, but did I really need two? Was the relief they provided even as good and necessary as I had believed?

Without them, my life had sometimes seemed jagged and raw, a precarious, high-strung balance on a thin, shaky wire. But maybe there was good reason for the depression I experienced. Maybe it came from something real and painful I needed to look at. Maybe, instead of smoothing out the rough edges with medication, I needed to feel them, let them cut into me, allow myself to bleed for a change. Without consulting my doctor or telling my husband, I tapered off Lexapro, just to see what would happen.

What happened was that I became unleashed. Within days, it became clear that my twin doses of antidepressants had been keeping my marriage intact. I had managed to tolerate my husband only by taking drugs. Now, everything he did irritated me, even the way he breathed. Perhaps it was mutual. Tensions between us mounted to new highs, exacerbated by the presence of my older son—the one he'd never gotten along with—who had moved home for a few months to save money. Watching the churlish way he interacted with my son brought into sharp focus the blunt truth that I needed to free myself from this man, sooner rather than later. In the bathroom at night, I sat in the quiet of my little stall and sighed, *Even if I have to live in a trailer, it will be better than this.*

Then, something else shook loose, released from its medicated numbness. I knew Lexapro had dulled my libido. But this was a surprise, an aching desire from a place deep within, a place that had nothing to do with my husband.

One Friday, alone in the house after a morning yoga class, I took a bath, telling myself a long, hot soak would help me settle down to write afterward. I lay back, letting the water soothe sore muscles, relinquishing myself to its warm embrace, and the hand sprayer became my new lover, a gentle lover who knew what I wanted, how to touch me, when and where.

The bath became a Friday morning ritual, me and the hand sprayer, the warm force of it kneading and plying me to exquisite tension, shattering, and release. It was delicious and satisfying that I could do this myself, my own way, in my own time, and then soak in the pleasure of my body. It was not that I'd never done this before, but it was different in the way I regarded my body—not as an instrument of sexual release, but as companion and friend.

And different because one day, I imagined a touch that was not my own but that of another woman, the one I couldn't stop thinking about. I imagined unbuttoning my blouse to her, closing my eyes as her fingers reached in to lightly brush my left nipple—the sensitive one—just a whisper of touch. I touched myself there, need and want spiraling through me, down into the deepest part of me. I imagined her hands moving over me as I reached for her, drunk with desire, saying *yes, go ahead, I am yours*. I had never imagined kissing another woman, but now I did, wanting to know the gentleness of soft skin, the taste of female, this female.

This is crazy, I told myself. A diversion. A backlash against my husband. A secret, wicked little fantasy that will pass. *What are you doing? Carolyn Heilbrun has titillated you with her talk of female friendships and women loving each other.* I might have been offended by these ideas two years before, six months before, maybe last month. But now they seemed wondrous, at least with Trish, and I felt myself wanting to go there, to experience it for real.

◦◦

That fall, for a road trip to visit my parents in North Carolina, I checked out a book on CD from the library. The title was *She Is Me* by Cathleen

Schine, and I knew nothing about it except what the turquoise cover revealed: three women, a mother, daughter, and grandmother, and a line about the unexpected twists and turns of their lives. What unfolded as I made my way through Virginia and across my home state proved so uncanny, I longed to bypass my exit and drive to the end of the story.

I was spellbound as the story unfolded: Greta, age fifty-three, married, unexpectedly falls for another woman. It was as if a benevolent voice was speaking to me through the story, offering reassurance that my new feelings were okay, normal even. Greta spoke my own fears: *What is happening to me? I'm not a lesbian—am I? How can this be? What would my family say if they knew?*

Back at home, tensions were so high "divorce" might as well have been scrawled all over the walls. Separately and without discussion, we each took off our wedding rings. I hoped Trish would notice, see me as available. I wanted her to know I was interested, but I had no idea how to do that. *How do women flirt with one another?* I wondered. I was so afraid of making a fool of myself, I went the opposite extreme, friendly but professional, keeping the focus on teaching matters rather than anything personal. But I longed to know the details of her life. *How does she spend her nights? What does she eat? Where does she live? What does she do on weekends?*

She had no idea how I pined for her, how thoughts of her consumed me. When my noon class ended, I'd stop by the restroom to check my appearance, then dash up the stairs tingling with excitement, pausing outside the faculty lounge to collect myself. She always sat in the same place, opposite the door on the other side of the conference table, the place where my eyes went first. I felt like a giddy teen surging with newfound lust and extreme emotions. Later, I learned that a second adolescence is often brought on by the self-discovery of coming out to oneself.

Little by little, Trish opened up. She had recently split with her partner of nine years, confirming that she was both lesbian and unattached. She, too, was a writer—a poet and playwright. She knew more about teaching than I did. She worked in her family's business and devoted her free time to rescuing animals; she even traveled to Mississippi after Hurricane

Katrina to help care for homeless cats and dogs. She was eleven years younger than I. She had always wanted children but it hadn't worked out. With every new detail, I adored her more.

All the while, I watched myself with detached fascination, safe in the secret of my longing. Was I crazy to think that anything could ever happen between us? I had no idea, but I wanted to find out, letting this newfound desire take me where it would.

The Tuesday before Thanksgiving, our conversation lagged, offering me little to hold on to during the week that would pass until I saw her again. After she left for class, I slumped in my chair, bereft. I fiddled at the computer, checked my email, then succumbed to the horoscope link on my home page, as if in search of answers.

You thought the two of you were just friends, and you've been conducting yourself accordingly. While you've been worried about discretion, caution and not jumping the gun, they've been thinking about how to lure you closer. If either of you happens to be unavailable at the moment, however, be very, very careful, even if you're sure you're just flirting. You know how quickly an attraction can take off.

I wasn't one to take horoscopes seriously or even read them on a regular basis. But this one spoke directly to me, lifting my sagging spirits. I stared at it, taking it in, and then suddenly, Trish reappeared.

"You're back!" I blurted out. She sat, explaining she'd left her students to complete their class evaluations in privacy. We talked, more animatedly this time, trading stories about how we'd spend Thanksgiving. I listened, unable to take my eyes off her face, my own cheeks warm and prickly with the excitement of her. I wondered if I was blushing, if she could sense the elation that flooded every part of me. I knew she felt it, too. She had to. How could she not? It swelled in the air, flying about, palpable, almost visible. We spoke quietly, yet I was certain everyone in the room knew I was swooning, madly in love. I didn't care.

She rose to leave, and my eyes followed her as she disappeared beyond the open door, something inside me stretching and pulling.

The night before Thanksgiving, my husband and I had the worst fight of our marriage. He was subdued and repentant for our Thanksgiving meal, but the next morning, he faced me in the kitchen and asked, "What do you want to do?"

It was his usual tactic for handling difficult topics. He put the question to me rather than stating his own position, a strategy that absolved him of any responsibility for the outcome. Nevertheless, I seized the moment.

"I want to get the house ready to sell, put it on the market, and split up."

By that afternoon, I'd typed up a list of all the work that needed to be done on the house and posted it on the refrigerator. I wanted to be ready.

As the term moved into its last weeks, Trish told me she didn't plan to teach the next semester. The days ticked away like a death march. I couldn't let her just walk out of my life forever. Then, a plan. We'd never had a real opportunity to talk about our writing, though once or twice one of us had commented that we should. On the last day of school, I would suggest we meet for lunch after grades were in to talk writing.

I waited anxiously as the last day approached, afraid of bungling this final opportunity to secure a connection with Trish beyond work, afraid I would sound foolish, afraid of rejection. But I awoke that last morning to an unexplainable sense of peace and calm, a feeling of certainty that the day's outcome was out my hands. It was as if a voice were assuring me that all would be well, that all I needed to do was relax and let the day unfold.

When Trish left the faculty room for her last class that afternoon, I didn't say goodbye or suggest that we get together later. I knew she would come back after the class was over. She did. We talked for a while, end of semester chat. Then she got up to leave.

"Thank you for being my mentor," she said, walking toward the door.

"I'll miss you next semester. You've been my favorite mentee of all time." My words sounded ridiculously corny.

Trish turned. Standing on the threshold of that open doorway, she looked at me and said, "We should get together and talk writing, maybe have lunch?"

Now, four years later, I still think of that fall as magical, miraculous, mystical even. *So much happened.* Yes, I left my husband for a woman, a woman who has claimed my heart with a love that is passionate, profound, soul-stirring. But the real story is about claiming my own heart. It is about the serendipity of circumstances coming together at precisely the right moment to find me standing before that door opening out to a self that is, at last, strong and safe and free.

We ~~Don't~~ ~~Do~~ Stereotypes

Sabrina Porterfield

ooking back on my formative years, I keep thinking I will somehow magically find that exact moment when I realized *Hey! I like girls!*

My fourteen-year-old self did get all breathlessly tingly whenever I watched the Eurythmics' Annie Lennox in the "Sweet Dreams" video; what with her angry orange buzz cut, sharkily seductive grin, and smacking pointer. However, I also spent much of the time I should have been studying algebra in Mr. McGlynn's class writing stories with my friends about our imagined love affairs with various members of Duran Duran. While this might explain why I could barely manage a C in most of my math classes, it doesn't really help me locate that stereotypical earth-shattering moment when I realized that girls were hot.

I didn't date in high school. Not because I was against dating, per se, but I had the distinct teenage disadvantage of being both a brainiac and an introvert. My poor mother—herself well known as a boy chaser in her days of purloined cigarettes and Catholic school uniforms—could not understand it. I think she was in a state of despair over me. "Relax," my father told her, "She's got other things going on. She'll date when she wants to."

Never mind dating a boy. Dating a girl in my tiny hometown of less than three thousand people was not really going to happen either. That would have been the mark of rebellion, and frankly, I was too busy trying to keep my grades up so I could get the hell out of Dodge to bother with any of that. I had places to go and things to see. The way I figured it, all of the normal teenage rebellious drinking and drugging and screwing hoopla could wait until I was safely away in college. The closest I ever came to being a rebel was going stag to my senior prom. No one asked me, and while I didn't care so much about going, I knew my mother would be dreadfully disappointed if I didn't go. (I didn't quite realize at the time that going stag would actually disappoint her even more than me not going at all, but we'll chalk that up to youthful naiveté.) As it turned out, I ended up having a blast, which is more than can be said from one of my friends who had a showy and hysterical breakup with her boyfriend, and later drunkenly vomited all over her prom dress.

Once I actually arrived at college, I found that there were so many things to see and do and learn that I didn't actually care too much about dating (or drinking or drugging or screwing, for that matter). I did go out on a single date with a fellow student who drove buses for the university, but he showed up late and automatically assumed he was going to get laid just because he bought me pizza. He learned the hard way that I've never been a woman that you want to assume anything about. There was also the roguish Brit in my Italian class whose charming accent and green eyes meant I spent less time on learning Italian and more on learning him (which again led to a less than stellar grade, and you'd have thought I would have learned by then to keep my head in the game, but alas). Sadly, I was far too tongue-tied to actually speak to the man, so that never got off the ground.

However, there was also my friend Angela. Ah, Angela. Adorable and sassy and funny and oh-so straight as can be. I was too uncertain of myself to even dream of approaching her romantically. Instead, I followed her around like a puppy dog, keeping my feelings most firmly hidden. I never tried anything with her, despite the torch I carried for her in my poor little gawky heart.

Do I regret my agonized silence? Oh, honey.

Here is the part where we interrupt our tale of my non-existent love life to make sure that you understand that I am notoriously clueless when it comes to the romantic intentions of others. My friends and family have, with a great deal of patience, informed me of numerous occasions when prospective romantic partners attempted (and failed) to attract my notice. I am always completely blindsided at the very idea that so-and-so might have had the hots for me. Really, I am that obtuse. To get my attention you'd have to be willing to hold a neon sign up over your head that reads "Sabrina U R Cute & Can We Do It K THX" or something. My lack of sexual entanglements is due far more to this cluelessness than any sort of frigidness or snobbishness toward potential partners. Or as one of my dearest friends put it, "For such a smart woman you are pretty dumb sometimes."

I met my would-be husband during my third year at college. He was a new graduate student in our department. After a few months of getting to know each other, he told me to my face that he liked me and asked me out directly (a necessary step, as we have established). He was smart and witty, along with a plethora of other qualifications that made for good boyfriend material. I was appreciative of the attention, and my neglected heart jumped at the chance. I wasn't aware that anyone else might have wanted me, and I was too inexperienced and too shy to ask anyone out on my own. I was, as they say, ripe for the plucking. He plucked me, and I plopped right into a relationship that would last me most of my twenties.

While it is true that we had a good relationship together for a few years, we never did have much of a sex life. I don't attribute that to me not enjoying sex with men, however. (Although, as I have only had sex with one man, I could be wrong on that account.) Mostly I attribute it to him not being as much of a tiger in bed as he seemed to think he was. For many years I just figured it was my fault. How would I know any differently? He was the first person I had sex with, so if, as he claimed, all of his former girlfriends were more than satisfied, the fact that I never had an orgasm must be my problem, right?

My boyfriend and I did get married after the inevitable moving in together, but it was a bad idea. My father died unexpectedly three months before the wedding, and I was devastated. My entire world was turned upside down, and I did not come out of the grieving period the same woman who went into it. Death changed me, and my husband never seemed very comfortable with the person I had morphed into. The post-parental-death Sabrina was blunter and less inclined to deal with other people's failings. I had become, as one of my friends so succinctly put it, the No Bullshit Woman. And the No Bullshit Woman? She was not altogether sure that having only one lackluster lover for her entire life was really going to cut it.

After some discussion and negotiation on the part of my husband and myself, I took a lover. A woman lover. And it was fun. I liked it. In retrospect, she was a pretty selfish and unimaginative lover herself, but I enjoyed getting to know a woman's body. I wasn't orgasming, but I was having a blast. After a few months, my husband suggested that she come and live with us, and we moved into a larger home to accommodate a third adult.

Because she was now living with us, I decided that it was time to "officially" come out to my friends and family. I drove up to my mother's house, nervous as hell, hoping that she would not freak out too badly at what I was going to tell her. I sat her down, and in my most serious voice told her that I needed to talk to her about something life-changing and important.

She looked very nervous.

I explained that what I had to tell her was difficult for me, and I hoped that she would listen and remain calm.

She started to look scared.

"Momma . . . I am a lesbian. Or at least bisexual. I am sleeping with a woman."

Her mouth dropped open, and she stared at me for a moment before leaning forward and walloping me a good one on my upper arm.

"JESUS CHRIST! I thought you were going to tell me you had CANCER. I don't give a shit if you are a lesbian! Don't you ever scare me like that again!"

And that was that. My mother was not keen on the whole idea of the threesome—she was afraid it was going to lead to nothing good, and of course she was right, in that infuriating way that mothers are—but the fact that I was sleeping with a woman? She just did not care. She still doesn't, and in fact, has photographs of my current family on her bulletin board at work. Coming out to my mother helped me to understand that all my mother had ever wanted for me was my happiness, and she did not care about my sexual orientation or anything else, so long as she knew that I was content in my life.

The rest of my family and my friends were fairly blasé about the whole thing. I come from liberal folk on both sides of the family tree, and if any of them discussed my sexual proclivities then they didn't do so in front of me. On the contrary, my maternal side made a special effort to be very welcoming to my lover, and I will always be grateful for that. My friends were also firmly in the bleeding-heart-liberal camp, and were already aware that I liked women, and were not at all fazed by it. The only negative reaction I had came from one friend, who tried to dismiss my attraction to women. She suggested that the only reason I was attracted to women was because I was sexually unsatisfied with my husband. She went on to further suggest that if I had the "right" man to satisfy me that I would no longer want and/or need a woman. You'd think that this sort of attitude would only come from the stereotypical macho blowhard trying to get into a woman's pants; but that's where you'd be wrong. The funny thing is that she's not the only woman who has suggested that to me. I'm not sure if it is due to plain old garden-variety homophobia, or if it is due to the mindset of the kind of woman who relies upon men to define her own self-worth; but it still throws me off whenever I hear it.

The downside of taking a lover was that my husband was not as comfortable with it as he said he was. After my lover moved in with us, we tried a threesome. That was a disaster. My lover was not bisexual, and wanted nothing to do with my husband sexually. He thought himself intellectually superior to her, and looked down on her. I was looking for someone who would take care of me both emotionally and sexually, and neither of them was up to that task. Our house fell apart, but I managed to drag myself out of the wreckage by sheer force of will.

When I made the choice to divorce my husband, I unsaddled the lover as well. Truth to be told, we were not suited for a long-term relationship. I had very little in common with her, and didn't even really enjoy her company all that much. Despite her violent and angry reaction to my news, she managed to find herself a new lover within weeks. In retrospect, if not for the insistence of my husband that she come to live with us, I think our affair would have been fairly short-lived. I was being ignored sexually and emotionally by my husband and was so gratified to have any kind of attention paid to me at that point that I mistook my own gratefulness for love.

It was after I had moved out and started the divorce proceedings that I met my current wife. We met on the Internet. Not only was it on the Internet, we didn't even have the decency to meet up on an Internet dating site. No, we met up on an *X-Files* fansite messaging board, and she was from Finland, of all weird places. She was straight. She was happily childless. She even had a former runway model turned psychology professor for a live-in boyfriend. But oh, she was funny, she was full of passionate justice, she flipped all of my switches and I hadn't even seen what she looked like yet. None of it mattered. I wanted her. I did. I wanted her, no holds barred. And me, shy little gawky Sabrina, Sabrina who never dated, Sabrina who spent all of her free time reading and rarely drank and who had never traveled or done anything remotely daring? I went for it. I went for it, and I used every single weapon in my arsenal: I used my humor, I used my intelligence, I used my charm as the No Bullshit Woman and I went after that woman until I had her turned upside down and inside out.

Who knew I had it in me? I was relentless. I ignored her when she told me she was straight and was not interested in women. I ignored her when she told me that it would be better for everyone if the former runway model and I got together and left her alone. I waved aside her insistence that she would rather die than ever be pregnant by assuring her that I would be responsible for the baby birthin'. I simply dug in my heels and waited out all of her protests and excuses and flashes of temper and finally, after nine months of a very, very bumpy ride, she gave in. She flew to California and right into my life. A year later, I followed her back to Finland.

So there I was, in an "official" lesbian relationship. No man around. We could go to Gay Pride and everything. I expected it to feel different than my straight relationship—and it did—but not for the reasons I was expecting. It felt different to be in a relationship where my partner actually loved all of my shortcomings instead of mocking them, where I was encouraged to be who I was instead of being molded into a person that made my partner look better, where the sex was mind-blowingly fantastic. It felt different to be in a relationship with someone who actually wanted children and was willing to work hard at parenting. The relationship felt different, but it wasn't because my partner was a woman. It was because my partner was Kia. It wasn't her sex or gender that made things different. It was because I had chosen the right person, the person who loved me for me, and who wanted to be with me.

I've heard other women say that they wished they had a wife. When I've asked why, they've said it is because they want a good coparent, or someone who is emotionally available, or someone who will be nurturing, or any number of things that have far more to do with socialization than biology, in my opinion. There is no denying that men and women are socialized into certain roles. However, I've known men who were fantastic parents, who do the cooking and cleaning, who are emotionally available. We associate those qualities with women, but my wife will be the first person to admit that she isn't one to be pigeonholed into the good wife category. Neither am I. While to outside appearances my wife may seem to fall into the more "butch" role while I take on the "femme" role, that's only via a casual glance. Anyone who knows us well knows that she's the hands-on parent, the gentle one, the one who looks out for everyone's safety, who feeds and nurtures the children, the one who keeps all of our finances in place and makes sure appointments are met, and who will spend hours on the floor playing. I'm much quicker than she is, full of drive and impatience, the hands-off parent who cleans and occasionally bakes something decadent and delicious, who sings lullabies and makes fart jokes and can't remember what day it is, no less when the kids need to go to the dentist. A friend of mine has asked me on several occasions who the "boss" is in our family. The answer is that there is no boss. We don't do stereotypes well in this house.

Over the years, I've come to understand that I am attracted to people regardless of their biological sex or gender identity. The commonly accepted parameters of sex and/or gender are simply not important to me. They aren't really all that important to my wife, either, which is probably why we are not part of the local lesbian parenting scene. We attended a few meetings, but we never felt like we fit in, so we stopped going. So much of the focus there was on the lesbian part of the relationship, and since we've never focused on that, we're outside the sacred circle. In fact, my "yeah, okay, whatever" attitude toward identifying myself first and foremost as a lesbian has resulted in some lesbians claiming that I am not, in fact, a "real" lesbian. If living with a woman for ten years and having sex with her and kids with her and going to the courthouse and getting legally hitched and going through the process of having her adopt the kids doesn't make me a "real" lesbian, then I am not sure that wearing a T-shirt that says, "I HEART PUSSY," and forswearing men forever and ever amen is going to really make all that big of a difference. In some circles, the fact that I would not kick Hugh Jackman out of bed for snoring is the deal breaker. I am just never going to be lesbian enough. I find I can live with that.

We've come across very little in terms of discrimination in Finland. Same-sex civil unions, adoption, and immigration are already legal here, so we don't need to go out and fight for those rights. It's already against Finnish constitutional law to discriminate based on sexual orientation, and the one time that we experienced homophobia on an official basis, we complained, and the person in question was immediately required to undergo sensitivity training and we were assigned to someone else, with official apologies. Nothing to get worked up about there. On a cultural level, telling someone that God doesn't approve of their relationship is considered unspeakably rude in this country, so I've never had anyone but American missionaries or immigrants from more conservative developing countries spout religious dogma at me. Most Finns I come across don't seem to care one way or the other that I am a lesbian, and it's not like everyone doesn't know. We're not exactly in the closet. The neighbors have pretty much figured it out, my coworkers at the community college where I teach English know, and Kia's family is so grateful for the grandchildren they never thought they'd get that they practically worship at my feet. We are not, as a family, in the fight-or-flight mode that so many lesbian couples find themselves in all over the world. Because of that, we find we are, for the most part, able to just live life like everyone else.

It may not be possible to pinpoint the sudden realization that I liked girls—or boys, for that matter. It's just always been a part of me, and it's never caused me undue trauma. I know who I am, and I'm good with it. I've been lucky enough to have an accepting and open-minded family, and I got rid of any friends who didn't accept me for who I am. I had the opportunity to relocate to a country where my sexual orientation is legally protected and accepted, and I don't have to worry that my lesbian family will be legally treated any differently than if we were a straight family. So long as I am left alone to live my life in peace, I don't give a rat's ass whether others think I am not straight enough or gay enough or even thin enough. The death of my father taught me that life is too short to spend living it constantly worrying about whether or not others approve of me.

Annie Lennox, though? Yeah. *Whooo.* I'd still hit that.

Counting Down from Ten

Candace Walsh

You know, the last thing I wanted to do was like Jill.

"Jill is a goddess," said Sam. "She's an incredible artist, she goes to Vassar, and she's really, really smart."

Sizzle went my jealous streak. I had met Sam in the bathroom line of my first college off-campus party. Fall semester, freshman year. Homecoming weekend. Parents tucked into their sleigh bed at the cutesy bed-and-breakfast downtown. Little did they know that at the same time, I was drinking keg beer from a big plastic cup, within a gaggle of my shiny new dorm-hall friends, about to embark on a disastrous and knotty romantic endeavor.

Sam wore a charcoal J. Crew rollneck sweater, a shaggy bowl haircut, and a huge incandescent grin. We were both English majors. He was a sophomore. I was a goner.

We had a fling, but I kept on getting flung out and back, like a boomerang, by the something that aligned within me and decided he was it. It. My seventeen years had delivered me to that bathroom line, a hatched chick ready to imprint, hard, on the first tall, lanky, preppy, vaguely literary, sardonic, honey-haired, blue-eyed boy to cross my path. Reckless public necking ensued.

Shortly after he quizzed me on my musical tastes, and I both named the Smiths and was able to list an actual album, he brought me back to his dorm room. As we walked across the chilly, postwar, upstate New York campus, he clinched it by correcting my use of the word "anachronism." I spent the next several years trying to make up for that error, and countless others registered by his gimlet-eyed gaze. At the time, striving for loving acceptance in the face of disapproval felt like home to me. But he was not impressed by my idolatrous show-offery. Additionally, his heart belonged to Jill.

The balance of freshman year, I jejunely fluffed my naturally curly hair, carefully applied the right amount of Dee-Lite inspired eyeliner, and pulled on my John Fluevog boots, because I had been taught that the prettiest and most decked-out girl got the guy. Maybe back on Long Island. Not here. I was chagrined.

As far as Sam was concerned, Jill, of the unkempt, slightly witchy home-bleached hair, who disdained makeup and wore a uniform of faded jeans and black T-shirts that came in a three-pack, left me in the dust. She had been his first back in high school. Every time we left college for breaks, he hung around her like a puppy dog, even if she had a boyfriend along. I only knew what she looked like from a photograph.

I went out with boys. And dumped them for Sam. He literally went for me the way a woman will binge on chocolate when she's PMSing, and then completely avoid it until the next perfect storm of hormones rolls on through. He was only consistent in the way that he both reeled me in and dispatched me. Our crowd of friends steadily lost respect for both of us as we engaged in this particular two-step. But I think they lost more respect for me, because at the end of the weekend, he was a guy and his behavior could fall under the category of laddish. I should have had more self-control, more self-respect.

Poor me, I know. I was entirely complicit. I was stubborn (*I would get him to love me*), threw good money after bad emotions-wise, and I did capital-L love him, or my idea of him. I come from a long line of passionate Spanish and Greek, throw-everything-under-the-bus-for-love women, and once we're in, we don't do anything halfway. So I threw myself under there, too.

It would have been highly useful for me to get therapy, instead of working out my childhood wounds so unproductively. Especially since instead of being cathartic, it ripped the scabs off those childhood wounds and gave them a good fresh repetitive pick-axing.

I went once. The campus therapist I was assigned looked like the police sketch of the guy who had raped and killed a dorm-mate of ours. Plus it was $30 a session and I was broke, so that didn't last.

One weekend during my junior year, Jill came up to visit. Turns out Sam had been talking me up to Jill the whole time he had been talking her up to me. Turns out I could be praised and lauded by him, but just not to my face. Jill and I ended up drinking forty-ouncers beside each other in the circle that wound around a campfire in the dark backyard that Saturday night. I was no longer the freshman girl Sam met in the bathroom line. My preppy wardrobe had gone bye-bye, replaced with raggedy Seattle grunge jeans and flannel shirts over camisoles. I had chopped off my long, thick hair, and dyed it crayon-red. My dad thought I was on drugs. What had happened to his track-running, wholesome-looking, church-going girl? I *was* admittedly engaged in the kind of osmotic collegiate drinking that lands you an F on an "Are you an alcoholic?" test. But I digress.

Talking to Jill felt like a giant dose of soul medicine. This threat wasn't scary at all! She had cute, slightly gappy teeth, burbling unguarded laughter, and bright blue eyes under quizzical eyebrows. She was funny, and clever, and a great listener. She threw back beer and smoked cigarettes like the beautiful no-nonsense German girls I remembered from my junior-high summer abroad—without any posturing or vestigial sheepishness. She had paint on her fingers (not her fingernails), and her rolled-up jean hems revealed muscular cyclist's calves.

Tacitly, Jill and I progressively talked more and more exclusively to each other, mirthful grins revealing what we didn't come out and say: out of the corners of our eyes, we saw that our connection to each other was slowly driving Sam apeshit. Pacing around our periphery, he veered in sideways to lob carefully casual non sequiturs our way. They bounced, gnat-like, off our bubble; and so did he.

When nature called, we went to the bathroom together, as chicks do. We took turns peeing, then, in a flash of devilry, we decided to ditch the party. She opened the bathroom window, climbed out, and I followed her. We ran off laughing into the night.

We walked to my apartment and sat in the candlelit dark, cross-legged on my settee, facing each other, like Jake and Andie at the end of *Sixteen Candles*. The phone began to ring off the hook.

"It's Sam," she said, with a grin.

"I know," I said, and disconnected it with theatrical aplomb.

I was intoxicated, only as the until-recently impotent are, on the power of it all. I had run away with Jill. Now what?

Well. We both knew what would make for a really good story. It was just a question of how we were going to get there. I took her foot in my hands and began to rub it. Her foot was callused and rough, but I was used to that, given that I'd been hooking up with guys for two years. Probably mainly to stop me touching her manky feet, she grabbed my hands, leaned over, and kissed me. Her lips were delightfully full, although she'd later confess that she thought they were ugly, thanks to middle-school boys who told her so. I wish I could say that we kissed in that way where we forgot to breathe, everything fell away, and we melted inside. It wasn't like that. We were kissing because we had run away from Sam. We ran away from Sam to break whatever spell we thought he had on us, and to rub his face in it. Hooking up with someone to get back at someone else is complicated because they're still at the center of it, even if they're not there. It wasn't a soul connection, it was an act of defiance. In the defiance was burgeoning power; action in place of feminine passivity. That was hot. As was she—whether the chemistry was there or not. And as I leaned in, and our hands moved to each other's waists, I was very aware that I was kissing a girl. Setting a certain power dynamic on its head. Kissing a girl. With a faint dusting of blond hair on her arms. Her ample breasts—minimized under two running bras, because she was so not a big-boob person—were a magnificent surprise when they came tumbling loose like Uma's in *Dangerous Liaisons*.

Although Sam probably gnashed his teeth and pulled out chunks of his lustrous hair thinking of us having full-on sex—and without him(!)—Jill kept her jeans on. "I have my period," she said, and that was that. It was booty enough to have kissed and held her for hours, to have bedded Sam's goddess.

Additionally.

Underneath a pile of very powerful reasons I felt driven to date and be in relationships with guys was a simple truth, like the princess's pea under all of those mattresses—here comes the cliché—lesbian porn turned me on way more than straight porn ever had, at high school sleepovers, when the Playboy channel inevitably got switched on and we got giggly and quiet and still. "Eeew," we said, rolling our eyes, ostensibly waiting for the straight porn to come on, but *come on*. It was during the early '80s. The male porn actors were not yet buffed-out Adonises with waxed chests and butts and fluffers. They were mustachioed, cheesy, and had to get the job done while *boom-chicka-bow* music played in the background. Not hot. I was all about the beautiful girls getting it on . . . without Dorky McDorkerson happening to drop by with a bag of plumber tools in hand. I thought I would have liked hetero porn more if the guys were good-looking. I was wrong about that, but that was my self-reassuring little note to self.

So back to the very powerful reasons I felt driven to date and be in relationships with men, not in any particular order:

1) There was the fantasy of lesbians on Playboy, but my sheltered, fundamentalist born-again, and homophobic Long Island childhood (albeit in the shadows of Manhattan and Fire Island) showed me no lesbians. Not one that I knew of, although they were probably all over the place, closeted and/or under the radar. The only, only idea I had of lesbians was an unfortunate one. They had hairy upper lips, rhombus-

shaped bodies, looked mannish in a bad way, and wore unfashionable, dreary clothing. If they were lesbians, well, they didn't do it for me. And would admitting I was a lesbian morph me into such a creature?

2) People made gay jokes. It was not okay to make racist jokes, but it was acceptable to make jokes where the punch line had to do with people being gay.

3) Telling someone they were gay or a faggot was an insult. "That's so gay" was an acceptable dis. I used it all the time.

4) When someone anonymously wrote a letter to my high school paper about being gay, the school exploded into a violent fervor. "Kill the Queers" became a commonly seen piece of graffiti. We had to have an assembly about it. And I'm not sure that during the assembly, anyone onstage came out and said that being gay was actually okay.

5) My church pastor preached sermons against being gay.

6) I was afraid of losing my parents' love, and the ability to inspire pride in them.

7) Oh wait! Let's not forget that I thought that I needed to prove that I wasn't one of those pathetic women who ended up with another woman because no men wanted her.

8) I wanted a fancy wedding like my cousins had. With the plastic figurines on top of the sugary cake with Doric columns. In a church, with a reception afterward that included my entire extended family and friends, all awash in a glow of uncomplicated familial pride.

9) I couldn't handle being identifiable as any more different than I already felt. I was already the child of a woman who witnessed about

Jesus to people in parking lots on the way out of Sears Surplus. My family had too many kids, we moved a lot, and my parents got divorced. My mom remarried a tall weirdo way too soon after the divorce. He said "terlet" instead of "toilet" and had bad grammar and a gray front tooth. I was also ashamed that everyone in my community was Catholic and we were (emphasis on *were*) born-again Christians. Different. I also felt ashamed that my step-dad got mad one day and grabbed me by the neck and almost broke it, and that right after that I was thrown out of my house and had to go live with my dad. I couldn't bear to be embarrassed or uncomfortable about one more thing. I could barely leave the house each morning as it was.

10) I liked guys. I mean, I was attracted to them. I was. They were usually feminine in one or more significant ways. But that just meant they were in touch with their feminine side, right? Which would make them more sensitive and emotionally available. Because that was really important to me.

⟶⟵

Jill and I did not have the happily-ever-after story you might expect, although something else transpired. She woke up the next morning, all smiles (she's a morning person). Unruffled, she made coffee and hung out with me for a little while before she ran off to do Jill things like paint, make soup, and talk about Teilhard de Chardin.

The following fall, she decided to go to grad school at my university, and after my housemate pulled out at the eleventh hour, and she needed an apartment, we sheepishly agreed to move in together. I with trepidation and excitement, she with pragmatism and boundaries already in place.

"I'm not gay," she said to me matter-of-factly. "I hooked up with you because it was an excellent prank on Sam."

Right. Me too. Yeah. Thus began the year of bittersweetly living with the straight girl I was in love with. Isn't that a lesbian rite of passage? I got to notice exactly how gay I was, as I plangently yearned for the missing piece of an otherwise ideal domestic relationship. We ate cheap soup made from a bag of dried peas, an onion, and water. We drank jugs of Carlo Rossi wine. We wound a string of white Christmas lights into a ball and hung it from the ceiling as a light fixture. We bought a piece of sunflower-printed fabric and placed it, unhemmed, on our kitchen table. We dropped acid that Jill's MIT-student friend cooked up and sent our way, and lay on our bellies and did charcoal and pastel artwork on huge pieces of paper for hours. We played Shawn Colvin, and the Story, and *Beleza Tropical.* And Belly. We read each other stories and poems that we had written, and I dressed her and put makeup on her if we went out on the weekends. We were such perfect lesbians, except we weren't. She had boyfriends, and I didn't. I put up with them gamely, although seeing her with a boyfriend felt like my heart was being rapped with the business end of a cat hairbrush. But.

It gave me a model of living together with someone in such a way that everything else since has not measured up. There was unspoken understanding, an alignment and a harmonious hum. For me, we did being alone together, and being together together, best. I know now that women do feel that way with men, and vice versa. I just so happen to be a woman who feels that way only with women. It cradled my spirit, so I could thrive.

Not feeling that way, as I left college, moved to New York City, lived alone, lived with boyfriends, and then with the man who became my husband and the father of my children, was the missing ingredient to my deepest contentment. As I got married, and danced with my groom, by the cake with the plastic duo on top; as I fit in to society as a half of a conventional heterosexual couple; as I got pregnant and had a girl and a boy; and did the rotating dinner party thing; and got my career back on its feet, I was not embarrassed and uncomfortable. But I grew to a point where that was not, not, not my goal.

Uncomfortable. I got the full dose of averted uncomfortable (like the interest that mounts when you ignore your student loans) when I broke up the family to move out because I fell in love with a woman. Like Jill, this woman was not the answer, but she was the catalyst, leading me out of my settling, misguided life and into an open space. There, when I was ready, I fell both riotously and quiescently in love with a woman who loves me back, just as much, and cradles my heart every day, while livening my senses in ways both torrid and soothing. "More than yesterday, but not as much as tomorrow," she wrote to me, early on, and it still stands, in all the best ways.

Jill and her husband just had a baby, and I sent her a blanket that happens to be edged in blue silk the color of her eyes. She's friendly, but keeps her distance, and that's okay. I understand that it must all seem like an embarrassing sidenote in her life—us climbing out the window of an off-campus bathroom, running away, laughing like the young, unencumbered fillies that we were. No idea that the impulse was a seed that would foster my later escapes, back to recover the self I lost when I first understood that in order to be loved, I couldn't be me.

Marriage Mirage

Ruth Davies

*M*oment of persuasion: I am standing at the kitchen sink, Jeff Buckley and I are singing "Last Goodbye," and my hands are burning in dishwater. The kids (five-year-old twins) are in pre-school, and in a minute I will look in the mirror as I arrange my face into a suitable expression before I go down to collect them, along with the other stay-at-home wives whose husbands are working in the mine. *You will remember this moment,* I say to myself, *because you're going to need it in the future.* Has it come to a checklist of pros and cons? No. It's inevitable. But I know that there will come a time when I'm not sure if I did the right thing, and I'd better have it clear in my head how I got to where I am.

Ten years later, I've been in relationships with four women, the kids are living with their dad, just down the road from me, and I've forgotten the details of that morning, although I can still remember that I was wearing a light summer dress and was barefoot.

If I look back on this journey, I see a collection of moments, occasional lights along the dark path of memory. My mother, responding to my question, "What would you say if I told you I were gay?" says, perfectly calmly, "I think I wouldn't want to know." Years later she swears she would never have said such a thing to me, but concedes she may have said it if my brother had asked that question. I think she thinks this will make me feel better. (And then, just recently, as I am going through my mother's drawers after her funeral, I find a book, underneath piles of underwear, called *Get Used to It!* It's a guide for children of gay parents, and I wonder if she had intended to give it to my boys.) Another memory is from my boarding school. When I am in Year 12 and worried about final exams, a girl three years younger than me is expelled for forcing a kiss on another girl. It unsettles me, but I don't have the language to challenge authority on their double standard, and remind them that a boy who did the same thing to a girl last year was merely counseled about consent. The brightest memory from school is that white page of a diary note, torn to shreds in my wastepaper basket in the dormitory, which had written on it the single question "Am I a lesbian?"

I grew up in a mining town, in northern outback Australia, where the class and gender roles were very clearly marked. The few jobs for women went to wives of men who worked in the mine. The only women who had their own careers were teachers, and they were single. (Men wouldn't follow a woman to a teaching job; she might get a teaching job wherever she followed him to, if she wasn't having babies.) There was no shortage of single men, however, and single women consequently never stayed single for very long. My own aunt, visiting us from England, was snapped up by a young engineer within a few months of being there. There were no gay men, nor lesbians—at least none that I knew of. And it wasn't a great surprise that when I finished university and returned to the town I found a nice, young man. We got on well, talked for hours, argued articulately, and laughed generously. In the space between meeting and marrying, I told him about a crush I had on a woman in our social group. He was quiet for a few days, but he believed me (and I believed it myself) when I said that these crushes on women never required any action from me and they would never amount to anything.

A few years later, with postpartum depression pressing me flat to the floor, I told a psychologist that I thought I might be gay. I asked her why this pesky festering feeling would choose now to rise to the surface after my successful years of 'keeping a lid on it.' She said that the PPD wiped out whatever resources I was using to suppress it and that I should do something. It took a few years, but eventually I did make it out of the marriage, carrying with me one of the two bookcases, one of the two beds, and a great weight of guilt about the broken man and tiny children I was leaving behind.

That year was the first time I financially supported myself. It was a time of struggling with a new sexual identity, for which I was prepared; and also a time of struggling with a new feminist identity, for which I was not. It was the first year that I saw how entrenched the gender roles of childcare are, with the boys' dad quite prepared to hand over childcare responsibilities to the next available woman (his new partner), in spite of the conversations we'd had about "equality" early in our married life. It led me, despite years of antipathy toward women who whined about their men, to start saying, "I'm not a man-hating lesbian, but sometimes I am." Those arguments with the boys' dad over childcare made me feel lost. He felt my demands were excessive, evidence of my new fierce lesbian politics. I just wanted to make sure the father of my children took day-to-day care of them and taught them that men are capable of working *and* parenting, just as are women the world over. I am still surprised that the father of my children is so locked into these gender roles that he will not tolerate my view on this at all. It reminds me of Rebecca West: "I only know that people call me a feminist whenever I express sentiments that differentiate me from a doormat."

There were some light moments along the way. As is common in small towns, the scandal filtered down through other families, into the flapping ears of their own children. In that first year I visited the boys for their birthday, and was walking about the garden supervising the small groups of seven-year-olds that had congregated under trees and on the trampoline. A bunch of them had their heads together over some secret, and I overhead one of them say, "Their father? He's a lesbian." I was in such foreign territory—kids I didn't know talking about me, my boys' birthday party that I hadn't organized—that I walked away, giggling to myself, without setting them straight. Another time, I was sitting with someone at work who was a colleague of a colleague. While trying to make small talk she said automatically, "So, what does your husband do?" I stuttered something about not having a husband, but I was struck afterward by how acceptable it was to open a conversation that way.

In the first few years I found myself learning a new kind of militancy, a new understanding of how ingrained societal roles are. I was learning about the connections and differences between lesbian and feminist politics, which seemed to be like a sisterhood: a deep-rooted affinity marred by occasional instances of back-stabbing and much sniping. My politics, although much bolder than previously, were far too timid for those rabid lesbian women who wouldn't let me bring my sons—by then eight years old—to the Reclaim The Night march. The way some of these women spoke about men disgusted me, and this reception from the "true" lesbians was the most surprising thing about coming out.

I moved to a town in Australia that is famous for its lesbian population, but I found it hard to make friends. At first, there didn't seem to be any other women who had children, but in my years there many lesbian couples conceived, using friends or formal institutions to provide sperm. It became such a phenomenon that one disaffected woman, reciting her poem at an open mike night, described the town as being full of "sperm-hungry lesbians." It got a laugh, and some women made cat-claw motions in half-jest. Although I was surrounded by the people I had been looking for all those years, I still couldn't find myself reflected in those faces.

About halfway through my time there, I spent a few months in England and managed to find the local group of women who met for coffee once a week. That group was entirely different. Many women had come out of marriages and had children. I really identified with conversations about how to negotiate these past relationships, and I enjoyed not having the "analysis to paralysis" and pop psychology I had seen at home.

They were a stark contrast to the hometown women, who had another language, and a whole system of categorizing people that I had known nothing about. It was eye opening when they told me about butches, femmes, baby dykes, hippie dykes, OWLs, lipsticks . . . but it was also limiting. If you couldn't be placed immediately into a category then there just wasn't a place for you. You had to sell yourself, bedazzle them, to fit in. My partner, who I met in that town, also remembers the feeling of having exactly one and a half minutes to pass the test to get into the clique. She was smart enough to realize immediately that she didn't want to be part of a group that operated that way, but it took me a bit longer. I understand the need for identity tags, I just expected that lesbians would be able to use them to include people, not exclude them. I feel old enough now to see how naive that was of me.

It's a small cost for all that I've gained. It was such a revelation for me to have sex with a woman, to touch and smell a woman, to feel so connected. I still remember a dinner scene from the boarding school days, when I was in grade eight and almost the youngest at the table, and two girls were "eeewww"-ing and "grroooossss"-ing over the question "Can you imagine what it would be like to kiss a girl?" I remember thinking to myself, *Anything you say now is going to get you in trouble. Just shut up.* I could very well imagine what it would be like. I'd had some practice at imagining it by then. The stress of maintaining that facade, of watching what I say, who I look at, and how I respond, has gone.

I look back to that day at the kitchen sink, and I wonder now what was on that list of points in my head that I needed so badly to remember. I think they had something to do with not allowing cancerous secrets to eat me away, something to do with modeling courage for my children, and a conviction that people have the right to be who they are. The beauty of remembering that moment now is that it doesn't matter what was on that list. I got here.

Falling for Leah

Amelia Sauter

The first thing I noticed in Leah's apartment was the photo of the smashed-up white Dodge Daytona on her refrigerator. The front end was wrecked and twisted. Leah explained matter-of-factly that she had intentionally driven into a bridge railing six months ago after she caught her then-girlfriend in bed with another woman. Of course she didn't want to kill herself, she told me, she just wanted her girlfriend to see her die, which was totally different because the act was intended to make her girlfriend feel bad, not to hurt herself. I began to wonder if coming here was a good idea. When Leah opened her lower kitchen cupboards to show me how all five of them were brimming with empty cheap vodka and Gilbey's gin bottles, I was sure I'd made a mistake.

"Maybe I should go home," I said, referring to the ashram-turned-wellness-center where I was living and Leah was working in the kitchen.

"I'll walk you," Leah said.

Two months earlier, in the cold belly of winter, I had landed at Kripalu Yoga Center, not long after the guru jumped ship when he was caught doing the hanky panky with some big-bosomed disciples. My arrival in the Berkshires marked the end of a year living out of the back of my bright yellow pickup truck, which was decorated with flower power stickers and a fat padlock to keep out other wanderers.

During most of my travels, my boyfriend, Spud, accompanied me. I was only twenty-five, and I did not know how to be alone yet. But I wanted to explore the country with someone. He didn't know how to drive and eventually he drove me crazy, so I finally I ditched him on the last leg of my trip, which included a four-month work-study at Kripalu, where I planned to (insert cliché here) find myself.

I noticed Leah right away. She had chin-length strawberry-blond hair that fell into her face when she placed the food pans in the buffet, and she carried herself confidently, like, well, a lesbian. For a straight girl, my gaydar was spot on. Attending an all-girls Catholic high school in the 1980s did not encourage alternative thinking, but from an early age all of my friends were girls, and starting in college, they were all lesbian-identified or bisexual. I, on the other hand, was boy-crazy. Sure, I fooled around a couple times with girls to see what it was like, but everyone does that, right? Right? I even slept with a close friend after college, which pretty much freaked me out and simultaneously wrecked our friendship. Each awkward experience with a woman made me more certain that I was just a curious straight girl, cursed to spend her life in bed with the guys. Those lesbians had it made.

Leah followed me down to the laundry room one night at the ashram and offered to carry my laundry basket back to my dorm for me. On the stairs, she turned and said, "You wouldn't want to go out with me sometime, would you?"

"Okay," I responded hesitantly. She was so cute in the way she asked, expecting that I would reject her, I just couldn't say no. I would tell her I wasn't gay later.

And I did. On our first date the following week, I blurted out at the Dos Amigos Mexican restaurant, mid chip-dip into the salsa, "I'm not gay, and I'm not going to sleep with you."

Leah paused for a moment, then said, "Who said I wanted to sleep with you?"

Leah asked a lot of other questions, too, about my family, about my upbringing, about my hopes and desires, about my slew of boyfriends. I was flattered by the attention, but after I saw her apartment I was sure she was crazy, or an alcoholic, or both. And then something happened. I got the flu, and lay in bed with her for ten days, and well, I found that I *liked* crazy. Maybe it was the doting, or the high fever, or her most excellent round, perky breasts, or her impulsive nature—but I *liked* her. She said that she wasn't a psychologically damaged drunk—that it was just a phase—and I wanted to believe her. We watched B-movies in her one-room apartment, on her futon that dangerously doubled as both a couch and a bed. A few weeks later, she was dropping me off at the ashram in her no-longer-smashed-up car and she asked if she could kiss me. I said yes, and experienced the most sensual kiss of my life. I floated to my dorm room.

Cut to the climax: we slept together and it was fantastic. "You should have warned me that you were a screamer," Leah said, as we lay on her futon and listened to the couple upstairs snickering.

"I didn't know I was a screamer," I said honestly. It had never happened before in the six years I had been having sex with boys. This was my first clue that my life was changing. At the same time, I had an ex-boyfriend back in Ithaca who still thought he was my boyfriend and was waiting for me to change my mind and come back and make babies with him. I did want to go back to Ithaca that summer, but not to Spud. Either way, I let myself dive into the relationship with Leah since it was safely temporary. The end was already in sight, so why not have some fun, because, damn, the sex was good.

We had been dating (read: having daily sex) for only six weeks when Leah blurted out she was in love with me. I could not say it back. I felt like a freaked-out adolescent in turmoil, newly discovering and exploring my sexual identity for the second time. I was fascinated by the differences between men and Leah. Men's bodies were hard and resistant. Leah's was soft, and it made space for mine when I pressed up against her. Men felt like foreign creatures from another country, or another planet, and Leah felt so familiar. Men smelled like sweat and gym shorts. Leah's sweet scent reminded me of peaches and honey.

I decided to postpone my exodus to Ithaca until the fall. Instead, I took an evil slave-like job at a bed-and-breakfast in Provincetown for the summer, three and a half hours from Leah and Kripalu. I was eager to live in a community that would support my newfound relationship. Leah came with me to help me move. I still can't explain what happened the day we said goodbye on the beach. We were sitting side-by-side as the sun set, tasting the salty air and listening to the waves crash. I was building spirals of pebbles and seashells on my bare thigh when suddenly our connection hit me in the head, in the womb, and in every nerve of my body like a bolt of lightning. It was like a floodgate opened inside of me, a gate that I didn't know was there, holding back waters that I didn't know existed. With seagulls and surf as the soundtrack, I started to cry. I realized I was madly in love with Leah. In three short months, I had gone from A (a hopelessly straight girl) to Z (hopelessly in love with a woman). I was ecstatic and overwhelmed and terrified.

I don't remember swimming in the ocean that summer, or eating fried oysters at the Lobster Pot, or getting ice cream in the middle of the night at Spiritus, or anything else I might have done in the few hours each week that I wasn't working. All I remember is having sex. On the beach. In my truck. In the tiny closet that masqueraded as my bedroom, kitchen, living room, and love den. Leah and I saw each other every weekend. She drove a hundred miles an hour in her speedy sports car to make the three-and-a-half-hour trip in two and a half hours, and I tried to do the same in my ancient pickup truck that staggered along at sixty miles an hour and left me stranded on the side of the road twice.

When I wasn't with Leah, I worked. Kathy and Kathleen, the cranky lesbian couple who owned Smuckers Bed and Breakfast, were in their mid-forties and retired from their day jobs as lawyers. They were thrilled that a college graduate had applied to clean for them and had hired me on the spot, but my brain would not be required for the rest of the summer.

I spent my mornings tidying up after happy vacationers and making up advertising slogans for the B&B like, "Fuck Her at Smuckers." My sink, shower, and hot plate were down some back stairs in a dank, windowless basement that had low ceilings and a bulb hanging in the center of a bare room, giving it the homey feel of a jail cell.

I had never met so many wealthy people before, nor had I ever been surrounded by so many gay people. But I was an outsider looking in. Women tended to visit Provincetown to vacation with their lovers, and gay men came to Provincetown to pretend women didn't exist.

I met one single, older woman who was vacationing alone at Smuckers. She paid attention to me, sympathized about coming out, and bought me pizza and Corona. I told Leah over the phone, "At last, I made a friend."

Leah flipped. "She's hitting on you!"

"But she knows I'm with you," I argued. "I talk about you all the time."

"She doesn't care! Lesbians have no boundaries with friends, don't you know that?" Clearly I had a lot to learn.

Now, let's pause for a minute to talk about being young and gay in the Berkshires, which was where I moved at the end of the summer so I could be near Leah. What seemed to be true was that kids ran off when they turned eighteen and did not return until they could start collecting Social Security. The snobby New England towns were dominated by elderly, art-gobbling senior citizens who visited for the summer and drove so slowly that you felt yourself aging as you sat behind them in bumper-to-bumper traffic. Homosexual sightings were uncommon. The gays were either in the closet, at the theater, or in the dive bars.

Leah liked to tell me that I wasn't a lesbian. I didn't notice hot girls, but I was acutely aware of how men interacted with me. She told me I was a "Leah-bian," and I wondered if she was right, that I was not gay but rather a straight girl with a girlfriend. She also liked to tell people that when she met me, I was a vegetarian, non-drinking heterosexual and that she corrupted me, turning me into a meat-eating, imbibing lesbian, which was essentially true. But I could not relate to her lesbian friends who were smoking-drinking-cheating-swearing-lying softball players, a couple of whom I rented a room from. I did not have any of my own friends. I tried to start a coming-out peer support group but the only people who showed up were middle-aged, transgendered men who looked like they'd been accepting fashion tips from Tootsie. I found a lesbian support group an hour away in Northampton, but I turned around and left when I realized the facilitator was the woman that my housemate was having an affair with behind the back of my other housemate. I was in love, and I was terribly lonely.

Fast-forward two and a half years: Leah remained impulsive, zooming through life in the fast lane, and I was still madly in love and lonely. Leah and I were now living together, renting an artsy, renovated barn in the country. I graduated from SUNY Albany with a master's degree in social work (I had started a boring grad school program shortly after relocating since I did not want to admit I was moving to the Berkshires just for a girl). Coming out to my parents was awkward and required an adjustment period, but they were not surprised. They told me they suspected I was gay for a long time, which was funny, because *I* hadn't known yet. Most everyone else in my life (none of whom lived in the Berkshires) took the news that I had a girlfriend as if I had informed them I got a new haircut.

Coming out to people I didn't know was much more complicated. I never knew when or how or if I should tell them. Inevitably, I had to come out, to landlords, x-ray technicians, employers. As a therapist at an all-girls residential treatment program, I was expected to keep my sexuality a secret, though the other staff had spouses and children who would visit them at work and interact with the girls in the program. Was I married, the girls would ask me, or did I have a boyfriend, and I would feel the frustration and awkwardness of not knowing what to say and having no one to help me find the words.

Then Leah bought a motorcycle. My first big a-ha moment of self-acceptance unexpectedly struck on the back of that bike. Leah decided we should ride with the Dykes on Bikes in New York City's Gay Pride parade. Leaving at 6:00 AM, we blapped down the Taconic Parkway on a sweltering ninety-degree day and joined a quarter of a million people cheering for each other, cheering for us, cheering for me. I got it. Pride. Everything was going to be okay. Everything was already okay. I was okay.

I think I made you wait long enough to find out if we lasted or if I went trotting back to boys. Leah and I have been together for almost fourteen ·years and I've never looked back. I'm still in love, and I'm not lonely anymore. I eventually dragged Leah back to Ithaca with me, where she channeled her crazy, creative energy into convincing me to quit social work and open a cocktail lounge with her. Yep, she's feisty and unpredictable, and she turned out to be a kick-ass entrepreneur and artist, inspiring those same traits in me. Our life is a whirlwind of adventure. And no, she's not a drunk.

Back in Ithaca, I successfully avoided Spud for seven years. He heard through the grapevine each time I got a new job, and always called and left his phone number with the receptionist, but I would just throw it into the trash. If I spied him walking on the street, I would duck into a store until he passed. He finally cornered me in the public library, in the periodical section, where he yelled at me and cried. He said he was attached to our year together and that we needed to reconnect. "History is important," he said. I did not feel the same way. The door to that part of my life was closed. I turned my back and walked away again, leaving him standing by the piles of magazines, staring after me.

You won't find me rewriting history to say that I was gay all along. I was straight. Now I am gay. I won't insult my past self by saying I was in denial or confused. I am a textbook example of the fluidity of sexuality. I always thought I couldn't change. I was wrong, and that freaks out a lot of people who are scared to imagine that one day everything they think is true and permanent could change. I found my knight in shining armor, and she's a girl.

I'd love to tell you I don't miss a darn thing about being straight, but I do achingly yearn for one thing: a wedding. After Leah and I had been together for five years, my conservative older sister, Judy, got married to a guy she'd met a year previously. My dad stood up at her wedding shower and got choked up as he announced that it was the first family wedding and how happy he was and how proud. He and my mother gave my sister their cake knife that was originally a wedding gift from my dad's parents to them. Next to "Fred and Gerry 1966" it now read, "Matt and Judy 2001." My sister, being fiercely competitive, waved the knife in my face and bragged in a sing-song voice, "I got the cake knife and you-oo-oo didn't. Ha-ha-ha-ha-ha."

I had never felt so left out.

When I dated men, I couldn't have given a shit if we got married. In fact, I told them all I would absolutely never marry them. But now I want what I can't have. My sister said Leah and I should just have a commitment ceremony ("and then it'll be acceptable to share a bed"), but the concept of pseudo-marriage doesn't work for me. I want the full package. In 2004, Leah and I joined the "Ithaca 50," the twenty-five couples that sued New York State for the right to marry—and lost.

Recently I emailed my mother: "If gay marriage ever becomes legal in New York, then dammit, I'm getting married. I'd love to wear your wedding dress." But I was too late. She had given her 1960s white lace wedding dress to the Salvation Army a few years earlier. I'm sure she checked with me first and that day I probably wasn't feeling so nostalgic. I wish I had asked her to keep it. I wish I had a reason to wear it. I wish I could get married to the woman I love.

Mirror Image

Leigh Stuart

"See that woman over there? See how she shakes hands like a man? She's a lezz-bian. Be careful." My mother was talking about Effie, the female tennis pro who was about to give me a lesson. Maybe it was the delivery—a slow, low, forceful whisper across the table at the tennis club—or maybe it was Effie's suntanned, well-developed arms, but that admonition frightened me. If I was careful, though, nothing bad would happen. After my lesson, my mother instructed me to wash my hands and I wondered if Effie was contagious. I did what I was told, kept a safe distance from the gays, and didn't catch anything during my formative years.

I was a good girl who did what she was told and didn't upset anyone, especially her mother. A short time after gagging my way through Robert K.'s "passionate" tongue kiss in the high school darkroom, I very secretly realized I would have rather kissed the lips of Susie L., the swimmer with the long blond hair and the pretty face. Kissing Susie L. instead of Robert K. would have definitely displeased my mother, her mahjongg friends, and the generations upon generations of ancestors who were watching me from their respective graves.

I graduated from college and law school with honors, married a lovely man, and had two beautiful children. My family was proud of me, and I was proud of making them proud. After almost twenty years of an unremarkable marriage (aside from my husband's hidden cocaine problem and the nagging fact that I had recurrent dreams of making out with Ellen DeGeneres in a rustic Spanish house in Santa Barbara), my husband suggested I get some interests and stop putting him under a microscope. I decided to sign up for spinning classes.

The exercise studio I chose was home to a colorful assortment of Venice Beach locals, and was definitely outside of my cloistered, private-school soccer-mom element. That's exactly why I went there. After spinning regularly for a few months and building a toned physique, I felt strong, confident, and brave enough to sit in the front row with the experienced spinners. There was one person in particular who always captured my interest. She had a broad inquisitive forehead, dominant cheekbones, and a statuesque neck reminiscent of European royalty. Brownish blond hair was gathered in a worn red band at the crown of her head, dreadlocks spilling down to frame her angular face. Her velvet skin contrasted the rough dreads, and her long dark eyelashes emphasized the flecks of amber in her eyes. "Hello," she'd say as she passed by, and then took a seat on the opposite side of the room. At the end of the forty-five-minute workout, I'd be sitting on the ground changing out of my cleats and she'd pass again. My eyes would scan her muscular legs and, more often than not, when I looked up she'd be smiling down at me. No one noticed, though.

Many more spinning classes. Months of hellos and goodbyes. Looking for something new. Seeking something different. Legs circling furiously. Not moving an inch.

This woman's presence in the room became as invigorating as the exercise. Over time and without specifically acknowledging one another, we shifted to side-by-side bikes. While ostensibly keeping occupied with class-related preparations, I listened to her conversations. Her melodic accent flowed into me; I exercised it out of me. I'd never met anyone

German before; I was sure my fascination stemmed from the many hours I'd spent watching The History Channel.

Nothing more.

Nothing at all.

When our friendship did form, it was built on exercise. An evening spin, followed by yoga three times a week, can really cement a connection. At forty-two years of age I was, at last, an athlete. We spoke of plans to train for the Los Angeles Marathon or do a mini triathlon. One day she invited me to dinner at one of her favorite restaurants. I was thrilled to be taking our exercise friendship to the next level. That's when she said it.

"I've been spinning since my girlfriend Tory and I bought the loft next door to the studio about a year ago. How about you?"

Tory? Girlfriend?

I was struck with an unfamiliar feeling akin to an errant dagger to the chest. No. She couldn't be. A few months ago, I'd seen her at the Venice Art Festival walking arm in arm with a tall dark-haired man, no doubt her handsome boyfriend.

Now what?

Four margaritas later, mine blended no salt, hers on the rocks, I realized that there was nothing to fear. Talking to Verena was like talking into a mirror. I saw myself reflected in the almost unbelievable beauty of her eyes, and for the first time in my life, I wondered who I'd become and how much I'd been missing.

I needed to buy a Jeep. Wrangler. Red. I'd always wanted one but was told—and therefore believed—it was too dangerous. I drove a Volvo. Safe and sound. I even wore sensible shoes. It was about damn time I finally took some risks.

"Waiter, excuse me, waiter?" Waiving my arms as if the bus were leaving without me, "I'd like another margarita, this time on the rocks, with salt."

That felt good.

"Verena?" I swallowed hard. "Would you mind if I touched your hair?"

She swiftly looked up.

"Not many people you know have dreadlocks?"

I promptly looked down.

"Next week I'll be cutting them all off, bleaching the spikes, then leopard spotting them."

Well then, since time is of the essence . . .

I removed the dreads from their tether and down they tumbled, down below her shoulders. They weren't as hard as they looked. In fact, they were soft and kept in neat, symmetrical sections. I investigated from where they grew and inhaled the faintest scent of Jil Sander. She responded to my touch, leaning her head into my hand wherever it traveled, offering herself fully to my sensual absorption. She then took hold of my hand, brought it up to her pink lips, and kissed it. I stopped breathing as a bolt of lightning traveled down to my toes, awakening something somewhere in between that had gone to sleep in high school.

We started hanging out, reveling in our differences: I, a conservative, middle-aged wife and mother with two children, planning a puppy party for my daughter's twelfth birthday; and she, a wild German lesbian, running a successful production company, and taking a class in concrete flooring.

We also discussed our similarities—women with traditional values who were close to our families, who looked for the best in people, and who wanted to be understood. We wrote volumes upon volumes of email welcoming each other into the deepest parts of ourselves. We went to the Getty Museum, took long walks on the Venice Boardwalk, and, mostly, talked. We talked for hours while the light changed in her loft, the shadows grew, and the earth continued to revolve on its axis. I wasn't doing anything wrong, just spending time with Verena.

I told myself that an immoral person, as opposed to me, is a person who has sordid secrets and doesn't tell the truth. My life was an open book. Some called me malignantly honest; I considered that a compliment. I informed my husband about my growing physical attraction to Verena and told him every single time I went to her house before, or after, spin. He even said to me, "All I want is for you to be happy. Whatever happens is gonna happen. I just hope I don't end up homeless." Well, of course he'd never end up homeless. He was my husband, for goodness sake.

Did I mention her new hairdo? She actually did cut off her dreads, leaving short, bleached blond spikes that exposed a thin line of dark roots, just at the hairline. Somehow that contrast, along with subtle black and brown leopard spots, magnified the almost impossible golden-greenness of her eyes. With shorter-than-short hair, delicate feminine features, defined bone structure, and a strong, fit body, she suddenly defied description. Verena was both, *all*, everything—a handsome man and a gorgeous woman neatly contained in one package. This ambiguity was entirely foreign to me. I couldn't take my eyes off of her.

There was certainly nothing immoral about looking.

I'd spent my entire life not upsetting anyone and I wasn't about to start now. Instead of keeping our intriguing acquaintanceship separate from the fabric of my life, I gradually brought her into my family. Over time and a few poker nights, Verena became friendly with Mark and the kids. I took her to a girls' dinner with my eighty-year-old mother, who called to tell me how lovely my new friend was, "She has such a pretty face, wouldn't a little hairclip on the side do wonders for her look?" I pictured one of those pink plastic clips that I wore when I was a teenager, this time adorning the center of a brown leopard spot.

Our special friendship progressed effortlessly. She even broke up with Tory, citing irreconcilable differences. But that had nothing to do with me. Really. One weekend I attended a meditation retreat. I had asked her to join me, but she couldn't. Halfway into the first day she surprised me by showing up, although I wasn't really surprised at all. I'd been in a garden meditating on love and she appeared right beside me. Since I'd been working in a higher plane of consciousness and had expanded my boundaries well beyond my physical body, I knew that earthly limitations should no longer restrict our soulful connection. After all, I'd been studying meditation off and on for almost two weeks and recognized those sorts of things.

So.

We got naked in the hotel room and didn't come up for air until well after dinnertime.

Being with her was the most natural, beautiful experience I had ever known. I'll say that again another way because it bears repeating. Being with *a woman* named Verena was the most natural, beautiful experience I had ever known. I couldn't tell where my body ended and her body began. We cried tears of connection and held one another. I held on for dear life, finally grasping what I'd been missing for over two decades.

From that day onward, the air I breathed smelled of sweet heavenly jasmine (although it could have been Jil Sander) and my heart and mind were certain of the following truths: 1) I was at long last entitled to feel this good, and 2) Somehow, some way, I would figure out how to be this free and not upset anyone. The details of that figuring were irrelevant at the time though, because I was ravenous for her. I ate well, filling myself with gratitude, excitement, relief, and a hearty helping of denial that I might be, ahem, *gay.* Whenever I wasn't with my family, I was with Verena, pushing away the unspeakable details of our connection and pulling her soft body into my arms.

Life moved forward and I clung to the heterosexual-good-girl version of myself so tightly that my hands went numb. I was falling in love. With a woman. And I'd been married to a man for nearly twenty years. The doctor said the numbness and tingling came from a stiff neck and I should try to be less stressed. *Less stressed?*

A manic daily schedule that included speeding to and from Verena's workplace during any free moment clouded my transparent communications with Mark. I convinced myself that vague references to my whereabouts and feelings would spare him unsubstantiated concern that our marriage was in trouble. It wasn't. He was my husband and I loved him; everything else would fall into place. Somehow.

One evening Verena and I went to a blues club and I enjoyed a tad too many double vodka cranberries, light on the ice. I was so used to being isolated and scared and nervous that when I heard the music, I started reeling and feeling and knowing such deep down, low down, center of the earth molten hot blues that the good girl inside of me moved over and made way for a standing up, undulating, helicoptering her napkin above her head, sexually aroused goddess of seduction. Shocked by my out-of-character (she said humiliating) effusion, Verena became furious, and insisted we leave. She said I wasn't who she thought I was.

That made two of us.

Verena referred me to a psychic. I didn't ask why. This woman was a friend of a friend visiting California for a very short time and had recently given Verena a "shocking, yet accurate" reading. I was thrilled to share her experience. Of course I made an appointment and put up $150 for the hour. One can't put a price tag on happiness, as they say.

She asked for my name and birthday and went into a trance, ultimately envisioning Verena holding a jagged piece of broken mirror and slicing me all the way down my center. The next image she saw was me lying on a dirt floor with a gaping, bloody, wide-open gash. I told her Verena would never do that and asked if perhaps it were a metaphor for something good. She explained, "Your higher selves are inextricably entwined and you have spent many lifetimes together in this 'Earth School.' Yet, in the current cycle, your lower selves might be incompatible. Your souls are definitely mates, though."

Our souls were definitely mates. $150 well spent.

I straightened my curly hair, wore my two-carat diamond wedding ring, and smiled pretty for the pictures. I attended piano recitals, soccer games, dinner parties, PTA meetings, and black-tie functions as a happily married mother of two. But when I dared think about the predicament I was in, I envisioned myself as a fraying rubber band stretched much farther than my capacity. Despite my best efforts, I couldn't continue to deny that I was living two lives and I found myself on the verge of one big *snap*. Horrifying thoughts haunted both my sleeping and my waking hours. Wife and mother Leigh had a lesbian lover. *It couldn't be.* Lesbian lover Leigh had a husband and children. *That's impossible.* The existence of one life negated the legitimacy of the other, and I was rapidly losing my grip on both of them. That meant only one thing: a shitstorm loomed on the horizon.

One day without any specific warning (it could have been as simple as my little boy asking me to make spaghetti for dinner), the torrent came. The sky broke open and inundated me with fear. Obsession. Urgency. Need. Doubt. Shame. More Shame. Tears. More Tears. Self-loathing. Physical pain. Mental pain. Hair loss. Shingles. Isolation. Hopelessness. I ended up hiding in a ball under my desk rocking back and forth, and settling on a perception of myself as a filthy lesbian adulterer who should burn in the fiery pits of hell. It didn't matter that I was Jewish and wasn't supposed to believe in those pits. It didn't matter that I told my husband (almost) everything and he said that I should explore my feelings. It didn't even matter that no one was mad at me, yet. None of it mattered because I was a married woman in love with a woman. I was bound to upset everyone around me, and consequently, I didn't deserve to live.

Some might have said I was suicidally depressed. Or at the very least, unhinged.

There was one redeeming thought that kept me barely tethered to life. Although I'd lost my identity, I'd found my soul mate. Someday, when everything was worked out, and my husband had a girlfriend of his own, and our kids were grown, Verena and I would live in a bougainvillea-covered cottage overlooking the Mediterranean. (We wouldn't keep any sharp objects in the house.) The grandkids would visit us frequently and our lives would be full of love and laughter and family.

Then.

Verena told me she was thinking about taking a solo road trip in order to wrap her mind around our "non-relationship" because *what we had* wasn't real. News to me. *What we had* was the one true thing in my life. I was sure her need to get away grew out of my need to loathe myself. I would have wanted to get away from me too, given the mess I'd become.

She was gone for a few weeks, incommunicado. My cells ached for her. I had blond chunk highlights dyed into my dark brown hair. I got an ear cartilage piercing at Tattoo Asylum in Venice. I even leased a red Jeep Wrangler, yet still couldn't settle into my own skin without her in my zip code.

When she finally returned to Los Angeles, glass shard in the hand I longed to hold, she informed me she'd ended up connecting with the red rocks in Utah and had found her place in nature.

I was thrilled for us. "That's great, Verena. When can we go see them together?"

But wait. There was more "really exciting" news. "I've bought a house there."

"Where?"

"In Utah."

"What??"

"I'm going to move there."

"Where?"

"To Utah. With Tory."

"What?"

"I'm going to move to Utah with Tory. You can come visit us, if you want."

"Us?"

They packed their cars and left the next week.

Yes they did. Just like that.

Then there I was; whoever *that* was. Sliced wide open and left for dead. While Verena was in Utah holding Tory's hand looking at the red rocks, I was in the wake of the storm holding a mirror looking at a stranger. The woman I saw was tired and scared, yet remarkably athletic for her age. I couldn't take my eyes off of her and wanted to know more.

That's where the story really begins.

Epilogue

Jennifer Baumgardner

*N*ow that you are done reading, I want to talk to you about why you picked up this book in the first place. I imagine you may have gotten it in order to support or understand a loved one who has a story similar to those found in *Dear John, I Love Jane*. Or, more likely, you are living a story similar to those found in *Dear John, I Love Jane* and sought out this book to learn that you are not alone. Far from alone, in fact.

I could have used a book like this when I was twenty-three, when I fell in love with a woman for the first time. After heterosexual relationships throughout high school and college, I was surprised, thrilled, and freaked out by a radical shift in the direction of my affections. There were all the typical signs leading up to my change, I suppose—way too much interest in the lesbians at my office, obsessive listening to Ani DiFranco, contriving ways to drunkenly make out with friends but have it not "mean" anything. But this new love affair came saddled with associations that felt unfamiliar and itchy to me. Was I now a lesbian? Had I always been gay but was just too homophobic or repressed or out of touch with myself to understand my sapphic ways? I was in love but scared; the relationship was glorious and disturbing. I, like the first essayist in this book, searched online for the whereabouts of old beaus to remind myself of who I was or am.

I was devastated (yet relieved) when that first relationship broke up and soon found myself with a guy—a writer, like me, who was funny and sad and, *whew*, a guy. But that scary, exciting question ("Am I a . . . ?") was still burning in me and, so, not so long after meeting the guy, I met a girl. Correction: I met a great, sexy, strong, passionate, talented, ethical, amazing, and irresistible woman. I left him for her.

I recognized my story in these essays: in the tales of having sex with a woman for the first time, how great it feels to be making it all up, how disorienting it is to have a new identity (lesbian) descend on you like a Civil War costume. If you're unsure that the new identity fits, you wonder if you're just scared, or you are, in fact, on to something?

The beauty of these stories is how clearly they demonstrate that working through those types of questions is part of the journey. And it is a particularly significant journey for a female in this society. Falling in love with a woman, as a woman, is deeply linked to feminist endeavors. By that I do not mean that you are a better feminist if you are gay or bisexual, but that falling in love with a woman enables you to overcome, and perhaps heal from, some of the worst wounds of patriarchy. It challenges the voice that says women's bodies are disgusting, the sexual persona that is passive or must be desired rather than desire, and provides an avenue to sexual pleasure for the body that has been exploited or violated. Falling in love with a woman can free you from the trap of reflected glory—if you once saw yourself as valuable because you landed a certain kind of man, this new state of affairs forces you to derive your sense of worth from yourself.

While I see political energy all over these stories, the dominant power in this book is love. You read the word over and over on these pages. These stories are not just about finding that perfect person to love, but finding yourself and loving her. It's being connected to something between women; feeling that you are on the side of all of the women who ever wanted something more and who wanted to be bigger or different than the narrow silhouette of traditional womanhood. It's chafing against the idea that women could only love or be loved in a certain way and proving that assumption dead wrong.

These stories speak to change. In my own life, the rich relationships with women came in the middle of my life story. I now live with a man and have two sons. My life continues to grow and I labor to remain alert to my desires and not fear change. I'm not always successful, but stories like these help me remember that love—especially loving ourselves—is bigger than our fears.

Bios

Jennifer Baumgardner

Jennifer Baumgardner is the co-author (with Amy Richards) of *Manifesta: Young Women, Feminism, and the Future* (Farrar, Straus and Giroux, 2000) and *Grassroots: A Field Guide for Feminist Activism* (Farrar, Straus and Giroux, 2004). She is the author of *Look Both Ways: Bisexual Politics* (Farrar, Straus and Giroux, 2008) and *Abortion & Life* (Akashic Books, 2008) and the producer of the 2005 film *I Had an Abortion*. A co-owner of the feminist speakers' bureau Soapbox, Inc., Jennifer also teaches writing at the New School and writes for magazines such as *Glamour*, *The Advocate*, and *Bitch*. She is currently working on a film and advocacy project about rape, and a book of essays about feminism. Originally from Fargo, North Dakota, Jennifer now lives in New York City with her two sons, Skuli and Magnus, and her boyfriend, BD.

Trish Bendix

Trish Bendix lives in Chicago, where she is the blog editor of MTV & Logo's AfterEllen.com, a site about lesbian and bisexual women in media and entertainment. She has also written for *Bitch*, *Time Out Chicago*, *OUT*, Gay.com, and *The Village Voice*. Find out more about her at www.trishbendix.com.

Audrey Bilger

Audrey Bilger teaches literature, gender studies, and yoga at the Claremont Colleges. She is the author of *Laughing Feminism: Subversive Comedy in Frances Burney, Maria Edgeworth, and Jane Austen* (Wayne State University Press, 1998), and editor of Jane Collier's 1753 *Essay on the Art of Ingeniously Tormenting* for Broadview Literary Texts (2003). She is a regular contributor to *Bitch: Feminist Response to Pop Culture*, and her work has appeared in *The Paris Review, Los Angeles Times*, and ROCKRGRL.

Katherine A. Briccetti

Katherine Briccetti's first book, *Blood Strangers: A Memoir*, from which "Wedding Gown Closet" was excerpted, is available from Heyday Books. Her work has appeared in literary journals, magazines, and in several anthologies, aired on public radio, and was nominated for a Pushcart Prize. She was awarded a residency at the Vermont Studio Center and is at work on a second memoir, *A Buswoman's Holiday*, about working with children on the autism spectrum while raising a son with Asperger's Syndrome. She lives in the San Francisco Bay Area and can be reached through her website: www.kathybriccetti.com.

Aprille Cochrane

Aprille Cochrane currently resides on the West Coast. She has a successful career in education. Her critically reviewed work has been published on multiple websites. She has published a collection of poetry, *Poems from the Girl Next Door: Imaginations, Illusions, and Images* (BookSurge Publishing, 2007), and is working on her second book of erotica.

Ruth Davies

Ruth Davies lives in Brisbane, Australia, with her partner and cat. Her teenage sons share their time between her house and their father's, just down the road. In her day job, she works for a research organization, editing reports and trying to convince scientists that they, too, can learn to appreciate the finer points of hyphenation trends. Nighttime finds her dabbling in speculative fiction (both the reading and writing thereof), post-graduate study, and various amateur arts activities. She is hoping to learn how to build phrases like Neil Gaiman, paragraphs like Hilary Mantel, and plots like Sarah Waters.

Kami Day

Dr. Kami Day is a retired college composition professor, partner, mother, grandmother, and queer activist. After her twenty-three-year traditional marriage ended, she entered graduate school, where she met her partner, Michele. They have shared their lives for sixteen years, and together have written and published an academic book and several articles and book chapters. They now live in Norman, Oklahoma, where Michele is on the OU faculty, and Kami fills her days with writing, reading, cooking, volunteering with a veteran's organization, and finding ways to raise awareness about LGBTQ lives and issues.

Lisa M. Diamond

Dr. Lisa M. Diamond is Associate Professor of Psychology and Gender Studies at the University of Utah. Dr. Diamond is an internationally recognized expert on female sexuality and specifically on *female sexual fluidity,* which describes the phenomenon of women periodically developing attractions and relationships that run counter to their overall sexual orientation. Dr. Diamond is best known for her unprecedented fifteen-year longitudinal study of one hundred lesbian, bisexual, heterosexual, and "unlabeled" women. Her 2008 book, *Sexual Fluidity,* published by Harvard University Press, describes the changes these women underwent in their sexual identities, attractions, and behaviors, and has been awarded the Independent Publishers Book Award and the Distinguished Book award from the American Psychological Association's Society for the Study of Lesbian, Gay, Bisexual, and Transgender Issues. Dr. Diamond has received numerous other awards for her work from the American Association of University Women, the Society for the Scientific

Study of Sexuality, the Society for the Psychological Study of Social Issues, and the American Psychological Association.

Holly Edwards

Holly Edwards has previously written for *The Skinny*, a Scottish lifestyle magazine, and *The Sofia Echo*, the English language newspaper in Bulgaria. She lives in Westcliffe-On-Sea, Great Britain, with her wonderful girlfriend, where she enjoys baking and eating baked goods.

Vanessa Fernando

Vanessa Fernando is a writer and many other things, too. Born and raised in Vancouver, Vanessa is currently working toward a degree in History and Gender Studies at McGill University in Montreal. She is grateful for her family (both biological and chosen).

Susan Grier

Susan Grier's work has appeared in *Maryland Magazine*, the *Charlotte Observer*, and the 2006, 2008, and 2009 editions of *Women Writers Read*, a publication of St. Mary's College of Maryland. Her essays have also been published in several anthologies, including *Trans Forming Families: Real Stories About Transgendered Loved Ones* (Oak Knoll Press, 2003) and *Thanksgiving to Christmas: A Patchwork of Stories* (AWOC.COM, 2009). She earned an MFA from The University of Southern Maine/Stonecoast and is writing a memoir about growing up Southern, raising a transgender child, and discovering her inner lesbian at age fifty-one. She lives in St. Mary's City, Maryland, and works as an editor.

Micki Grimland

Micki Grimland, LCSW-ACP, is deliciously and delightfully married to Sharon DePierri and has three cherished daughters and one precious son-in-law. They live in the suburbs of Houston, expanding consciousness of the suburban white picket fence society. Micki loves rock climbing, nature, the arts, having conversations, and enjoys exploring the intersection of spirituality and psychology. She is a therapist in private practice for thirty years and helps people along the path of full personal actualization. Her family appeared on *Oprah* on a show about coming out in mid-life, she is frequently on the *Great Day Houston* show, and is a mental health consultant with Channel 11 and 13 in Houston, Texas. Her life will be summed up on her epitaph by this quote: "She sucked the marrow out of life!"

Crystal Hooper

A Pennsylvania native, Crystal Hooper moved to Nashville, Tennessee, after graduation hoping to find her place in the country music industry. Ten years later, still looking for that place, Crystal found herself on an unexpected back road that would change her course of direction. In processing the pain, guilt, and fear she felt in falling for another woman, Crystal found that love and personal growth overrides the perception of success. Crystal is currently in a committed lesbian relationship, and with her ex-husband, they are all raising their six-year-old daughter together in a loving and peaceful environment.

Lori Horvitz

Lori Horvitz's short stories, poetry, and personal essays have appeared in a variety of literary journals and anthologies, including *The Southeast Review*, *Hotel Amerika*, *13th Moon*, *The Dos Passos Review*, *Quarter After Eight*, and *P.S.: What I Didn't Say* (Seal Press, 2009). She has been awarded writing fellowships from The Ragdale Foundation, Yaddo, Cottages at Hedgebrook, Virginia Center for the Creative Arts, and Blue Mountain Center. A native New Yorker, Lori now makes her home in North Carolina, where she is an Associate Professor of Literature and Language at UNC-Asheville.

Jeanette LeBlanc

Jeanette LeBlanc is a photographer, writer, poet, and dreamer. She regularly consumes ridiculous amounts of dark chocolate, craves the sound of crashing waves, and wishes people would stop putting mushrooms on pizza. She has a love affair with words (all of them, especially the bad ones) and is inspired by the intersection of shadows and light. Hopelessly idealistic and impossibly pragmatic, Jeanette fully believes that she will one day earn a very good living with her camera and her writing. In the event that Plan A doesn't work out, she is willing to settle for a huge lottery win, or the generosity of a very rich benefactor. Either way, she has no intention of being a starving artist. Jeanette lives in Phoenix, Arizona, with her girlfriend and three delightfully unruly children. Jeanette writes about life at www.peacelovefree.com, and chronicles her coming out journey at www.awakeningsblog.com.

Erin Mantz

Since her childhood days touting pigtails and well-pronounced ad copy while auditioning for TV commercials, Erin understood the power of communication. Today, Erin's articles have appeared in the *New York Post*, *Washington Parent* Magazine, *Tango* magazine, and more. Erin authored *Dads, Teach Your Child (Ages 2-6) About Computers* (WonderDads Publishing, 2008). She has also built her career in communications for major corporations in the Washington, DC, area. Erin grew up in Chicago and attended Ithaca College in New York. She resides in Potomac, Maryland with her partner, two sons, two "stepsons," and two dogs. Her published clips are on www.erinmantz.com.

Meredith Maran

Meredith Maran (www.meredithmaran.com) is an award-winning journalist and the author of several best-selling nonfiction books, including *Dirty* (HarperOne, 2003), *Class Dismissed* (St. Martin's Griffin, 2000), *Notes from an Incomplete Revolution* (Bantam, 1997), and *What It's Like to Live Now* (Bantam, 1995). Her work appears regularly in anthologies, newspapers, and magazines. The mother of two grown sons, she lives with her wife in Oakland, California. Her next book, *My Lie: A True Story of False Memory*, was published by Jossey-Bass in September 2010.

Veronica Masen

New York native Veronica Masen is a self-employed costume designer, mother of two, dog lover, and avid gardener. She is a voracious reader, devouring everything from chick-lit to the classics, and writes fiction, poetry, and screenplays in her spare time. This is her first published piece.

Amanda V. Mead

Amanda V. Mead is a writer and teacher in Washington state, where she lives with her partner and their dog and cat. She is currently working towards her MFA in poetry at the Inland Northwest Center for Writers of Eastern Washington University. Amanda is an assistant poetry editor for *Willow Springs* literary arts journal. Her poetry has been published in *Opsis Literary Journal* and *Read This: Montana State University's Literature and Arts Publication*. She is also a political activist for LGBT causes, and works with LGBT youth in the Spokane area.

Libbie Miller

Libbie Miller's life was not particularly interesting until she finally came out to her husband of ten years. It was then that she decided she had a story worth sharing. She's now engaged to be married to her best friend, who not only rivals her Converse collection, but is equally neurotic (in a cute, *When Harry Met Sally* kind of way). When she's not at her day job churning out corporate copy, she's concert hopping with her fiancée, learning to play more than two chords on her guitar, or hanging out with her four animals in Phoenix, Arizona.

Sabrina Porterfield

Sabrina Porterfield's essays have been featured in the anthologies *Ask Me About My Divorce* (Seal Press, 2009) and *Labor Pains and Birth Stories* (Catalyst Book Press, 2009). She loves her Jane so much that she moved eight hours south of the Arctic Circle to be with her (and that's love, baby). She spends her time mothering twins, teaching English to Finns, and wearing lots of warm clothing. When she can grab a quiet moment, she does a little writing on the side.

Sara C. Rauch

Sara C. Rauch is a poet, a writer, and an aspiring kombucha harvester. Her poetry has appeared in *The Berkshire Review, upstreet, Inkwell, Earth's Daughters*, and *The Black Boot*. She lives with her partner and their four big-boned cats in Northampton, Massachusetts. When she isn't writing, she is tending her community garden plot, riding her bicycle, and figuring out new and exciting ways to cook kale. Visit her blog at www.cactusroom. blogspot.com.

Michelle Renae

Michelle Renae is a writer and spoken word artist who makes her home in Chicago. Her work focuses primarily on feminist issues and spirituality as explored through her own life and sexuality. Michelle is also the co-founder and president of Organa Wellness Inc., a Chicago-based organization that helps women harmonize body, mind, and soul through a range of holistic services. She lives with her husband and their energetic three-year-old son. To contact Michelle and learn more about her work, please visit www.michellespoken.com or email her at michellespoken@gmail.com.

Amelia Sauter

Amelia Sauter is a writer, cartoonist, martini lounge owner, marketing consultant, and musician living with her dynamic partner, their simple-minded dog, and their needy old cat in Ithaca, New York. Yes, she really does all those things, and yes, it pretty much makes her crazy. Back in the old days when newspapers thrived, Amelia wrote a regular cocktail column for *The Ithaca Journal*. Her cocktail blog can be found at www. feliciaspeakeasy.com and her freelance blog is www.drinkmywords.com. Amelia is currently writing a humorous memoir, *Small Town, Big Cocktails* (working title) about leaving a stable social work career to open a wild cocktail lounge, when she didn't even know how the heck to make a gin and tonic. She is seeking a publisher for the book.

Rachel Smith

Rachel Smith was born in Chicago in 1970. She is the mother of two children: a son (eleven years old) and a daughter (three years old). She holds a Bachelor of Arts degree in Sociology and an MBA in Healthcare Management. Currently, she's employed as an administrative assistant at a large teaching hospital in Chicago. She got married in 2005 and is currently separated from her husband, although he lives close by in effort to maintain a strong relationship with their children. She is still with her lover, K.

Sheila Smith

Sheila Smith was born into the Depression, came of age during the McCarthy era, but became a political radical and a gender queer anyway. She's lived in the same town, Corvallis, Oregon, for fifty years. She worked in biology labs, and turned dog trainer and lay minister in retirement years. She writes for much fun and little profit. Her work has been published in *Spirit of Corvallis* (Donning Company Publishers, 2008), *A Cup of Comfort for Divorced Women* (Adams Media, 2008), two animal shelter newsletters, and PETCO's electronic newsletter.

Leigh Stuart

Leigh Stuart lives in Los Angeles with her two teenage children. In addition to being a devoted mother, she is a partner, daughter, freelance writer, attorney, and former wife. Recognizing her personal truth while simultaneously uncovering her longtime husband's secret life is the subject of her nearly completed memoir, *Revolution*.

Susan White

Susan White, originally from eastern Tennessee, received her master's degree from the Bread Loaf School of English and her MFA from

Stonecoast. She has published short fiction in *River Walk Journal*, *Pisgah Review*, *Front Range Review*, and *Fresh Boiled Peanuts*. Her nonfiction essay, "Night Run," will appear in *A Daughter's Story* anthology. She teaches high school English in Asheville, North Carolina. When she's not grading or writing, Susan enjoys running on the mountain trails with her dogs, Zora, Callie, and Hooper.

About the Editors

Candace Walsh is the editor of *Ask Me About My Divorce: Women Open Up About Moving On* (Seal Press, 2009). She is also the features and poetry editor at *Mothering* magazine. She co-founded and edited *Mamalicious* magazine. Her articles have appeared in *Travel + Leisure, Sunset, Food & Wine, Natural Solutions, Newsday, New York, Blender,* and *Details.* She also wrote, with John Morris, the book *Stone Designs for the Home* (Gibbs Smith, 2008). Candace lives in Santa Fe, New Mexico.

Laura André received her PhD from the University of North Carolina at Chapel Hill. She was Assistant Professor in the history of photography at the University of New Mexico from 2003 to 2007. Her essay "Not Otherwise Specified" appeared in *Ask Me About My Divorce: Women Open Up About Moving On* (Seal Press, 2009). She lives in Santa Fe and works for an independent bookseller specializing in rare and contemporary photography books.

Acknowledgments

*W*e'd like to thank Krista Lyons for supporting and signing this project, Andie East for promoting it, and Seana McInerney for handling the paperwork. We love the brilliant cover design, and send our most passionately heartfelt kudos to the book's cover designer, Kate Basart.

The rich variety of this book is entirely due to the many wonderful writers who sent in their stories—way more than could all be squeezed between these covers. Thank you for wading through the messiness of recalled personal history and sorting it out on paper for our appreciative consideration. We'd also like to thank all of the writing website moderators and blog writers (like Jen Sabella at AfterEllen.com) who posted our call for submissions. Jill Soloway was kind enough to give us some wonderful and accomplished writer leads.

This book has been generously graced with the eminent insights of Dr. Lisa Diamond and Jennifer Baumgardner, who have individually mapped the terrain of women's desire in new ways that are both intrepid and visionary.

We are grateful to Andi Zeisler for publishing Audrey Bilger's article on the changing meaning of the word "wife" in *Bitch* magazine, which sent us scrambling for her involvement in this book. Gretchen Van Esselstyn of mediabistro.com gave us one of our first mentions in a tutorial on writing for anthologies.

We also want to thank Jill McArthur for bemusedly hearing out our up-to-the-minute editorial dispatches and giving us each such great hair for our author photo.

Candace's children played nicely on many an afternoon when we had a deadline looming; Laura's dogs snored soothingly in the background. Thank you to the friends and family who cheered us on and joined our book's Facebook fan page; and thank you to the scores of complete strangers who joined it as well. Our book's proposal was drafted at Two Fools Tavern in Albuquerque, and we read submissions and hammered out the introduction there over many a Guinness and Cobb salad (Candace), and Bass and nachos (Laura). It's the quintessential, unpretentiously perfect writer's haunt and we hope to linger there over many future projects. We also want to thank Jill McArthur for bemusedly hearing out our up-to-the-minute editorial dispatches and giving us each such great hair for our author photo.

Selected Titles from Seal Press

For more than thirty years, Seal Press has published
groundbreaking books. By women. For women.

Ask Me About My Divorce: Women Open Up About Moving On, edited
by Candace Walsh. $15.95, 978-1-58005-276-4. A spicy, bracing, riveting
anthology that proclaims: I got divorced, and it rocked my world!

Sexual Intimacy for Women: A Guide for Same-Sex Couples, by Glenda
Corwin, PhD. $16.95, 978-1-58005-303-7. In this prescriptive and poignant
book, Glenda Corwin, PhD, helps female couples overcome obstacles to
sexual intimacy through her examination of the emotional, physical, and
psychological aspects of same-sex relationships.

Girl in Need of a Tourniquet: A Borderline Personality Memoir, by Merri Lisa
Johnson. $16.95, 978-1-58005-305-1. This riveting and dramatic personal
account gives us a glimpse of what it means to be a borderline personality
in a relationship.

Lesbian Couples: A Guide to Creating Healthy Relationships, by D. Merilee
Clunis and G. Dorsey Green. $ 16.95, 978-1-58005-131-6. Drawing from
a decade of research, this helpful and readable resource covers topics
from conflict resolution to commitment ceremonies, using a variety of
examples and problem-solving techniques.

P.S.: What I Didn't Say, edited by Megan McMorris. $15.95, 978-1-58005-
290-0. For the friend who's been there for you through everything, the
friend you've lost touch with, or the friend you've wished you could
help, this thought-provoking collection of unsent letters expresses the
unspoken.

The List: 100 Ways to Shake Up Your Life, by Gail Belsky. $15.95,
978-1-58005-256-6. Get a tattoo, ride in a fire truck, or use food as foreplay—
this collection of a hundred ideas will inspire women to shake things up
and do something they never dared to consider.

Find Seal Press Online: www.SealPress.com
www.Facebook.com/SealPress
Twitter: @SealPress